A Dangerous Innovator

Mother Oliver IBVM in her book, *Mary Ward,*
indicated that many of
Mary Ward's enemies saw her as
'a dangerous innovator'.

Others have written of Mary Ward, and have told the
amazing story of her life and the astonishing survival of
the Institute she founded. Jennifer Cameron makes a
valuable addition to this growing body of literature by
setting Mary Ward firmly in the context of Reformation
women: women among Mary's family and friends, and in
Europe other women who tried to achieve a new and
different way for women to live their commitment to the
Church and its universal mission. Their ideas and their
call were too novel and too radical to be accepted in their
own time. Most had to modify their projects. Mary Ward
would not, and could not – despite misunderstanding
and opposition from within the Church. It was this surety
of God's will for her and for her Institute that made her
the 'dangerous innovator' of the title of this book, and
'that incomparable woman' so praised by Pope Pius XII.

Sr Noni Mitchell IBVM, Superior General 1986-1998

My five daughters were pupils of Loreto, Kirribilli. Julia,
the youngest, became head of the school in her final year.
Each one has made a statement with her life – in law,
literature, nursing, art and working with indigenous
people in the western desert; such accomplishments, of
course, are shared by many of their schoolday peers. To
people of the grim Elizabethan age, as Jennifer Cameron's
wonderful book depicts, it would seem that Mary Ward
died a sad and lonely failure. Yet her spirit has not failed
us. I believe our 'dangerous innovator' is well and truly
abroad to this day, inspiring the many grand works of the
Institute which she founded.

David Burke, author

A DANGEROUS INNOVATOR

Mary Ward (1585-1645)

Jennifer J Cameron, IBVM

ST PAULS

A DANGEROUS INNOVATOR: Mary Ward (1585-1645)

© Jennifer J Cameron 2000

First published, September 2000

National Library of Australia
Cataloguing-in-Publication Data:

Cameron, Jennifer J.
A Dangerous Innovator: Mary Ward (1585-1645)

Bibliography.
Includes index.
ISBN 1 876295 28 7

1. Ward, Mary, 1585-1645. 2. Loreto Nuns. 3. Nuns - England - Biography. I. Title.

271.97092

Published by
ST PAULS PUBLICATIONS – Society of St Paul
60-70 Broughton Rd – PO Box 906 – Strathfield, NSW 2135
http://www.stpauls.com.au

Cover painting:
Mary Ward at about the time she went to St Omer in 1609.
From the *Painted Life* No 16.

Cover design by Isabel de Sequera

Printed by Ligare Pty Ltd

ST PAULS PUBLICATIONS is an activity of the priests and brothers of the Society of St Paul who place at the centre of their lives the mission of evangelisation through the modern means of social communication.

Foreword

God exacts a special tax from those who offer their lives through the Church. Martyrs are made by those outside the Church; but God's taxation office is staffed by God's own people. Mary Ward's life is a good example of this iron law of Church history. Certainly she suffered at the hands of antipathetic state officials, but her deepest, most interior sufferings, were at the hands of her own. Jennifer Cameron's book brings this out in sharp colours.

The book tells how Mary Ward bore her treatment with faith and hope and love. She did not despair of the Church, as Acton said of Erasmus. Handled roughly with insensitivity, deceit and even malice, she nevertheless refused to be deflected from doing God's will as she knew it. She seemed unsurprised that the Church of sinners was made up of sinners. This book demonstrates that it was also, and at the same time, made up of people on their way to being saints, even great saints. Nothing demonstrates Mary Ward's sanctity more than her passionate adhesion to the will of God, whatever the obstacles.

Well, the period between the sixteenth and seventeenth centuries which we call the Reformation century is a crowded constellation of saints and saintly endeavours. It is also a time of mysticism, when the frontiers between heaven and earth thin out and are easily breached. Think of the paintings of El Greco, the poetry of John of the Cross, or the music of Victoria or Palestrina. Jennifer Cameron shows that Mary Ward fits comfortably inside this mystical milieu. Her sayings are as authentic and convincing as those of Julian of Norwich: 'I remained for a good space without feeling or hearing anything but the sound "Glory,

glory, glory".' That is the genuine article. Her practicality and common sense underpin the reality of these revelations.

Other readers will want to emphasise other aspects of this book, such as its feminist perspectives. It is an important addition to the story of Catholic women. Here, Jennifer Cameron insistently quotes the papal apophthegm, 'Let women be governed by women', a saying which will bring wry smiles to those who know the history of women's institutes in subsequent centuries. There will be others too who will dwell on the necessary role of the Society of Jesus in this story. As in the Mary MacKillop saga, the Jesuit fathers enter at a different angle from the canon lawyers and curial officials... and save a work of the Lord.

Whatever the special interest, however, every reader will be captivated and, I believe, enlivened, by the personality of Mary Ward. This is her book and we owe Jennifer Cameron our gratitude for writing it.

Edmund Campion
Catholic Institute of Sydney

Acknowledgments

The Institute of the Blessed Virgin Mary for permission to reproduce the map on page 126, from Emmanuel Orchard (ed) *Till God Will* (Darton, Longman and Todd, 1985) p 4.

Sisters of the Company of Mary (Province of England and Ireland), for permission to reproduce the map on page 84, from Francoise Soury-Lavergne, *A Pathway in Education* (1984) p 397.

Tanner Werbung GmbH, publishers, for permission to reproduce the painting on the front cover and the paintings comprising plates 1-7.

P Hans Zwiefelhofer SJ, Secretary General of the Society of Jesus, for permission to reproduce plate 8.

*   *   *

My gratitude for the gracious support and encouragement of the following people in the research and writing of this work must be acknowledged: Dr Sophie McGrath RSM, who was a very wise and generous supervisor; Sr Sonia Dillon IBVM, who initiated the project and continually urged it on; Sr Anne Anderson IBVM, who steadily encouraged me and gave ready and competent teaching of computer skills; Dr Jeanne Cover IBVM, who lent me her doctoral thesis on the spirituality of Mary Ward; Sr Thérèse Daly IBVM, who sent me numerous stimulating articles; the Australian Provincial Superiors of the IBVM, and IBVM community members, who encouraged the pursuit of the topic for this work.

In addition, I wish to express my gratitude to the faculties and staffs of the various member institutes of the

Sydney College of Divinity where I pursued the different studies related to this material.

I should like also to acknowledge the work undertaken over many decades by Sister Immolata Wetter IBMV of the Roman Generalate. Historians interested in Mary Ward are deeply indebted to her for years of painstaking research on Mary Ward and her work. Dr Henriette Peters' recent, scholarly published work on Mary Ward has also been an invaluable contribution to the resource material used in the preparation of this book, and I should like to thank Sr Helen Butterworth, translator of the English edition, for correspondence about Peters' book.

We acknowledge with gratitude the financial gift that enabled the initial publication of this book to proceed. I should like to pay tribute to Mary Ward and all her Institute companions throughout the centuries who have been 'women for all seasons'.

Thank you also to the Managing Editor of St Pauls Publications, Father Michael Goonan, and editor, Chris Brennan, who undertook this publication and carried it to completion.

Contents

ILLUSTRATIONS

Plates

The plates appear between pages 150 and 151.

Maps

CHAPTER 1

Mary Ward in Historical Context

General Reformation Background

Mary Ward was born at Mulwith near Ripon in Yorkshire, England, on 23 January 1585 and died at Heworth Hall outside the city of York, on 30 January 1645. The map of 1622 on page 22 shows Ripon (spelt with two 'p's) where Mary was born. Her maternal grandparents, with whom she lived as a child, had their home near Welwick in the south of Holderness. In order to make an assessment of Mary Ward as a woman of the Reformation period it is necessary to situate her within the context of those times.

Mary Ward's lifetime, set in the historical period called the Reformation, spanned a period of great change, great turmoil, and great challenge. The Reformation was not just an isolated religious upheaval, but one which affected the entire European culture.

The Church has always stood in need of reform and this need was accentuated in the social and politically disturbed times of the late Middle Ages and early modern period. At this time the clergy were generally poorly educated and Church leadership was too frequently corrupt. Church offices as well as indulgences, Masses and pardons were frequently bought. Immorality was common among the priests. Throughout the Christian centuries there had always been individuals and groups who worked for reform and, during the fifteenth century, as the need for reform from the papacy down became more patently evident, the call for reform became more persistent.

It was, however, the Saxon Augustinian, Martin Luther, who was to become the first significant focus for reform at this time. Political, economic and social circumstances favoured Luther's protest against the papacy which was triggered by a papal campaign to promote funds for the Vatican which involved the sale of indulgences. Luther's breach with the Church was promoted by the incompetency of the incumbent Pope, Leo X, and the inadequacy of his advisers and envoys concerning his dealings with Luther and his followers.[1]

Luther's successful revolt against the papacy soon stimulated the other two significant Reformation leaders, Zwingli and Calvin. The teaching of these reformers aided the political and economic aspirations of the aristocratic leaders and developing middle class of the emerging nation-states. They were anxious to be free from the onerous taxation and interference of the papacy and the holy Roman emperor, who was theoretically supported by the pope.[2]

In 1521 Luther was excommunicated from the Catholic Church and in the same year the *Edict of Worms* formally proclaimed him a heretic. The passionate confrontation that followed this break with Rome precipitated such disasters as religious wars and the peasants' revolt in Germany. It was indeed a most chaotic and challenging time.

Eventually 'The Religious Peace of Augsburg' was proclaimed in September 1555. This Peace Formula proclaimed that each prince had the right to decide which religion (Catholic or Lutheran) his subjects would follow. An immediate consequence was an uneasy fusion of Church and State which was to affect the work of Mary Ward later when she was establishing schools on the continent.[3] Not unexpectedly, the Peace of Augsburg resulted in an unstable peace which erupted in 1618 into what is known as 'The Thirty Years' War', and this was to be the background of Mary's European endeavours.

The Reformation in England

The Reformation in England, Mary Ward's homeland, was different from the Reformation in continental European countries. The English Reformation was essentially political in origin. The resulting changes in religious loyalties, attitudes and practices were officially implemented from above by statute, proclamation and royal commission.[4] However, although the Reformation in England was proclaimed by King Henry VIII himself, the continental situation had created a precedent that made Henry's move less blatantly revolutionary.[5]

Henry had initially strongly supported the papacy against Luther, but by 1529 his support was waning rapidly. This about-turn was accelerated by his unfulfilled desire for a male heir - a legitimate heir who was able to continue the royal lineage. Since his wife, Catherine of Aragon, had failed to give him this heir, Henry was anxious to obtain an annulment of his marriage to her, but Rome refused to comply. Following this turn of events Henry attempted to legitimise his own position by making himself head of the Church in England and bypassing papal authority.

In 1531 Henry VIII required the English clergy to acknowledge him as 'the protector and only supreme head of the Church and clergy in England'. By 1534, in the *Act of Succession*, Parliament required all English subjects to swear an oath of loyalty to their king in his new role as head of the Anglican Church and to accept Elizabeth over Mary Tudor as the true heir to the English throne.[6]

It was for refusing to take this oath that Sir Thomas More and John Fisher became English Catholic martyrs in 1535. Both Fisher and More held on doctrinal grounds that no parliament could abolish the pope's power. More declared at his execution that he died 'in and for the faith of the Holy Catholic Church'.[7] Fifty years later, when Mary Ward was born, the tradition of English Catholic martyrdom for those who would not conform to the Anglican Church was well established.

The recusants

Henry VIII was in need of money and now, as supreme head of the Church in England, the easiest way to recharge his coffers was by the dissolution of the monasteries. A facile justification for seizing the wealth of the monasteries was to declare that the religious men and women in the monasteries were not leading good lives. In fact there was little hostility towards the monasteries. As the Protestant Reformation historian, Owen Chadwick, commented: 'for the most part the monasteries were neither fervent nor disgraceful. They were pleasant, half-secularized clubs for common and comfortable living. Some of the smaller (monasteries) were little more than farms.'[8] Knowles also states that it would seem clear that there was no animosity towards the religious on the part either of the local gentry or of the monks' neighbours.[9]

Nevertheless, in January 1534, commissioners were appointed to visit the monasteries. Before the visitations could be completed the Act of Suppression was passed in 1536. By this Act religious houses with a net income of two hundred pounds per annum were chosen as the first to be dissolved.

From November 1537 the bigger and wealthier houses had begun to dissolve themselves by agreement. According to Chadwick:

In May 1539 Parliament passed an act vesting in the crown all monastic possessions surrendered after the Act of 1536. None of the abbots present in the House of Lords protested against it. The dissolution was a peaceable process, with the bloodshed only of the few who refused the royal supremacy. The last house, Waltham of Essex, surrended to the King on 23 March 1540.[10]

Although many, including abbots and monks and some nuns, did not apparently resist the closure of the monasteries, there was a significant number of Catholics - clerics and laity, men and women - who did resist the new religious trends.[11] They became known as 'recusants' (refusers). Indeed these same Catholics resisted strongly - even to the point of war.

The biggest and best organised revolt of the recusants was in the north. This took place in the autumn of 1536 and concerned almost the whole of the northern provinces of England. It was called 'The Pilgrimage of Grace' and was a protest on behalf of the old religion - against the divorce of Henry VIII and his claims of royal supremacy, particularly targeting the Act of Suppression. The rising was quickly put down, although it had support from all classes and was directed by men of substance and education. It has been said that: '... the high character and ability of the Yorkshire leaders and those who joined them gave a colour and a significance to the whole rising which it might otherwise have lacked'.[12] Both families of Mary Ward's parents were part of this resistance.

In January 1547, Henry VIII died and was succeeded by his nine-year-old son, Edward VI. On Edward's early death he was succeeded by Mary Tudor, daughter of Catherine of Aragon and Henry VIII. She became Queen in 1553. Mary tried to re-establish the Roman Catholic religion and three hundred Protestants were put to death for defending Anglicanism. Mary's attempt to restore Catholicism included the restoration of Roman authority in Church matters, but this was not acceptable to Parliament. The laity, who now owned monastic lands, were not in favour of a reconciliation with Rome, lest they lose those lands. After five years of a sad reign Mary Tudor died in November 1558.

Elizabeth 1 (1558-1603) succeeded Mary Tudor. This new English Queen was the daughter of Anne Boleyn and Henry VIII and so had Protestant leanings. She had also witnessed the Protestant persecutions under the reign of Mary Tudor. Both Catholics and Protestants had become hardened into their positions by persecutions under Henry VIII and Mary Tudor, and the challenge for Elizabeth was to steer a course between the two extremes in an effort to unite her realm.[13]

With this end in view Elizabeth I had two very important Acts of Parliament passed, *The Act of Supremacy* and *The Act of Uniformity.* The Act of Supremacy in 1559 abolished the pope's jurisdiction within the queen's domain. The death penalty was imposed on those who twice defended the pope, or twice refused the oath.

Although Elizabeth eschewed the extreme position of the Puritans (English Calvinists) she sought to unite the country under Protestantism. This strategy involved an anti-Catholic stance. *The Book of Common Prayer* had been promulgated in 1552 in the reign of Edward VI and through the Act of Uniformity Elizabeth I imposed the rites and prayers of *The Book of Common Prayer* as the only lawful form of worship, and not to use it also carried penal provisions.

The official policy of Elizabeth and her Government was firstly, to determine the number of Catholic recusants; secondly, to keep the more important and active ecclesiastics and laymen under surveillance or in prison and, thirdly, to prevent manifestations of Catholic life. Much of this depended upon the installation of new bishops, the chief agents in each diocese in establishing the Elizabethan settlement.[14]

Elizabeth succeeded in establishing the Anglican Church not only by persecuting Catholics, but also by the growth of Anglican theology. The publication of the *Thirty-Nine Articles* represented 'something of a compromise between traditional Catholic theology and the more radical doctrine of the Swiss reformers'.[15] Elizabeth thus aspired to win her Catholic subjects to the new faith.

As a result of Elizabeth's efforts many drifted into the practice of Anglicanism, but the Act of Supremacy acknowledging Elizabeth as head of the Church in England was the stumbling block for conscientious Catholics. Indeed some 50,000 of the Catholic 'recusants' (refusers) adhered to their faith. At this time the population of England and Wales was estimated as five million, with the majority of the people being rural dwellers.[16] From these figures it is clear that the resistance to Elizabeth's attempts to impose her religious authority on the English people was carried out by a very small minority, but this minority was a very strong group. They have been referred to as a 'rejected minority' who do not follow the usual pattern found in studies of the sociology of religion.[17] The historian, Norman, comments that:

> The English Catholic 'recusants'- those who refused to conform to the laws of the unitary Protestant establishment - did not develop sectarian qualities, did not become political radicals (though a few sought revolution as a means of procuring a Catholic dynastic restoration), did not deviate from orthodoxy, and did not, above all, quietly slide back into an acquiescence with the new order. Theirs is a noble history of enormous self-sacrifice for higher purposes, and of a rooted determination to preserve both their English virtue and their religious allegiance in a sensible and clear balance.[18]

Mary Ward's family belonged to this group of northern recusants and so this atmosphere of political resistance was the culture into which she was born, and in which she grew up. Indeed there was another northern rising in 1569 and northerners were also involved in the 'Gunpowder Plot' to blow up the King, James I, and the Houses of Parliament in 1605. As a result of this plot the former statute of Queen Elizabeth against recusants was altered 'to include every English person who engaged a Catholic servant or gave a Catholic stranger hospitality; he had to pay 10 pounds per month per person'.[19]

Mary Ward's uncles, John and Christopher Wright, and Thomas Percy, Mary's uncle-in-law, were all killed in their encounter with the sheriffs at Holbeach as a result of their involvement in the Gunpowder Plot.[20] Mary was nurtured from these roots of the northern gentry Catholics; resistance to oppression was a meaningful part of her heritage.

The three women who were prominent in Mary Ward's early life had all been imprisoned as recusants. Her grandmother, Ursula Wright, had been imprisoned for fourteen years. Catherine Ardington, at whose home Mary made her first Communion, had been in York prison. Another relative, Grace Babthorpe, in whose home Mary spent seven years, had been in prison for five years. Mary's early women mentors were then strong women whose religious faith was central to their lives, and for which they were prepared to suffer.

In 1570 Pope Pius V had issued a bull, *Regnans in Excelsis,* which excommunicated Queen Elizabeth I. This had not helped the situation of the recusants, and the supposed Catholic link with King Philip II of Spain gave rise to allegations against Catholics of disloyalty. They were accused of treachery against their country. In fact the recusants were intensely loyal to England and their martyrs, such as Thomas More and Edmund Campion, protested their patriotism and claimed to be true servants of their country, but God's servant first.[21]

The fact that Elizabeth I's reign was so long (there were eleven popes in that time) enabled her to implement her policies firmly. In 1581 Parliament reinforced its anti-Catholic stance by passing stringent regulations which made conversion to Catholicism a capital offence. As Trimble records: 'To celebrate or hear mass now involved one in a crime punishable by fine and imprisonment; to reconcile or be reconciled to Rome became high treason; to fail to attend the services of the Establishment entailed a monthly fine of 20 pounds.'[22]

In general the difficulties of communication would have made Queen Elizabeth I a remote figure to most of her subjects. She would have been viewed as a woman of power who propagated that power through the portrayal of the monarchy. She was never seen as one who was concerned with the betterment of women - survival was her main concern - as it would have been for the majority of her poor women subjects. Some of the strategies Elizabeth I used to establish and maintain herself as a strong female English monarch illustrate her political influence as Queen of England. Mary Ward was growing up during the last years of Elizabeth's reign.

Clergy problems on the English mission

The priests who remained in England were known as Marian priests because they had been ordained during the brief reign of Mary Tudor. During the outlawing of the Catholic religion in England there was no possibility for Catholic priests to be trained as priests in England. The solution to this problem was the education on the continent of secular priests for England.

Cardinal Allen, who originally conformed to the Protestant Church under Edward VI, confirmed himself as a Catholic by refusing to take the Oath of Supremacy in 1561.

While on the staff of the new University at Douai, founded by Phillip II, Allen decided to finance a college to prepare priests for the English 'mission'. Consequently in 1568 Allen founded an English college at Douai and another college was founded in Rome in 1576. Seminarians in these colleges were being prepared for martyrdom, and by the end of the sixteenth century 123 priests had been executed in England, together with some sixty men or women who had been declared guilty of assisting them.[23]

The services of these secular priests were supplemented by the Jesuits who came to the English mission in 1580. They were the most hated of all priests by the English Government, although there were not many of them in England. According to Norman: '... by the end of the 16th century there were fewer than 20 Jesuits in England (and four of these were in prison)'.[24]

Robert Parsons, ordained a Jesuit in 1578, was the leader of the Jesuit mission to England. He was fired with missionary zeal as he took over the English mission after Allen's death. Parsons himself died in 1610 when he was Rector of the English College in Rome. The fiery missionary zeal of the Jesuits (many were young, adventurous Englishmen) and the more conservative approach of the secular clergy led to difficulties between the two groups. The Jesuits were very influential among the English laity as spiritual directors. Prayer featured strongly in the life of the recusant households. As will be seen, this conflict between the Jesuits and secular clergy was to be a significant element affecting Mary Ward's efforts to obtain approval of the Institute she was to establish.

Another cause of difficulty between the Jesuits and the secular clergy was that the English Catholic Church during the reign of Elizabeth I had become a church with much lay involvement.[25] Because the practice of the Catholic religion and the harbouring of priests were outlawed, priests had to be sheltered and hidden in the houses of Catholics. In this time of disruption in the life of the Church, the Catholic laity were in a position to exercise initiative - irrespective of the opinions of the secular clergy - and they were often influenced by the Jesuits. The autobiography of the Jesuit, John Gerard, *The Hunted Priest,* gives a comprehensive coverage to the stories of priests who were hidden by laity.

Obviously the former Catholic parish structure could no longer exist and so a Jesuit-run church was developing in England, and this did not please the secular clergy. The loss of parish funds for the secular clergy made it very difficult for them. Lay people became free to choose their pastors, and this was a great advantage for some Catholics as they engaged priests who were members of their families, or sons of their friends. They chose Jesuits to instruct them, administer the sacraments and teach their sons, and sometimes their daughters, because the Jesuits were more mobile than the secular priests and perhaps more prepared for the conditions of a persecuted church.[26]

The loss of finance and of ecclesiastical power were certainly not welcomed by the secular clergy. They appealed to Rome so many times that they became known by the group name of 'Appellants'. Theirs was a church political group and, according to Bossy, their 'fundamental argument was about whether England ought properly to be called a missionary territory at all'.[27] But English Catholics generally continued their lives without much direct involvement in the priests' differences.[28]

Mary Ward had first-hand knowledge about priests sheltering in hiding places. It is said that this is why she was sent to stay with relatives as a young child lest she inadvertently give information to the pursuivants about the priests' hiding places and the names of the priests.[29] Thus the political, religious and social situations in England touched in many ways the lives of Mary Ward and the young women from England who were to be her first companions.

Added pressure on Catholics

In 1581 Parliament enacted regulations that made the celebrating or hearing of Mass punishable by fine and imprisonment. Failure to attend the services of the establishment entailed a monthly fine of twenty pounds.[30] As Holmes points out: 'by opposing Elizabeth's religious policy, Catholics were obeying God in preference to men, disobeying bad human laws in order to obey good divine laws'.[31] The result was that many Catholics used 'equivocation'. This was the technical term used to describe what could be called lying that was employed in order to conceal a priest's identity, or that of other people, as well as one's own Catholic allegiance.[32] Mental reservation was also used by Catholics asked to swear allegiance to the Queen and the Anglican religion.

The Jesuit martyr, Robert Southwell, defended equivocation at his trial in 1595. However, casuists of the time were divided on the approval of equivocation and mental reservation in the face of death.[33] Despite these differences between Catholic moral theologians in the sixteenth century, equivocation enabled many English Catholics to survive in cases where they were destined for death.

Scarisbrick claims that the papists made a mockery of recusancy laws because '... priests were smuggled in and out of the country via a score of ports, while whole areas of the land remained virtually Catholic and gaols were as leaky as sieves'.[34] Many anecdotes in John Gerard's autobiography also attest to this. As will be seen, Mary Ward crossed to St Omer many times, often under assumed names. Marmaduke Ward, Mary's father, and other members of her family were imprisoned at times and on other occasions escaped even the monthly fines.

It has been asserted that the Catholic minority in the Elizabethan era consisted mainly of people from the upper classes, that is, those who had money to pay the fines. In many cases this was so. Mary Ward's father, a landowner, paid for his family's refusal to attend the Protestant services. The gentry certainly provided the Mass centres in their houses and brought the Jesuits from the continent. However, Catholics were not confined to any one class but came from all levels of society and all occupations - men and women included. The famous martyr, Margaret Clitherow, came from the lower middle class.

As indicated, however, the 'seigneurial' class had the advantages of money and education, and so it was from these upper class families that the leadership of the recusants naturally was derived. Initiatives for escaping persecution were part of this leadership, but education in the Catholic faith was another essential activity which was carried out by the upper class families, as will be seen in the case of Mary Ward and her Sisters.

Catholics who wished to return to the fold of Catholicism had to have their sin of apostasy forgiven by a priest with powers to forgive this 'reserved sin'. Priests from Mary Tudor's reign did not have the power. William Allen had it conferred on him by Rome and he could confer it on others. Catholics who required this kind of confessor had to know that a priest with such powers was required and then find such a priest - an added burden for those who were already confused about religious issues in a country which did not have modern communications! Mary Ward and her Sisters worked in England on these very difficult issues of reconciling Catholics back to the faith and instructing them in that faith. Sister Dorothea was one such sister who worked incognito in East Anglia. Her story will be told later.

So the obvious consequences of the Reformation in England were to drive the Catholics and their practices of religion underground - as well as making the public practice of the Protestant religion (Anglicanism) compulsory. Weekly attendance at church was now enforced by Church and State - a remarkable obligation for former casual, or non-church attenders. Pews were installed in Protestant churches. They were confining (people had to sit and listen to sermons), but they also filled the spaces formerly occupied by side altars and statues. The entire religious landscape of England had undergone great change.

Recusant women

The role of Catholic women, especially women of the gentry, was such a strong one in Counter-Reformation England that Bossy asserts that it was 'in effect a Matriarchy'.[35] He maintains that the average woman of the upper classes was dissatisfied because 'the Reformation had not been designed with her in mind'.[36] Women had lost their opportunity for religious life as nuns and in the Protestant Church the literacy necessary for reading the Bible was restricted to the upper classes. Bossy comments:

> All in all, I think the evidence entitles us to conclude that, to a considerable degree, the Catholic community owed its existence to gentlewomen's dissatisfaction at the Reformation settlement of religion, and that they played an abnormally important part in its early history.[37]

Bossy emphasizes the active role of Catholic women at that time. They were actively proselytising - not just being influential in their domestic spheres. Catholic women were active in communicating their faith and suffered persecution for it. They often endured long periods of imprisonment, as did Mary Ward's maternal grandmother, and they also suffered the conclusive act of faith commitment by being martyred. Scarisbrick records:

Of the thirty recusant women in Ousebridge gaol in York between 1579 and 1594, eleven died in prison. There were well known individuals, like Anne Line, hanged at Tyburn in 1601 for harbouring priests, and Mary Cole, in prison in the Clink at the age of twenty-one for non-attendance at church.[38]

Stories of great courage and ingenuity are told about the English Catholic women who resisted conformity to Anglicanism. Suffice it to mention a few. Grace Babthorpe spent five years in prison for her faith. After she was released and widowed she went to Louvain in 1617 to join a community of English nuns there and her son, a Jesuit, preached at her clothing.[39] One of her daughters, Barbara Babthorpe, joined Mary Ward's group of early companions. The Wards were related to the Babthorpes. Mary Ward herself had lived in the Babthorpe home in Osgodby, East Riding, from 1599 to 1606. Here an almost monastic life was lived with such customs as 'Mass at six o'clock in the morning and evening prayers before bed'.[40]

Dorothy Lawson came to her husband's deathbed in London in 1613. He had spent most of his time in London practising law but he was supposed to have been converted to Catholicism at that time. Dorothy Lawson was a strong advocate of the Catholic faith from her house on the Tyne River below Newcastle. Jesuit priests, such as Father Richard Holtby, who had guided Mary Ward, were known to have been hidden from pursuivants in her house.[41] Later on four of Dorothy Lawson's grand-daughters entered Mary Ward's Institute.

Another example of ingenuity is shown by Dr Thomas Vavasour and his wife, Dorothy. They were strong Catholics and the Vavasour home became a great centre for the education and strength of Catholics. Mrs Vavasour ran the equivalent of a 'Catholic maternity home'. When the 'goodman' (priest) arrived women were summoned and it was assumed that one of the mothers was in labour and needed assistance. In fact they went there for the celebration of the Eucharist, prayers and instructions.[42]

There was also Margaret Clitherow who, in 1587, was crushed to death for her persistent adherence to Catholicism. Margaret Clitherow's life and death illustrate many of the facets of the lives of the strong Catholic women of the North of England. At the age of fifteen she married John Clitherow, in July 1571. John was a widower with two sons and he was about twice Margaret's age. Margaret became a capable businesswoman who ran her husband's shop.

Margaret Clitherow was imprisoned for not attending Anglican services. This happened several times between 1577 and 1584. Not only were there strong Catholic communities in the prisons, but also Margaret Clitherow 'took advantage of the leisure which her adversaries had provided for her to read English and written hand'.[43] John Clitherow paid the recusancy fines for his wife and she was released. But both Margaret and John Clitherow were again taken to York Castle prison for having a hidden Mass room in their house in the Shambles in York.

Margaret refused to plead so that no others were implicated in the so-called treasonable offences. In fear of his reputation, the weak Judge Clench sentenced her. The judgment was that she would be pressed to death with her hands and feet tied and a sharp stone under her back.[44]

Because a pregnant woman could not be executed until the birth of the child (the baby had done no wrong), Margaret's friends said she was pregnant, but she would not affirm it for certainty.[45] After ten days the execution was carried out at the Toolbooth near the prison in York on 25 March 1587. Mary Ward, as a child of two years of age, was then living in the district of Yorkshire.

The life, and death by martyrdom, of Margaret Clitherow, illustrate much of the history of Reformation women who showed considerable initiative in promoting Catholicism, with men and women working together. Prison life was often a strong spiritual experience for recusants because prisoners were assisted by Jesuit co-prisoners such as John Mush and Francis Ingleby. Margaret Clitherow's example of heroism inspired young women of that time. One such woman who was influenced by this role model was Jane Wiseman. She was a widow from Essex, who also refused to plead when she was arrested and imprisoned for harbouring priests. She was released when James I came to the throne. Four of Jane Wiseman's daughters were professed in nunneries on the continent.[46]

Not only did the recusant women of Yorkshire have the courage to practise their religion, but they also dared to flaunt it. Such women showed a form of bravado and humour coupled with lively disrespect for social mores. It was thus within a lived tradition of strong women, active in the public sphere, that Mary Ward was nurtured as a child and young woman.

The so-called 'matriarchal period' of Catholic women in England came to an end about 1620, according to Bossy. He argues that there were two reasons for this:

1. There was a change in the administration of the recusancy laws because the collection of fines was rapidly declining. Husbands and wives were more likely to be of the one faith - marriages of those with different religions were more difficult. The state, not churches, was responsible for marriage laws, as Henry VIII could have reminded them.

2. The authority of the father of the family was strengthened. There was a patriarchal revival among the Catholic gentry. The role of the priest was also authoritarian.

Bossy asserts that the suppression of Mary Ward's Institute was a case illustrating how Catholics continued to assert paternal authority:

> It (Mary Ward's Institute) was both a product of the matriarchal era in the community and an attempt, if not exactly to prolong its existence, at least to ensure some permanent readjustment of the roles of man and woman. As such it had appeared at an unfavourable juncture, and in response to a wave of hysterical agitation had been suppressed by the papacy before the close of the 1620s. From this point onwards there is little to suggest that Catholics differed from the norm in their estimate of paternal authority.[47]

The Counter-Reformation

As has been indicated there was a very significant desire for reform within the Roman Catholic Church in the sixteenth century. This impetus for reform gathered momentum after Luther's break with the Church and despite the often poor leadership of the popes of this time. Reform was finally given official direction in the calling of the Council of Trent by Pope Paul III. After a series of false starts the Council of Trent met in twenty-five sessions over a period of eighteen years (1545-1563).[48] The bull announcing the convocation of the Council specified that the definition of Catholic dogma and the reform of the Church were the two main tasks of the Council.[49]

Protestant reformers came to the second phase of the Council (1550-1555) but they failed to be satisfied by its teachings. Through the Council of Trent however, the Church, according to Holmes and Bickers, 'established a firm foundation for the renewal of Catholic life, and it should be regarded as both the fruit of the Catholic reform movement which was now a century old and the cause of the Catholic Reformation which now enjoyed papal support'.[50]

The implementation of the Decrees of the Council of Trent was crucial to the effectivenesss of real reform in the Catholic Church. Successive popes took up the unfinished tasks of the Council. Pope Pius V concluded the revision of the Roman Catechism in 1566, the Roman Breviary in 1568 and the Roman Missal in 1570. The next pope, Gregory XIII, completed a revision of canon law and the publication of the Gregorian calendar, which was named after him. He also began the practice of having permanent papal nuncios resident in various Catholic countries as agents of papal authority. Mary Ward was to experience the benefits and the problems of having such representatives in countries outside Italy.

Reform of the training of the clergy was also an important part of the Council of Trent. Pope Gregory XIII promoted the establishment of seminaries. When it was impossible to establish a seminary in a particular country, a national seminary was opened in Rome. An example of this was the establishment of the English College in Rome in 1584, the year before Mary Ward's birth.[51]

While the renewal of the clergy was an essential part of the reforms of the Council of Trent, the reform of religious orders was not overlooked. A long decree on religious orders was issued at the twenty-fifth session. Jedin comments that 'as far as women in religious orders were concerned, the most important points were the safeguarding of personal freedom at the profession of vows and the tightening up of the regulations on enclosure'.[52] Mary Ward's insistence that enclosure was impossible for the active ministry of her Sisters was one of the contentious points which she would place before the Roman authorities.

With the revival of the Catholic Church through the Counter-Reformation there was a resurgence in religious orders. The origin of the Society of Jesus, the Jesuits, who were significant in the life of Mary Ward, had its roots in this period. The Spanish nobleman, Ignatius Loyola, was converted to a close following of Christ while recovering from a war wound in 1531 at the age of thirty. The next year, at Manresa, Ignatius had many spiritual experiences which gave rise to his spiritual exercises which, in 1548, were published as a book. These *Spiritual Exercises* express the charism of the Jesuits and it was upon this form of spirituality that Mary Ward and her Sisters were formed through the direction of Jesuit priests in England and on the continent.

The Society of Jesus was given approval by Pope Paul III when he accepted the Formula of the Society in 1539. Ignatius was elected General in 1541 and thus began to draw up the Constitutions of the Company. This laborious task was completed before his death in 1556. The Constitutions were approved by Pope Paul IV in 1558.[53] The apostolic mission of the newly formed Society of Jesus evolved gradually and the universal apostolic mission was indicated by the Fourth Vow through which the professed members of the Society oblige themselves to 'special obedience to the sovereign pontiff regarding missions'.[54]

O'Malley comments that this was 'a vow of mobility, that is, a commitment to travel anywhere in the world for the help of souls... The Fourth Vow was thus one of the best indications of how the new order wanted to break with the monastic tradition'.[55] This was a new, active order whose members were nourished by a strong spiritual life whilst working for the 'greater glory of God' - contemplation in action. Mary Ward was to envisage the same kind of life for the members of her Institute.

The Catholic response to the reformers was therefore twofold. One was the response which consisted of retreat into re-establishing Catholic tradition as epitomised in the sessions of the Council of Trent. At the same time there was also a second, creative response evident in the rise of new religious orders, such as that founded by Ignatius Loyola for men and that of the Ursulines established by Angela Merici for women. It was this second response that gave impetus to Mary Ward's endeavours and to which she was in turn to contribute new thinking about the kind of life appropriate for women religious, usually referred to as nuns.

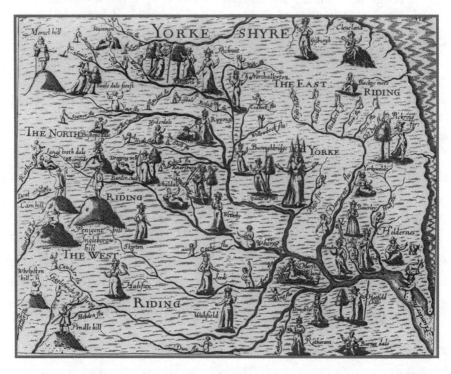

Map of Yorkshire showing Mary Ward's birthplace. (From 'Poly-Olbion' by Michael Drayton, 1622.)

CHAPTER 2

Women in the Reformation Period

In order to contextualise the work of specific women of the Reformation period, in this case Mary Ward, it is necessary to consider the situation of European and English women in general at this time. Although the finding and accessing of primary sources is difficult when studying the history of the women in the Reformation period, according to Wiesner, more has been written about women of this period than in previous historical periods.[1] This chapter then gives an overview of the situation of women in the Reformation period.

Although a not inconsiderable number of both Catholic and Protestant women left written testimonies of their beliefs, these are not often found in the public sphere, for as Wiesner explains: 'sources are arranged by male names, occupations, and places of residence, with women recorded sporadically and then often only when widowed or single'.[2]

As a result of her extensive research in the 1990s Wiesner asserts that women were not passive recipients of the Reformation. This too was the finding of Roland Bainton as a result of his earlier studies of Reformation women.[3] Such Protestant women as Katherine Zell, wife of the Strasbourg reformer, and the Bavarian noblewoman, Argula von Grumbach, are known to have defended, promoted and suffered for the Lutheran cause.[4] Not so well publicised is the active resistance of the Catholic women recusants in England.[5]

Religion

Women were much involved in the Reformation and the Counter-Reformation movements and also they were much influenced by them. Bainton asserted that 'the reform, in my judgment, had greater influence on the family than on the political and economic spheres'.[6]

Instead of celibacy being given an elevated status among the Protestant reformers, marriage was emphasised as being the superior way of life. The home became, and continued to be, the place where women could fulfil their religious calling because 'once the Reformation was established, most women expressed their religious convictions in a domestic, rather than in a public setting'.[7]

Martin Luther married the ex-nun Catherine von Bora (1499-1550) and they had six children. Although initially a marriage of convenience, Luther grew to love Catherine and she had a great influence over him. She was the first well-known wife in a Protestant parsonage and took her place with dignity, devotion to Luther, courage and determination.[8] On mutuality between husband and wife, Luther wrote: 'Let the wife make her husband glad to come home, and let him make her sorry to see him leave.'[9]

Nevertheless, women's place in the home, according to Luther, was an inferior one. As Douglass comments: 'All the reformers presume in Biblical fashion that the husband is the head of the household and that the wife should be obedient to him.'[10] There was however a contradiction between the theology and the practice. While Luther's wife was theoretically subordinate to him she was also very much her own person. As Bainton says of her: 'she discussed with her husband the issues of the Reformation and supported him in his polemical endeavours'.[11] Economically the household depended on her astute administration.

Lutheranism certainly gave esteem to woman in the home as wife, mother, nurturer and supporter. No doubt this advanced the cause of women in the private sphere. Women's involvement in public affairs was another matter. Katherine Zell (1497-1562) was a well-known Lutheran woman who felt called to public ministry and who resented being confined to the home. As one of the first wives of a Lutheran priest, Katherine, a gifted speaker, delivered a public address when her husband, Matthew, died in 1548.[12] She also visited and cared for the sick and published a collection of hymns. She was an active and zealous reformer - one who spoke, wrote and worked for the defence of the Reformed Church, but for this she was disciplined by the men leaders of her local church.[13]

Katherine Zell spoke strongly in defence of clerical marriage. When her husband was excommunicated for marrying her she resented the bishop's criticism and defended her position. She reminded them of St Paul's words that in Christ there is no longer male nor female, and said: 'I do not pretend to be John the Baptist rebuking the pharisees. I do not claim to be Nathan upbraiding David. I aspire only to be Balaam's ass, castigating his master.'[14]

Calvin had a happy marriage and good relationships with women. However, for him, women were naturally inferior to men, but like Luther, he also taught 'the priesthood of believers'. Calvin wrote that 'every member of the church is charged with the responsibility of public edification according to the measure of his grace, provided he perform it decently and in order'.[15] All people, men and women, within the reformed communities were then charged with the responsibility of the faith. Ordained ministry was for men only, but there was the teaching of co-responsibility in ministry and this included women in their own sphere.

The Scottish reformer, John Knox, was the toughest of the reformers in maintaining his stand on the inferiority of women.[16] The Scots believed in strong men and it was irksome for Knox to see women on the English throne. He said these queens were 'usurping men's authority in his day by ruling nations'.[17]

In the religious sphere, Reformation women were strongly influential in the area of piety. Bainton asserts that the Reformation groups placed more stress on piety than on dogma and this was 'congenial to women' especially since preaching was denied to them.[18] However, the Quakers allowed women to preach in the seventeenth century. According to Boulding: 'preaching in public was one of the worst things a woman could do in the 1600s, and Quaker women were continually preaching in public - in streets, in fields, wherever they could command an audience'.[19]

Women writers of the Reformation period arose from both Protestant and Catholic groups. Notable are: Argula von Grumbach (1492-1563), a Bavarian noblewoman who defended the Lutheran position; Marguerite of Navarre (1492-1549), and her daughter, Jeanne d'Albret (1528-1572), French women who defended the Calvinist position;[20] and Teresa of Avila (1515-1582), whose writings contributed significantly to the Catholic Counter-Reformation.

The pious writings of women both Protestant and Catholic were valued. Research reveals that 'sometimes ministers were actually instrumental in having pious women's writings published'.[21] Teresa of Avila's writing was promoted after having passed the scrutiny of the Inquisition. Mary Ward also wrote for the benefit of her associates and her manuscripts were copied and passed on for later publication.

While the writings of these women did not overtly challenge men, they did at times arouse criticism that such women were engaged in unwomanly activities. Many pamphleteers condemned women writers and preachers. While such women writers claimed that the Spirit was the source of their inspiration, they also stressed implicitly 'the spiritual equality of all men and women'.[22] In this way women challenged patriarchal thinking and the division between public and private life.

Wiesner remarks that most humanist women stopped studying and writing once they married.[23] Forward-thinking women were challenged by men, and other women, as being anti-women. Mary Ward also encountered this criticism and, in her famous 'Verity' speeches in 1617, she clearly refuted the words of the priest who said that her fervour and that of her companions would decay because 'when all is said and done they are but women'. Mary responded: 'There is no such difference between men and women that women may not do great things. And I hope in God it will be seen that women in time to come will do much.'[24]

As a result of her research, Debra Parish notes that the piety of women within their spheres of influence in home and community has been recorded and promulgated in the sermons at their burials. The sermons were delivered by church ministers, mostly Anglican or Presbyterian.[25]

However, there is ample evidence that women's 'weakness' and 'subjection' were preached from many Protestant pulpits. St Paul's words in *First Corinthians* (14:34-35): 'Women should be silent in the churches... it is shameful for a woman to speak in church', were often quoted to support the subordinate position of women in church matters such as preaching. Mary Ward was to meet this criticism of her work many times from her enemies, and it was also included in the Bull of Suppression in 1631, whereby she and her companions were condemned for undertaking works 'which are most unsuited to their weak sex and character'.[26] Wiesner also points out that 'Protestant teachings also rejected many of the activities which had given women's lives religious meaning such as Corpus Christi processions and lay female confraternities'.[27]

But this was not the only role for women in religious affairs. There were women 'prophets' who expressed themselves freely in the spirit. Many of these were regarded as witches and were dealt with accordingly. But the history of the witch-hunts, which were carried out in both Protestant and Catholic provinces, is complex and cannot be dealt with here. Suffice it to say that ongoing research shows that economic, social, political and religious changes were central to the causes of the witch-hunts and the position of women was affected by these movements.[28]

Education

Education is taken to refer to the development of the whole person, intellectually, spiritually and physically, and to include informal means and formal structures such as schools. Generally women in the upper classes in the Reformation period were literate, and educated in piety and the 'accomplishments'. The latter included needlework, dancing, calligraphy, drawing, painting, music and moral instruction.[29] They also had the knowledge of household economy and law, which was necessary for overseeing their households.[30] Universities were closed to women, but some women shared in the classical learning of the Renaissance through the bounty of their fathers who provided tutors for them, or permitted them to share their brothers' tutors.[31] Well-known examples of this in England were the daughters of Thomas More who were well-educated women.

The advent of printing and the accent on the reading of the Bible by the Protestants led to an increase in literacy among the rapidly increasing middle-class women.[32] The ability to read was not necessarily accompanied by facility in writing. Reading was considered part of religious instruction, but writing was considered a threat to males because those who could write would be able to express their own ideas, which may have been a challenge to men.[33]

Eileen Power claims that there were at least four different ways in which women of the Middle Ages were able to acquire literary education and these continued with various modifications into the early modern period of the Reformation.[34] The education of women and girls was the way Mary Ward envisaged the propagation of the faith and the enrichment of the culture for her time. Girls could be educated at:

Nunneries

Only some nunneries kept schools and these schools were not large. They took in girls (and sometimes little boys) as boarders. High fees were charged for this because the nuns needed the income for their survival. What was taught depended on the education of the nuns themselves. Power writes:

> Generally speaking in the early centuries of the Middle Ages the intellectual standards at many houses were quite high. But in the later centuries the education of the nuns themselves grew progressively worse, (as the centres of education moved from the monasteries to the universities) and Latin had died out of most convents in the fourteenth century, and French in the fifteenth century.[35]

Clearly, where the Reformation led to the closure of nunneries, as in England, it reduced this avenue of education for women.

Households of great ladies

Girls who were not educated at home were often sent to the households of great ladies. Here the children were given training in manners, and some were educated by tutors. Power claims that the correspondence of the time often showed that girls were unhappy in these circumstances.[36] This system persisted into the Reformation period in England as the children of Catholic recusants were often sent away from home for safety reasons. Mary Ward herself lived with her grandmother, Ursula Wright, from 1590 to 1595 - from the ages of five to ten. For about a year, 1597 to 1598, Mary lived with Mrs Ardington at Harewell. Later on, from 1599 to 1606 she lived with the Babthorpe family at Osgodby. Indeed until the early seventeenth century many children of the upper classes were not brought up in their familial homes. As babies they were sent out to live with wet nurses, and older children gained other experiences away from home, such as in some forms of apprenticeship.[37]

Private homes

Girls in the Middle Ages may have been educated by a tutor at home. This involved boys and girls being taught together. In England, tutors were obtained for the boys, and girls were often allowed to attend lessons - education for girls was an afterthought. Mary Ward was educated by a tutor in the Babthorpe household. She was one of the privileged ones who learnt Latin and French.[38]

Grammar schools

In the Middle Ages, grammar schools existed for boys and some also educated girls. In Paris in 1380 twenty-one schoolmistresses were registered as teachers with the masters.[39] In England there were reports of girls attending schools kept by old priests.[40] In the later Middle Ages there was an increasing accent on education in order to counteract heresy. However, few girls in the seventeenth century in England attended grammar schools and those who did were forbidden to take the ordinary public grammar course with its heavy grounding in Latin.[41]

There were also village schools which could teach girls to read. This was more the exception than the rule.[42] Women as a whole, however, displayed the same high level of illiteracy as labourers and husbandmen. A figure of ninety per cent illiteracy amongst women is given for London - the most favourable area - in 1600, declining in 1640 quite sharply to around eighty per cent; in East Anglia in the same period female illiteracy is given as nearly one hundred per cent.[43]

The less privileged woman was not in a position to command education. However, there were exceptions. Some women could read and they employed secretaries to write for them because reading and writing were skills which, as indicated previously, were not necessarily learnt together. Some also kept libraries of books. These books were generally devotional books, works of spirituality, and the Bible. Generally, however, Power says that 'it is certain that the overwhelming majority of peasant women or general domestic servants received no education at all'.[44]

Daughters of the poor did not require reading or writing to support themselves. Their education in motor skills such as knitting, weaving and sewing was obtained by observing their elders and by practice in the trades. Certainly, however, the Protestant practice of Bible-reading promoted literacy among the lower classes, including women.

In England, Thomas More was the great advocate of Christian humanism. He argued that instruction in the pagan classics combined with a study of Christian thought would educate people for a moral and enlightened society. More's daughter, Margaret Roper, became one such female scholar. However, humanist education for women was confined to a minority. As the recent studies of Warnicke point out:

Not only was an extremely small percentage of women ever offered an advanced classical or vernacular education but even by the end of Elizabeth's reign, less than five percent of them knew enough about writing to sign their names. In addition, the same dynamic process that gave rise to a variety of scholarly achievements gave rise to death and deprivation... Among pious Protestants, there was a pervasive fear that the advanced education of a woman would make her too proud to humble herself properly to her husband.[45]

Work

Domestic service was a common way of life for women in the seventeenth century. According to Fraser: 'between one quarter and one third of all households of the period contained servants'.[46] Such a life provided security but was not without its perils. Servants were welcomed into families and were often left money in family wills. They were given board and lodging and paid about two pounds per year.[47] Women domestics however were often exploited by the men of the household. This frequently resulted in pregnancy and dismissal.

Women's work then had a low status in the economy of the states.[48] Women's wages were lower than those for men. In England in 1563 the *Statute of Artificers* set women's wages at one third to one half of that for men.[49] Fraser gives examples of actual women's wages. Dairymaids received four pence a day, while maid servants received an annual wage of two pounds.[50] Nurses' wages were lower than the better class of domestic servant.[51] Young actresses were expected to work for nothing at the beginning of their careers and then would receive ten to fifteen shillings a week.[52] (But they would not have worked many weeks in the year!) Prostitution varied from six to eighteen pence per encounter according to the few sources which are available on the topic.[53]

Women of the increasing middle class supported their husbands in their work, especially when it was run from their home, and supervised their extensive household which often included apprentices. However, according to the extensive studies of Roper, when they became mistress of a workshop which was 'only through marriage to a craftsmaster, their economic opportunities were always circumscribed within a position of subordination'.[54]

Women of the upper classes, such as Mary Ward, depended upon a dowry from the family for their support and in Reformation England this dowry was the woman's means of securing a marriage partner. No longer was entry into a convent in her native land open to an English woman.

Marriage and childbirth

In the seventeenth century the average length of life was thirty-five years. This was the average life expectancy for all persons - women were not identified as a special class for analysis.[55] There was high infant mortality. Because of this, families were large, and devastating plagues required parents to have ten or more children merely to replenish the population.[56] Large families were also required as sources of labour, especially in rural families. The depiction of Reformation women in a warm, maternal glow as mothers or grandmothers is far from the reality. Women's lives were very difficult because of the perils of childbirth. Having survived childbirth, women were often widowed, as men were more prone to disease than women, and there was the continuous threat of death to men in wars at home or abroad.[57]

With such frequent and early deaths, remarriage several times was more the norm than the exception. According to Fraser in seventeenth century England: '... about one quarter of all marriages were a remarriage for either the

bride or the groom. Four or even five marriages in a lifetime were as likely to be achieved then in a society with a
high rate of mortality...'[58] There were many Catholic and
Protestant women in Europe and England who were widowed through persecution.

Remarriage was often a necessity for women who had
no other means of support. This is illustrated well in Mary
Ward's own family as her mother was twice married. Ursula
Ward's first husband, John Constable, was imprisoned in
York for recusancy in 1580 and died there in 1582.[59] Those
women who survived the perils of childbirth, disease and
hard work often lived to old age - sometimes a remarkable
old age of one hundred years or more. Fraser remarks: 'it
would not be so much the lack of aged persons as the lack
of a large middle-aged group which would surprise us about
the seventeenth century in contrast to our world today'.[60]

A problem for women in the Reformation period was
the crowded living space in which they experienced their
domestic lives. As we have seen, women did not have careers as we know them, and so worked at home in child-
rearing, cooking, cleaning, sewing, or working in the fields.
Remarriages, where both partners often had young children
from their previous marriage, led to crowded spaces in
which the melded households had to live. According to
Boulding: 'few working-class families had more space than
was needed for sleeping and eating'.[61] Domestic crowding
exacerbated psychological and physical pressures. This certainly gave way to domestic violence and there are accounts
of mothers beating their daughters.[62]

Wealthy widows were more fortunate in so far as they
did not need to remarry, and if they chose to do so, their
money was often a bargaining point in the choice of a new
marriage partner. Fraser notes that 'city wives were particularly well treated: by the Custom of London a wife had

the right to one third of her husband's property at death, and if there were no children, their one third also'.[63]

There was little outlet for unmarried women, especially those of high purpose wanting to be of service to the society in which they lived. The size of the dowry required for the middle- or upper-class woman to marry greatly increased the number who would have formerly chosen to join convents, but in England this was no longer an option and decreasingly so on the continent. The lack of this option increased the number of spinsters in the middle and upper classes.[64] As a child, Mary Ward had never seen a nun and only became aware of the existence of such a lifestyle through an elderly domestic servant. As will be seen later, this encounter engendered in Mary a high regard for religious life which imposed challenging demands on people and saw to it that they were upheld.[65]

This desire for the option of the equivalent of a convent life was to be forcefully argued for by the seventeenth century feminist, Mary Astell. In her first book, *A Serious Proposal*, Mary Astell proposed a scheme for an all-female college, a 'Protestant nunnery', with an insistence on a woman's right to a life of the mind, but in a due subserviency to the Almighty.[66]

Relationship with husband

The Reformers no longer saw marriage as a sacrament. Marriage laws were seen to belong in the public sphere. Luther opposed divorce, but Bucer favoured divorce when the conditions of marriage, especially love, were lacking.[67]

John Calvin taught that wives were subordinate in marriage and were to obey their husbands. However, he also stressed mutual respect between partners. Husbands' rights to rule over their wives were not enforceable in two exceptional cases: the wife may escape from her husband if she is in danger of death, and she should refuse to obey commands causing her to sin against God.[68]

Because the number of adherents to the Reformed religions was increasing there were many marriages between those of different religions and this frequently caused dissension between the partners. In England husbands often paid the recusancy fines for their wives and even moved their families into other dwellings to avoid detection.

The Reformers, like the Catholics, exhorted women to obey their husbands. Their obedience was to be cheerful, and women were to be silent when men were enforcing their authority. There were manuals for men giving them advice about how to enforce their authority and these often included physical coercion.[69] Wiesner notes that stories of husbands beating their wives do not commonly feature in the literature of the times, although other sources indicate that domestic violence was commonplace.[70]

However, wife-beating was common and as Osment points out: 'in the communities of Reformation Europe it was believed that marriage, family, and society could not long survive if the fathers of the house lost their nerve... Wife-beating and cuckolding certainly knew no religious confession.'[71]

Protestant writers, like the Catholics, cited the three purposes of marriage as: the procreation of children, the avoidance of sin, and mutual help and companionship. However, the ideal of mutuality in marriage was not an ideal of equality because the stress was on husbandly authority and wifely obedience.[72] While the Catechism of the Council of Trent says it is the duty of a husband to treat his wife courteously and with honour, she was not to be the mistress of, but rather subject to, her husband. The husband has the duty to provide necessaries for the support of the family, to keep his family in order, and to correct the morals of all.[73] In the same Catechism the next Question, XXVII, asks what the duty of a wife requires and the initial part of the answer quotes St Peter where he says: 'Let wives be subject to their husbands.' *(1 Pet* 3:1) The Catechism further enunciates the duties of wives:

> Be it also a principal study of theirs to train up their children in the practice of religion, and to take particular care of the domestic concerns. Unless necessity oblige them to go abroad let them willingly remain at home; and let them never venture to leave home without the permission of their husbands. Again, and in this the conjugal union chiefly consists, let them always remember that, next to God, no one is to be loved more than their husband... whom they shall also honour and obey with the greatest alacrity of mind, in all things not inconsistent with Christian piety.[74]

According to Scarisbrick, after the Reformation in England women lost an outlet for leadership in the Church when the various lay confraternities, usually in the form of guilds, were abolished. Formerly, women had been active in the guilds and even held office.[75]

The leaders of the Reformation accentuated the woman's role in the home as they denigrated celibacy and exalted the married woman above the nun, whose role they formally abolished through the closure of monasteries. But this limited Protestant women's scope to the private sphere and young Catholic women like Mary Ward and her companions, eager to participate in the wider community of the Church and society, sought again the structure of the religious life, though, as will be seen, adapted to changed conditions in society. They saw such a structure as providing authority, support, resources, freedom from the restrictions of marriage, and scope for service and leadership in the wider community - especially as educators in the faith.

Class

The social class in which women found themselves in Reformation times made a great difference to their lives. As has been indicated, opportunities for education was one such difference. For example, Queen Elizabeth I was educated by private tutors, among whom the famous scholar, Ascham, is named as the one who taught her to read Greek fluently and to speak it moderately well. Elizabeth was also fluent in Latin and sometimes astonished her hearers by a spontaneous Latin oration. She was also able to speak Italian, and, of course, French.[76] Elizabeth also wrote the Italic hand, which was easier to read than the Secretary script which was used in legal documents. Mary Ward, belonging to the upper class, was also tutored in several languages by her grandmother, Ursula Wright, and by the tutors who taught the Babthorpe children.

Being in the upper classes usually provided a woman with resources to further her personal interests. These resources, apart from those of a financial nature, also provided her with power through connections with influential relatives, friends and patrons. As will be seen, Mary Ward benefited greatly from such advantages connected with her class.

Class also brought certain responsibilities as the women of the upper classes had responsibilities in organising their households and, at times, their husbands' affairs, which involved their having authority over men of lower social status.[77] Women also had power through their status to act as patrons for both women and men - especially for those in the lower classes. Mary Ward was to benefit from the patronage of such women as the Infanta Isabella.

Law

The general position of European working women before the law in the late sixteenth century to the eighteenth century was summarised by Natalie Davis:

> Women suffered for their powerlessness in both Catholic and Protestant lands in the late sixteenth to eighteenth centuries as changes in marriage laws restricted the freedoms of wives even further, as female guilds dwindled, as the female role in middle-level commerce and farm direction contracted, and as the differential between male and female wages increased.[78]

By 1603, the year when Queen Elizabeth I died in England, women lived under common law. A woman was under the guardianship of her father and then her husband, if she married. An unmarried woman was protected by her father or another male. As Fraser explained: 'Legally, the position of the "feme sole" was equally ignored: her legal rights were assumed to be swallowed up in those of her nearest male protector.'[79] With regard to women and property the common law asserted: 'That which the husband hath is his own - that which the wife hath is her husband's.'[80] Formerly, the law of equity, which operated out of chancellery under the influence of the Church, had modified the harshness of common law.[81]

Fraser explains that for widowed women who did not remarry, or for those who were single (the term 'spinster' became the legal term in the seventeenth century for the unmarried female), a guardian had to be chosen.[82] This male guardian was to oversee their financial affairs and to appear for them in court. However, European court records show that women did appear in court.[83] Argula von Grumbach was a Bavarian noblewoman who defended the Lutheran position in court. Women certainly appeared in the English recusancy courts, as the case of Margaret Clitherow well illustrates.[84]

There is evidence that some women did not accept their situation tamely. They objected to having guardians because they believed that decisions within their households (which women were free to make) were as much in the public sphere as were the affairs of men. They argued that households were taxed, not persons, and women were included in a household. They concluded therefore that women had a public legal right to act for themselves without guardians.[85]

The dependency of women on their husbands worked to their advantage when it was a matter of delinquency. Because the rights of women in law were technically their husbands', then a woman's husband was also responsible for her crimes; but a husband's crimes could not be attributed to the wife. However, as Fraser remarks, although women were not responsible for their husbands' crimes, they endured '... all the same their practical consequences'.[86] Wives obviously suffered when their husbands were gaoled.

As indicated previously, up until about 1600 in England, many Protestant men had Catholic wives. The problems of recusancy fines or imprisonment for such spouses had confronted Parliament for many years. According to Bossy, Parliamentarians did not 'like to punish the innocent husband by upsetting his housekeeping and depriving him of services to which he was entitled'.[87] This certainly indicates the attitude that women were primarily the servants of men.

Nevertheless, it seems that women were not so easily controlled. In 1593 in England, the Council of the North tried to put a bill through Parliament which would have imposed on husbands a fine of ten pounds a month - half the recusancy fine - for having a recusant wife. In 1610 a new Act was passed whereby a husband would have to pay half a fine, or an equivalent in seized property, before he could get an imprisoned wife home again. It became a dead letter when justices of the peace refused to co-operate.[88] This could be interpreted that it was recognised locally that the control of a woman's religious adherence was beyond the sphere of the husband, and a corollary could be that there was a significant number of independently-minded women at that time.

Political influence

In Reformation times, women were involved in politics in that they could be used as political pawns in arranged marriages, if they belonged to the governing class. They could also at times exert personal influence on the leaders through their personal charm and force of personality.

However, women did not always submit to politically contrived marriages. For example, Jeanne d'Albret was the only child of Marguerite of Navarre and Henri d'Albret and, in a merging of politics and religion, her uncle, Francis I, imposed on her a marriage to the Duke of Cleves, a relative of Anne of Cleves, one of the wives of Henry VIII. Although she was only fourteen, Jeanne protested and had to be carried to the altar. The marriage was soon annulled.[89]

A second marriage of Jeanne d'Albret to Antoine de Bourbon followed. It was an attempt to consolidate territories in the north and south of France. Although they appeared to love one another there was an eventual rift over religion when Jeanne embraced Calvinism in 1560. Destructive religious wars in France followed and Jeanne was caught between Catholics and the Reformers.

As Queen of Navarre, Jeanne had considerable political power. Concerning the religious conflict she took a conciliatory stance, but she was a Huguenot believer and this influenced her decisions. When the Catholic ecclesiastical revenues were being dispersed Jeanne argued, according to Bainton, that 'the money should not go into the coffers of the state but should be used for the Reformed ministers, schools - she established a university - and the relief of the poor. But she did allow some funds to be used for the expenses of the war.'[90]

Some points about the latter mother and daughter are worth making in the context of the Reformation women and their education. Marguerite was the elder sister of Francis 1 of France. When Francis was away at war or imprisoned (he was a prisoner of the Spanish in 1525) he entrusted the administration of the kingdom to Marguerite.[91] Certainly, national security was involved here, and elder sisters were supposed to be trustworthy, but Marguerite was an able woman for this position. She is described as 'a lady of the Renaissance who read Dante in Italian, Plato possibly in Greek, and Luther to a slight degree in German'.[92] Francis and his sister favoured the new learning and this led her into favouring the Reformed Church. Marguerite wrote poetry and prose - all religious writings. At her death in 1549 it was said of her that 'she so hallowed the soil of Navarre, that it became the most fruitful field of the Huguenot movement to be spearheaded by her daughter, Jeanne d'Albret'.[93]

Mary Ward benefited from the support of politically powerful women. Such a one was the Infanta Isabella Clara Eugenia. The Infanta helped Mary with the foundation for the English Poor Clares in Gravelines, Brussels, which was then Spanish territory. She also wrote a letter of introduction for Mary and her associates to Pope Gregory XV.[94] Again the Infanta Isabella advised Mary to wear pilgrim's clothing on her journey to Rome. She also supported the Sisters in Rome by sending money to them via the Spanish Papal Ambassador, Cardinal Vives. At the Infanta's insistence, Vives obtained a papal audience for them in 1621.

The Electress Elisabeth of Bavaria was another of Mary Ward's politically influential noble friends. She and her husband, the Elector Maximilian I, gave the Sisters the Paradeiser House in Munich and supported them for years. Elisabeth sent a carriage to take Mary home from the Anger prison in 1631, even though there were strained relations between them at this time because of the Church's bull suppressing Mary's Institute.

Pope Urban VIII's sister-in-law, Donna Constanza Barberini, was a friend and supporter of Mary Ward. When the Roman house was ordered to be closed in 1625 the mothers of the pupils made representations to Donna Constanza for a stay of these proceedings.[95] Donna Constanza also recommended Mary to the Papal Envoy in England, Carlo Rossetti, who arrived there in 1639.

On Mary Ward's side of their friendship we have the account, in Chambers, of Donna Constanza's request to Mary Ward to receive a marchesa into the community for two or three months. Although this was inconvenient for the Sisters, Mary Ward consented and the marchesa lived with them. Chambers comments: 'Whatever inconvenience the Princess caused the English Ladies by her charity in this instance, her friendship became life-long and publicly known.'[96] Indeed Mary was not loath to seek the assistance of noble ladies and it was given generously many times.

Men of lower classes also depended on the patronage of such women. Ignatius Loyola, as a religious leader, sought and enjoyed the patronage of women as he was often dependent upon the largesse of noblewomen for the initiation or continuation of the mission of the Jesuits. Indeed, as indicated in the times of religious upheaval of the Reformation period, women were frequently powerful protectors of the clergy - the new Reformed clergy and Catholic clergy - depending on the circumstances.

Queen Elizabeth I (1558-1603) was another royal woman who had a strong influence on political affairs. She was an extraordinary woman of the Reformation. Elizabeth I even created a public festival for her Accession Day. Catholic festivals had been suppressed by Protestantism and Elizabeth attempted to replace them by her own celebration.[97] It has been assessed that she 'presented herself to the nation as both man and woman, queen and king, mother and firstborn son'.[98] The representation of herself in this androgynous form was her ploy to boost the concept and image of a female monarch.

Strategically, Elizabeth I presented herself as a male when she required strength over the males in Parliament. She used this appeal in 1563, and again in 1566, in response to a petition that she marry and declare a successor. Marcus commented: 'On one such occasion early in her reign she held up the hand bearing her coronation ring, seeming to portray herself as the nation's wife.'[99] In her Armada speech before the troops at Tilbury in 1588 (when Mary Ward was three years old) Queen Elizabeth presented herself in the dress of a king saying: 'I have the body of a weak and feeble woman, but I have the heart and stomach of a king, and of a king of England too.'[100]

How did this royal androgynous view of the English monarchy affect the lives of other English women? Marcus claims: 'the male-female heroine's capacity to revive and renew, died along with Queen Elizabeth I'.[101] This conclusion could be questioned in the light of the strength of subsequent English women, among whom were the recusant women, including Mary Ward, though it is highly unlikely that her role models began and ended with Elizabeth I.

In Italy there were still monasteries and nunneries. In the latter some of the women were there as 'forced vocations' because the only options for 'respectable' women were marriage or the nunnery. Much of the life in the nunneries was described as 'vitiated by worldliness, relaxation and coldness in their apostolic work'.[102] However, in general, in Italy the Reformation failed and much of its energy was used ultimately in the Counter-Reformation.[103] The influence of women in this country appears to be more that of the influence of the princesses and noblewomen. They were influential with their money and their persuasive powers with men, including cardinals and popes. Mary Ward was to experience their political influence, as we have noted above.

Parish, as a result of her research concerning Reformation women, is of the opinion that, instead of women appearing in 'silence' and 'subjection' (St Paul's words), they are shown as actively participating in political and religious debate. Their pious lives and strong defence of their religious beliefs bring into question the historical assumptions that female religious influence was confined to the household sphere.[104] Mary Ward certainly moved beyond the household sphere and became politically involved.

CHAPTER 3

Mary Ward: Beginnings

Family influences and education

Mary Ward was born in 1585 at a time when Protestantism was led resolutely by Queen Elizabeth I. The English sea victory over the Spanish Armada in 1588 reinforced Elizabeth's position as a powerful head of both state and Church, and helped her to gain a firmer hold on the English nation.

Mary was born into a recusant family in Yorkshire where Catholicism remained firmly entrenched. Marmaduke Ward and his wife, Ursula Wright, had six children (four girls and two boys) in ten years. The strong Catholic background of the family is reflected in the fact that the four girls were to enter religious orders and one of the boys was to become a Jesuit.

Mary was the eldest of the six children. Her sisters Barbara and Elizabeth entered Mary's Institute. Teresa (Francis) became a Carmelite in the Netherlands. John (David) married, but was tragically killed in a duel. George entered the Society of Jesus in 1619 in St Omer. He worked on the English mission and died in London in 1654.[1]

The early biographies give Mary's baptismal name as Johanna or Joanna. But where was Mary Ward baptised? Peters says that the Ripon parish registers are incomplete and that it is possible that Mary was baptised secretly, though the early sources do not hint at that.[2] However, the early biographies say that the name of Mary was added by her at confirmation. This choice of name clearly indicated her love of Our Blessed Lady. Mary was the name by which she was known from then on.

As the last Catholic archbishop of York, Nicholas Heath, had already been removed from his see by 1559, it is unlikely that Mary Ward was confirmed in England. Peters hazards that she was confirmed in Flanders as records show that the Bishop of St Omer confirmed young girls in the Englishwomen's chapel some years later, in 1619.[3] In Mother Immolata's writing on Mary's devotion to Our Blessed Lady she claims that Mary was confirmed at St Omer some time after Whitsun 1606.[4] Mary would then have been twenty-one years old.

Ursula Ward's marriage to Marmaduke Ward was her second marriage. Her first husband, John Constable, had been imprisoned in York for recusancy in 1580 and died there in 1582.[5] Peters asserts that Marmaduke Ward and Ursula Constable were married sometime between July 1582 and April 1584.[6]

Questions are often asked about the social status of the Wards. Peters points out that while the Ward family was one of the oldest families in the county, they did not belong to the nobility, but were armigerous landed gentry. On the continent, such a family might be reckoned minor nobility, but not in England. The Wards obviously belonged to the upper class in England, because they had resources to pay the recusancy fines and they lived in large family homes.

Early biographers assumed the continental way of describing them and referred to Marmaduke Ward as 'Lord', or 'Gentleman'.[7] If Marmaduke Ward bore a coat of arms it has not been displayed, although it was claimed by Chambers that the Ward shield bore a cross patonce Or on an Azure field, which was seen on the choir screen in Ripon cathedral.[8] Peters claims that this was the coat of arms of Ursula Wright and her first husband, John Constable. On the continent, Mary Ward and her Sisters were known as *virgines nobles*. However, Mary never used a personal seal that would have shown a family coat of arms. When she later sealed important letters, her sign of authentication was as similar as possible to the seal of the Society of Jesus.[9]

About Marmaduke and Ursula Ward, their daughter Mary wrote in 1617: 'My parents were both virtuous and suffered much for the Catholic cause.'[10] Recusants had to pay fines for not attending Anglican services. It is recorded in the Recusant Rolls held in the Record Office in London that Ursula Ward was fined forty pounds on two occasions for such recalcitrant conduct.[11] Marmaduke Ward likewise paid many such fines.[12]

When Mary was five years old she was sent to live with her maternal grandparents - Robert and Ursula Wright - on a large estate, Ploughland, near Welwick in Holderness, East Yorkshire. Mary recalled: 'I was now full five years old when by what means or procurement I know not, I was sent to my grandfather and grandmother, parents of my mother to be brought up.'[13] According to Peters, it was possibly a case of security - security for Mary as a Catholic child, and for the Catholic household where Catholics (especially priests) were often sheltered. A small child could unwittingly give clues to their Catholic practices.[14]

At her grandparents' home Mary came under the powerful influence of her grandmother, Ursula Wright, of whom she wrote:

> My grandmother was noted and esteemed for her great virtue. She had in her younger years suffered imprisonment for the space of fourteen years together; in which times she

had made profession of her faith before the president of York, Huntingdon, and other officers... When I came to her, she had been released for a few years and had come to live at home.[15]

Also present in the household were her mother's younger sisters, Martha and Alice. It appears that Alice was about Mary's age and somewhat frivolous.[16] Mary reacted against this as she responded to the strong moral and prayerful example of her grandmother. Again of her grandmother Mary recalled: '... so great a pray-er was she that I do not remember in that whole five years that I ever saw her asleep, nor did I ever wake when I did not perceive her to be at her prayers'.[17] Ursula Wright senior appears to have been a woman of steadfast faith and one of the great English 'matriarchs'.

As an educated woman, Ursula Wright directed Mary's studies during the five years she was with her. It is recorded that 'beside the instruction usually given to children, she [Mary] learned Latin, in which she was sufficiently proficient to be able to write it fluently in after life, and also to be well read in the writings of the Fathers'.[18]

After the death of her grandfather, Mary returned to her parents who were living at Mulwith where they stayed until a fire burnt down the family home. After this they spent a short period in Newby before moving to Northumberland. By this time the position of Catholics was becoming increasingly difficult. Mary was sent to reside in the house of Mrs Catherine Ardington, who was the daughter of Sir William Ingleby of Ripley Castle. The Inglebys were related to Mary through her mother's family, the Wrights. Mary made her first Communion there at Harewell on 8 September 1598.

In the person of Catherine Ardington, Mary once again came under the influence of an heroic Catholic English woman of whom it is noted by Peters:

In 1586/7 and in 1594 she [Catherine Ardington] had been taken from her home in Nidderdale and put into the ill-famed prison of York, but she remained steadfast in her Catholicism. The house had a hiding-hole, reached by a secret passage where priests took refuge from pursuivants. Mrs. Ardington offered help to other recusants, and Marmaduke found her ready to accept his daughter into her household.[19]

Mary Ward's next move was to stay with the distinguished Babthorpe family at Babthorpe and Osgodby from 1599 to 1606. The Babthorpes lived on these two estates a few miles apart. They had owned them since the reign of Henry V. Edmund Campion, the noted English martyr, is known to have been at Osgodby.[20]

The Babthorpes were related to Mary through her mother's family, the Wrights. Mary explained that she went away from her home on this occasion because her parents' move to Northumberland was considered to be a threat to her health, since the climate there was too harsh. Joining the Babthorpe household was also a move designed to give Mary a better opportunity of finding a suitable marriage partner.[21]

Here, Mary was under the influence of still another strong woman who had suffered for her faith. Grace Babthorpe had spent five years in prison for adhering to her Catholic faith and her husband, Sir Ralph, had been under such great pressure that he had attended Anglican services. They were ultimately ruined financially and later migrated to Louvain.[22] Mary was greatly influenced by the spiritual life and practices of the deeply religious Babthorpe household.

With her cousins, the Babthorpe children, Mary was educated by tutors. She learnt further Latin, French, Italian and German - languages which she would use in subsequent years. This was an instance (as in the case of Sir Thomas More) where the family had tutors who taught both boys and girls because the parents thought it important to educate the girls also.

It was during this time that Mary met Margaret Garret who was described as 'an old, simple but very devout maid who looked after the chapel and probably did light work'.[23] Through stories which Margaret Garret told her about life in monasteries and nunneries in England before their dissolution, Mary Ward became greatly interested in religious life. Indeed this was a key time for Mary as she became possessed by a strong resolve to be a religious. She was fifteen years of age. Concerning this resolve she writes in her autobiography:

> This affection to the religious life was in general, for I had no inclination to any Order in particular, only I was resolved within myself to take the most strict and secluded, thinking and often saying that, as women did not know how to do good except to themselves, a penuriousness which I resented enough even then, I would do in good earnest what I did.[24]

Mary's desire to be a religious was soon to be tested. At first there was the opposition of her parents. She recorded: 'My parents, though otherwise extraordinary pious, would not for any consideration give their consent, for I was the eldest child and much loved, especially by my father. I was therefore obliged to remain in England six years and some months longer.'[25] Marmaduke Ward had marriage plans for this much-loved daughter.

Marriage offers

Historical sources list several suitors for Mary's hand. One suitor is reputed to have offered to marry Mary when she was thirteen and living at the house of Mrs Ardington at

Harewell.[26] Mary refused them all. Her vocation was tested thoroughly by the offer of marriage from Edmund Neville. He had claim to the title, Earl of Westmoreland, and would have inherited extensive estates. This union with Mary would have established another Catholic family in the north of England - a family which was urgently needed to bolster the cause of Catholics in the north.

Neville appeared ideally suited to marry Mary. According to Peters:

> Edmund or Edward Neville was born in 1563 and therefore was about forty years old when he sought Mary Ward's hand. He was a schismatic until he was 28, attending Anglican services, although without inner conviction. He became a convert... He had sworn, should Mary Ward refuse him, to seek no other wife. His claim to the title and possessions fell into Anglican hands. In 1606 he entered the English College in Rome (alias Eliseus Nelson) and became a Jesuit. Neville died in 1648 on the English mission.[27]

Mary's confessor at the time, Father Holtby SJ, advised her that even if she had already been a novice in a Convent it would have been her duty to leave it and marry Edmund Neville. Still, Mary would not consent. She made her own discernment about going abroad to become a religious - not an easy choice since there was pressure to remain and support the Catholic cause at home through marriage to Edmund Neville. However, Mary discerned that it was her duty to become a religious.

Eventually Mary's father relented and looked more favourably upon her desire to be a religious. It has been suggested that the harsher laws against Catholics that followed the discovery of the Gunpowder Plot in 1605 may have contributed to this change of attitude.[28] Father Holtby SJ, Mary's confessor, also withdrew his opposition to Mary's desire to follow a religious vocation after he accidentally spilt consecrated wine from the chalice at Mass in London in 1606. This brought about such a change in him that, after the Mass was finished and she handed him the towel to dry his hands, he said to her with flowing tears: 'May it be far from me to hinder your religious project any further. Rather I will endeavour to further it.'[29] The incident is depicted in the fourteenth painting of *The Painted Life* and was thus obviously considered an important incident in Mary's life.

Continental endeavours (1606-1609)

In 1606 Mary was twenty-one and, as an adult Catholic, she was subject to the recusancy fines, so it was an appropriate time for her to go to the continent to follow her religious vocation. She travelled to Flanders in the company of Mrs Catherine Bentley who was the great grand-daughter of St Thomas More, her grandmother being Margaret Roper, Thomas More's favourite daughter. Mary Ward travelled as one of Mrs Bentley's daughters. Of this occasion Mary wrote: '... we went to Dover, a port town of England, and then passed the seas in four or five hours and arrived at Calais, and from thence to the city of St Omer'.[30]

Archduke Albrecht of Austria, grandson of Charles V, had been chosen by Phillip II of Spain to marry his daughter, the Infanta Isabella Clara Eugenia and he gladly agreed. The marriage was happy but childless. Isabella had received a good education at the Spanish court. Her father gave her the Netherlands as a wedding gift on condition that it would revert to Spain if she remained childless, though this secret pact was not generally known. The Spanish Netherlands therefore remained Catholic, despite the Dutch Calvinists in the north, the influence of the French Huguenots in the south and centres of the Reformed Churches of the Rhineland to the east. It was a land in which Catholics could live free and peaceful lives, but it was an uneasy peace.[31]

The town of St Omer, Mary's destination, was about thirty kilometres inland from Calais. It contained six parishes at this time. Jacques Blaes was bishop there from 1601 to 1618. He had been Provincial of the Franciscans and promoted education in his diocese. He had enlarged the Douai seminary for diocesan priests and this had become a training place for secular priests for the English Catholic Church. He specifically encouraged the education of girls. In 1615 he completed the building of a house for Marie Aubrun, daughter of Councillor Aubrun, who was instructing poor girls in her own home.[32]

Bishop Blaes was very supportive of the English Catholic refugees. Of him it was said that 'He was a man of great character; a man of principle, learned in many disciplines and experienced in ecclesiastical matters.'[33] He was to prove a good friend to Mary and supported her in later years.[34]

When Mary arrived in Flanders in 1606 there were several institutes that followed the Rule of St Francis and had some members who were emigré English Catholic women. These institutes were popularly known as Grey Sisters; Black Sisters; the Poor Clares; and the Rich Clares, who were called Urbanists, who did not beg for a living. Those following the Rule of St Dominic were the Sisters of St Catherine, the Sisters of Sion and the Sisters of St Margaret.[35]

The English Jesuits conducted a well-known boys' school in St Omer. During the French Revolution this school transferred to England where it was known as Stonyhurst.[36] Mary Ward had letters of introduction from England addressed to Father Flake SJ at the Jesuit College, but Father George Keynes, Professor of Moral Theology at the English Seminary, was the first to greet her. He assured Mary that she was expected at the Convent of the Poor Clares. He declared, however, that she could not be a choir sister there since the convent had reached its limit of thirty Sisters per house. She was expected to be a lay Sister.

Father Keynes assured Mary that both choir and lay Sisters followed the strict Rule of St Clare. In fact this was not so because the lay Sisters were tertiaries of the Third Order of St Francis. The Poor Clares urgently needed an outsister and Mary accepted that it was God's will that she should undertake this.

Extern Sister to Poor Clares

As an outsister it was Mary's duty to walk the streets begging and carrying back to the convent the heavy baskets of food. However, she was entirely unsuited to this work because of her upbringing and frail health, but she continued to do it in a spirit of obedience despite her own anxieties and queries about her from ladies of the town who 'asked the abbess why such a gentle and delicate young girl had been given this sort of work'.[37]

On St Gregory's day in 1607 Mary was summoned to speak to the Franciscan Visitor, Father de Soto. He told Mary that she was not suited to the life in the Poor Clare convent. Then strangely, but also providentially, Mary had the insight of establishing a separate convent for English Poor Clares. The difference in language was a problem for Mary as well as for other English women seeking to become religious on the continent.

Mary left the Poor Clares as an outsister in April or May 1607. After a year, during which little is known of her activities, Bishop Blaes wrote a letter of recommendation for her to the Archduke Albrecht. The Archduke's sister was a Poor Clare nun in Madrid.[38] Subsequently a house and a piece of land for the English Poor Clares was given to them by the Governor. This was at Gravelines on the coast between Calais and Dunkirk. Gravelines was a fortified town and the Council of Trent had offered the advice that new foundations of nuns should be in fortified towns in order that the Sisters be given some protection.[39] The English Sisters dispensed with begging - they would be supported by their own dowries and by the governor.

New convent for English Poor Clares

The English women eventually moved to Gravelines after the resolution of the many difficulties and intrigues that arose between the Bishop of Ypres (the diocese in which Gravelines was situated) and the Governor of Gravelines. In November 1608 an English Jesuit, Father Roger Lee, gave the thirty-day Spiritual Exercises of St Ignatius to the professed nuns who had moved from the Walloon Poor Clare house, and then to the new candidates among whom was Mary Ward. Mary was later to secure English Jesuit confessors for the Sisters - the English language was the main reason, but Jesuits directing Franciscans was an innovation.

Mary's former Novice Mistress, Mary Stephen Goudge, was appointed by the Franciscan Bishop Blaes as Abbess. She refused Mary Ward permission to make her vows as a Poor Clare. Mary's sister, Frances, was clothed. Mary was to have further formation as a Poor Clare. This was providential because without this intervention Mary would then have been professed as a Poor Clare Sister.

On St Athanasius' Day, 2 May 1609, Mary had a decisive revelation. She says of it: '... Here it was shown to me that I was not to be of the Order of St Clare; some other thing I was to do. What or of what nature I did not see, nor could I guess, only that it was a good thing and what God willed.'[40]

All this caused Mary great pain. After another six months, in order to discern her options, Mary left the Poor Clares in the autumn of 1609. She recorded that before Father Roger Lee she made a private 'vow of perpetual chastity and another to obey him in this particular, that if, or when he should command me to enter into the Teresians (Carmelites), I would obey'.[41]

The Gravelines convent was subsequently returned to Franciscan direction and the Jesuit influence disappeared. The English Jesuits had been keen to have a convent to which they could send English women refugees. It is significant to note here that the Jesuit General, Father Claudio Aquaviva, had written from Rome to the Flanders Provincial saying that the Jesuit Constitutions forbade a Jesuit to direct or meddle in the affairs of women's orders.[42]

The Gravelines convent survived until the French Revolution, when the nuns withdrew and settled in their homeland, England. Mary Ward maintained a cordial relationship with those in her first foundation.[43]

Return to England. Revelation

Mary Ward returned to England in 1609 and appears to have stayed with family and friends in various parts of the country. While in England at this time she had the first of the three pivotal experiences which were to point the way for the foundation of an active religious institute for women. According to Mary she was doing her hair before a mirror after making her 'meditation coldly' when she had a profound spiritual experience. In her autobiography Mary describes what she then understood intellectually:

> It was shown to me with clearness and inexpressible certainty that I was not to be of the Order of St. Teresa, but that some other thing was determined for me, without all comparison more to the glory of God... I did not see what the assured good thing would be, but the glory of God which was to come through it, showed itself inexplicably and so abundantly as to fill my soul in such a way that I remained for a good space without feeling or hearing anything, but

the sound, **Glory, Glory, Glory.** ... returning to myself, I
found my heart full of love for this thing, accompanied by
such glory that not yet can I comprehend what it was.[44]

This spiritual illumination came to Mary to enlighten her
as to the future, but not to give her clarity as to what she
should do. By this time she had received these revelations:
- to found a house in Flanders of English Poor Clares;
- to leave that order, and therefore her own foundation;
- to abandon the idea of becoming a Carmelite, and therefore the idea of a contemplative life.[45]

About this time in England, Mary Ward was joined by
companions who wanted to assist Catholics in this dangerous and crucial period of their history. Of this group Peters
comments: 'The impetus towards forming a community at
the end of 1609 may have originated from the first people
who worked with her in England, and not from Mary Ward
herself.'[46] That her companions wished to live in a community with Mary was typical of English Catholics who
grouped together at this time for support, and for the nurture of their faith. Mary had shown herself a strong, attractive leader by her foundation at Gravelines.

When Mary left England several companions travelled
with her to St Omer. It is not known whether or not her
first companions were all with her then, or joined her later,
but it is known that they were: Winifred Wigmore, Mary
Poyntz, Johanna Browne, Susanna Rookwood, Catherine
Smith, Barbara Babthorpe and Mary's sister, Barbara
Ward.[47]

All these women were from a recusant background and
belonged to families from the north of England. In the picture from *The Painted Life* (Number 22) it is notable that Mary
and her first companions are depicted in a semi-circle with
no apparent sign of hierarchy. Mary would appear to have
emerged as the first among equals. It can also be noted that

this circle arrangement may have been just a convention used in painting at that time. People were mainly represented in *The Painted Life* with their faces to the front, perhaps because these paintings were to be an historical record for Mary's Institute, and the key people needed to be shown.

Mary knew St Omer well from her previous begging experiences for the Poor Clares. She and her companions acquired a house in what was then known as Rue Grosse. Their pastoral work was among adults who were mostly English refugees. Mary and her companions were soon called the 'English Ladies' - a name which is still used for them on the continent.

Mary Ward wrote of their intentions at this time: 'Amongst other goods to her neighbour a chief one was to employ themselves in education of youth, not only of our nation, of which there were a great many, but also those of the place where they lived, who were taught gratis, that all become good Christians and worthy women.'[48]

At this time she and her companions would also have known other groups which devoted themselves to the education of girls in the region associated with St Omer. These included the Daughters of Our Lady of the Angels, as well as the newly founded group of Marie Aubrun called Our Lady of the Garden.[49] It has already been mentioned that Bishop Blaes encouraged Marie Aubrun by building a house for her work. Another community of women in St Omer (they were spread throughout Belgium) was known as the Devout Daughters of St Agnes. At that time they were a modern pious association which followed the Augustinian rule, like that of the Ursulines in Paris. They devoted themselves to the education of girls of all classes and in 1626 they received episcopal approval.[50] Indeed, the Flemish tradition of pious women networking together was well known to Mary Ward and her companions.

English emigrant girls boarded with Mary Ward's community. Some were there for educational purposes as well as to find a place of refuge from the persecution in England. A number of these young women joined Mary's group, or the English Poor Clares, but this was not the main purpose for accepting them as students. Later accusations against Mary and her companions would be that they encouraged girls to join them and not other religious orders, and that they did not teach the native people - only the English. The accusations were unfounded as we have Mary's words (quoted above) about educating the local women, and this was achieved in St Omer as Chambers states: '... they had a day-school for the young girls of the town, and this without any remuneration'.[51]

The annals of the English Jesuits for 1610 record: 'In the town (St. Omer) are living certain young Englishwomen of high birth and excellent education. They intend to devote themselves to the spiritual life and are waiting for a suitable moment to fulfil their wishes. With general consent they left their house, and they will be helped by some of ours (the English Jesuits), because their motives are excellent.' [52] This contact with Jesuits on the continent was to be the source of later troubles for Mary Ward.

The accusations of recruiting companions were unfounded because Mary had encouraged many other women in England to enter some of the continental orders known to be in St Omer. Also by September 1611, they had still not decided on a rule. There was no lack of advice about taking a rule as Mary wrote in her autobiography: 'Great instance was made by diverse and spiritual men that we would take upon us some Rule already confirmed, several Rules were procured by our friends, both from Italy and France, and earnestly urged to make choice of some of them.'[53]

Early companions and biographers

As indicated pictorially in *The Painted Life,* Mary was the first among equals. Two of Mary Ward's early companions and first biographers were Mary Poyntz and Winifred Wigmore. According to Peters, Mary Poyntz (1593-1667) returned to St Omer with Mary Ward in 1609.[54] However, Orchard notes that she probably joined the group as a candidate or pupil as she was only sixteen at that time.[55]

Chambers reports that the Poyntz family ancestors had come to England from Normandy with William the Conqueror. Mary Poyntz' mother was Maria Wigmore and thus Mary Poyntz and Winifred Wigmore were first cousins. Mary Ward was said to be related to the Poyntz family, but the relationship is not detailed.[56]

Chambers also notes that Mary Poyntz was a very gifted person and a staunch friend of Mary Ward. It appears probable that she had one sister, Frances, who also joined her Institute. Her Jesuit brother, John, was on the English mission in 1624. He was subsequently Rector of the English College in Rome from 1659 to 1663.[57]

The Poyntz family lived in Gloucestershire and Mary Ward apparently stayed with them in 1609, on her return from St Omer. It seems that Mary Poyntz was so attracted to Mary Ward that she determined to follow her. Chambers also reports that Mary Poyntz was to be married to a cavalier of rank, but she refused him when she met Mary Ward. He asked her for her portrait and she eventually gave him a portrait with one normal side of her face and the other side in apparent decay, as in death. It is reported that the cavalier was so shocked that he later entered a religious order.[58]

Mary Poyntz accompanied Mary Ward on some of her long journeys and was present at Mary Ward's death. Mary

Poyntz was Superior at Munich from 1637 to 1642 and was also Superior of the Roman House in 1633 when Mary Ward returned there to live under the eyes of the pope and cardinals who had condemned her.

According to Chambers, Mary Poyntz returned to England in 1637 with Mary Ward and Winifred Wigmore. After Mary Ward's death, Mary Poyntz again became Superior - this time of the community that moved to Paris. Mary Poyntz was elected Superior General in 1654, the second Superior General after Barbara Babthorpe. She founded the house in Augsburg in 1662 and died there on 30 September 1667.[59] She was buried in St John's Chapel in the Cathedral of Augsburg - a great honour.[60]

Mary Poyntz devoted herself to 'perfecting the work of the existing houses of the Institute as well as advancing the spirit of the individual members'.[61] She continued Mary Ward's work and spirit and her administration advanced the confirmation of the order which was given in 1703.

Winifred Wigmore (1585-1657) was the same age as Mary Ward and was her dear friend and companion. Winifred was the daughter of William Wigmore of Herefordshire and Anne Throgmorton, daughter of Sir John Throgmorton, President of Wales.

Winifred's father was a recusant Catholic. The family was numerous and six children became religious - three of them Jesuits.[62] Winifred could speak five languages and was therefore a great asset when Mary Ward founded new houses in different countries. A French obituary of her states that 'there was no business nor undertaking of Mary Ward's in which she did not take part, sharing also in her many troubles and difficulties'.[63]

Such was the calibre of the women who shared Mary Ward's ideals and supported her endeavours. As will be

seen in the next chapter they had singularly strong and re-
sourceful forerunners and contemporaries.

CHAPTER 4

Significant Initiatives of Catholic Women in Europe

In order to understand Mary Ward's work more clearly, it is helpful to know of the previous attempts to make education available to women. Mary Ward built on these initiatives, but she held to the ideal of active, non-enclosed religious. Christian women coming together for mutual support in living out their ideals was not a new phenomenon in the history of the Church, and some of these women and the groups they formed are examined here.

The Beguines

As immediate predecessors of the women of the Reformation the Beguines of the Middle Ages belonged to this tradition of Christian women living in community. The Beguines began about 1175 in Liège (in present-day Belgium) and spread quickly throughout western Europe. The form of the movement evolved gradually. The first stage consisted of individual women living strict religious lives and practising evangelical poverty in their own homes. These women lived on the income from their own labour - they made lace, gardened, taught school, nursed and even managed shelters for women and children who were employed in the cloth industry.[1]

In the second stage of the Beguine movement the women lived together, and in 1233 the Bishop of Liège obtained Papal consent from Pope Gregory IX for them to continue in their own self-regulated communities. In the third stage, there was enclosure for the small groups which grew up around infirmaries and hospices where the women worked. In the fourth stage, the Beguine enclosure became a parish with a church, a cemetery, a hospital, a public square, convents and houses. Their spirituality emphasised the humanity and passion of Christ with special devotion to the Eucharist.[2]

Associated with those that did not become incorporated in a regular form of religious life was the suspicion that they were connected with heresy. As a result of official Church opposition, the Beguine movement declined. Some suggest that it was perhaps because they became too wealthy, or too strong for some Church authorities. As in all movements there were pious and impious Beguines. Concerning them Marygrace Peters OP makes the summary comment:

> The Beguines yearned for God, sought a lifestyle and a lay spirituality that would be in the service of the church. Their presence in late-medieval society was a challenge to the assumed notions of the society itself. Assumptions about women and their 'place', ideas about Christian lay spirituality, and notions about the authentic apostolic life had to be reconsidered in the light of their presence on the scene.[3]

Other groups of women followed in the wake of the Beguines. The initiatives of the religious women who immediately preceded Mary Ward, and of those who were her contemporaries, indicate strong movements towards promoting the education of women and girls in the Reformation period. Mary Ward was an heir to these movements and in turn was to contribute towards their further development and promote them significantly.

Frances of Rome (1384-1440)

Another group of religious women in the pre-Reformation period relevant to the situation of Mary Ward was the Congregation of Tor de Specchi. This congregation was founded by Frances of Rome in the 1430s. According to Chambers this group had a mitigated form of the Benedictine Rule, but were not cloistered. Pope Eugenius IV had approved their rule in 1433 which was the year of its foundation. Members took no vows but promised obedience to the superior. They had their own pensions, two servants, and could leave the congregation to marry. Their work involved many charities with a special attention to prisoners. There was only the one flourishing house in Rome, as they never made other foundations.[4]

The Congregation of Tor de Specchi lived in direct dependence on the reigning pope as Pope Eugene IV had arranged when confirming the government of the order in 1433. But then there arose the subject of enclosure after the Council of Trent.

In May 1566 Pope Pius V promulgated his apostolic constitution, *Circa Pastoralis*. This constitution directed that the decree of the Council of Trent on enclosure be implemented. As a result, women who were living together without enclosure were forbidden to receive novices unless they were willing to take solemn vows and to observe enclosure. According to Dortel-Claudot:

> ... by force of this Apostolic Constitution, Institutes of women which already existed were compelled to take solemn vows with the obligation of assuming strict enclosure, and evidently of relinquishing any works of charity. Otherwise they were condemned to suppression or slow death through the prohibition of receiving novices. In fact, new initiatives of women without enclosure were prevented.[5]

As a result, doubts were expressed in Rome as to whether the Convent of Tor de Specchi was exempt from enclosure. The question was submitted to the great theologian, Martinus Azpilencta, the Navar Doctor. The solution was that the Sisters could not be obliged to strict enclosure as they were not moniales (having solemn vows) but oblates (having simple vows).[6]

When Mary Ward's plan for her institute was being examined by a congregation of cardinals in 1622, Cardinal Bandini, whom Mary regarded as a friend, suggested that the confirmation of the order could be granted if the English Sisters were prepared to accept the kind of enclosure practised by the Tor de Specchi. Grisar further elucidates:

> We have no exact information about the freedom of movement granted to the Oblates; but we know that the noble ladies were permitted to leave the house in order to visit the 'Church of the Olivetaner' in the Forum, with which their community had a special connection. They could also, in individual cases, visit their relations with a companion. They accepted pupils into their houses but did not have as their aim such a many-sided work for the education of girls; therefore, the same reason did not exist for them, as did for the English Sisters, who were claiming complete freedom of enclosure.[7]

This was an apparently friendly advance from Cardinal Bandini but Mary Ward could not be satisfied with such a solution. Mary and her Sisters always remained friends of the women of the Tor de Specchi Congregation, who gave hospitality to Mary and her companions. When Mary's sister, Barbara Ward, was ill in Rome in 1622 the Tor de Specchi offered their aid, and Barbara spent a few weeks with them in the hope that their care and nursing would entirely restore her, while she at the same time had an opportunity of being instructed in the Italian language.[8]

Angela Merici (1474-1540)

Angela Merici was a most significant predecessor of Mary Ward in the Reformation period. She was a very spiritual, celibate woman who gave her life to working for the good of people (especially women) in Brescia in Northern Italy. In her girlhood Angela had a vision of herself as foundress of a company of virgins. St Ursula, the martyred fourth century British princess, resembled Angela's vision and Angela's company came to be called Ursulines.[9]

Through her men friends Angela was associated with the *'Company of Divino Amore'* (Company of Divine Love) - a kind of secret, charitable society which cared for the sick and the poor - especially women in asylums, many of whom were affected by syphilis which had been brought into Italy by French soldiers. This Company was established in 1497 in Genoa to promote individual renewal and the restoration of Christian life in society.

Angela Merici was sixty years old when, on 25 November 1535, the Feast of St Catherine, in the Church of St Afra in Brescia, she assembled twenty-eight companions and recorded her name with theirs in the register of the Company of St Ursula. Although Angela was to die five years later her initiatives proved to be seminal.

In 1535 (the year of the execution of Sir Thomas More in England) in Brescia there were eleven monasteries of religious women in which there were about three thousand nuns, but their way of life did not suit Angela Merici's vision for women in the service of the Church. Her 'daughters' lived with families who needed their help, and were therefore uncloistered and uncontained by rigid monastic rules. Angela Merici 'sought, by a unique creative insight, to provide in an organised way for women who desired a spiritually dedicated life but did not wish, or were not able, to enter a monastery.'[10]

As the Ursuline scholar, Ledochowska, explains, Angela Merici divided Brescia into four areas. The government of the Company was as follows: the four most capable virgins of the Company were to act as teachers and guides in the spiritual life; four widowed matrons were to serve as mothers, full of concern for the good and welfare of their spiritual daughters and sisters; and four mature and upright men were to act as agents and fathers in the day-to-day needs of the Company.[11]

According to Ledochowska, a few years after the recording of the names in the Register of the Company in 1535 'her daughters in Brescia alone had risen to 400, in a population of 40,000 every tenth family counted an Ursuline under its roof '.[12]

An experienced woman, Angela Merici was wise enough to know that a new Company could not exist without ecclesiastical approval, so she worked to secure this approval with the aid of her secretary, Gabriel Cozzano, a canon attached to the Curia of the Cardinal Bishop. Cozzano was familiar with Roman authorities and as Caraman notes 'in choosing Gabriel Cozzano as her secretary she was securing the future of her work by placing it under the guidance of an ecclesiastical authority who was likely to outlive her'.[13]

So at Angela's dictation (it seems that she could not write) Cozzano wrote the Rule. In 1536 the Rule was approved by Cardinal Cornaro. At this stage there was no mention of General or Assistants - this was written into the Rule thirty-seven years after her death.

Like so many religious founders Angela did not intend to form a new religious order, yet that was the result. Hers was the first rule in the Western Church drawn up by a woman for women to live outside the cloister.[14] Another highly significant aspect of Angela Merici's initiative was that her order was a purely female initiative and had no male counterpart. Before this Ursuline Rule the older established orders for women were female counterparts of ones for men, for example, Benedictines, Carthusians, Franciscans, Dominicans.[15]

With time, as more experienced and educated women joined the association, the members of Angela's Company lived together and were governed by one of their own. Because Angela Merici did not have a preconceived idea of her company she always claimed that the plan came from God. Her strong spiritual life was attested to by those who knew her.

Angela Merici's dependence on men was shown in the organisation of the government of her Society - men were to act as their bursars and agents in the day-to-day needs of the Company. This was a very practical step! Angela also used a male secretary, Gabriel Cozzano, to write the rule at her dictation. It was also through Cozzano that the rule was approved by the local Cardinal Cornaro. However, the life and work of Angela Merici testifies to a pioneering spirit which was primarily concerned with bettering the lives of women.

Angela Merici's work as an educator began to take shape through the works of mercy carried out by her Company. She and her women friends began to take care of girls from the age of twelve upwards. The initial aim was to educate them in the faith through Christian living in families, but it was soon evident that girls required education in all aspects of their lives if they were to break out of their cycle of poverty and oppression. At that time there was little or no education for girls, except in abbeys, and this was usually for children of the nobility.

Later on in the seventeenth century the Ursuline charism was expressed through the opening of the first boarding schools. The first such school for girls was founded by the Ursuline Company at Parma in 1595.[16] By 1610 the Ursulines in France were involved in education for girls. They were in France earlier than this, but 1610 marked the foundation of the Paris Ursulines, with boarding and day schools.

Enclosure for religious women was a directive from the Council of Trent. Trent really reiterated earlier legislation, in particular the requirement of strict enclosure and the taking of solemn vows for canonically recognised nuns, mandated by Boniface VIII in 1298. In a decree, *Decori,* issued by Pope Pius V in 1570, situations in which cloister could be abandoned were defined as those in cases of fire, leprosy or an epidemic.[17] Hence enclosure was inevitable for the Ursulines if they wanted the full status of religious, and not just to be recognized as a pious association. The first official recognition of the Ursulines as nuns came in Paris with the Bull of 1612.[18]

Jeanne de Lestonnac (1556-1640)

One of the great Counter-Reformation women contemporaries of Mary Ward was Jeanne de Lestonnac. She was born in 1556, the same year in which St Ignatius Loyola had died, and she herself died five years before Mary Ward.

Jeanne de Lestonnac's father, Richard de Lestonnac, was a councillor in the Parliament of Bordeaux. Her mother was Jean Eyquem de Montaigne, sister of the French humanist philosopher, Michel de Montaigne. Jeanne's mother was well educated and spoke Latin and Greek. She was also a Calvinist. Jeanne de Lestonnac's Catholic faith was inherited from her father.

Jeanne married Gaston de Montferrat Landiras in 1573 and they were happily married for twenty-four years. Eight children were born and five survived (two boys and three girls). In 1603, when all the children were provided for, the widowed Jeanne entered a contemplative order, the Feuillantes, who were Cistercians. The severe life there was too much for her health and she had to leave after six months. She then devoted herself to charitable works in which she was joined by friends. From this group in

Bordeaux there emerged the Congregation of Mary Our Lady (ODN).

It was clear to Jeanne that the education of girls was the great need of the times. If girls were to be educated in the faith, it followed that they had to be educated in general. The example of the Jesuits in educating boys was seen as a model and the Jesuits were sympathetic to Jeanne de Lestonnac as foundress of such a congregation.

In 1606 the Formula of the Congregation of Mary Our Lady, together with a summary of the constitutions and common rules of the Company of Jesus adapted for women, was presented to Cardinal Sourdis. The Cardinal proposed that Jeanne and her followers join the Ursulines for whom he had a special liking. Jeanne de Lestonnac insisted that her work differed from that of the Ursulines.

With the aid of the Jesuit, Father de Bordes, the order was given approval quickly because it incorporated the Rule of St Benedict (an enclosed lifestyle ensuring women's safety) and a modified Constitution based on that of the Society of Jesus which was an already approved Constitution, as Father de Bordes pointed out to the Pope. By 1607 Pope Paul V had formally approved the new Institute of the Order of the Congregation of Mary Our Lady.[19]

The girls who came to the Sisters of the Congregation of Mary Our Lady in Bordeaux required flexible arrangements. Some only stayed a few hours (day scholars), while others came as boarders. As a result there emerged the enclosure for boarders and nuns, with permission for some Sisters to leave the enclosure to teach the day scholars. Girls taken for education in the medieval monasteries observed enclosure and lived with the nuns, hence Jeanne de Lestonnac adapted this long-established precedent (itself Benedictine). Thus was effected a melding of the Rules of St Benedict and St Ignatius.

The Calvinists had concerns for the education of girls and Jeanne de Lestonnac's work appeared to answer the needs of Catholic girls who might otherwise have been tempted to attend Calvinist schools. She considered that a boarding school was the best nursery after that of the family for Christian living. However, as mentioned above, she was wise enough to combine both boarding and day schools. Thus Soury-Lavergne comments that, while

> ... Day Schools offered a structure which favoured a certain democratisation of education and an embryo of community living, the Boarding Schools effected a certain selectivity and guaranteed an integral education for the training of agents of re-christianisation. Both formulae were put at the disposal of the cultural and religious aims of the Company of Mary Our Lady.[20]

Women had to bring a dowry on entering the Congregation of Mary Our Lady. This was in accord with both Church law and civil law in France which laid down that a monastery could not admit more than could be supported.[21]

Soury-Lavergne points out that Jeanne de Lestonnac showed a positive position with regard to girls by making little reference to the supposed evil in girls - they were not Eves. Under her direction girls were also given freedom from surveillance and emancipated from conforming to certain 'images' of women. Women were considered by her to be autonomous beings - contrary to many of the structures and attitudes of the times.[22]

According to Soury-Lavergne, Jeanne de Lestonnac's philosophy of education reflected her philosophy about women. Jeanne's experiences as wife and mother had given her many insights into women's lives and the image she entertained of women emerges as being '... not a question of a super-woman, nor of the woman-child, but there appear - in dynamic and serene harmony - the features of woman simply happy to be what she is'.[23] Jeanne's aim was to create 'a school of doctrine and holiness for the happiness of families'.[24]

In order to be able to learn and appreciate religion the students were instructed in the rudiments of reading and writing. But students were also taught numeracy and sewing and the general culture of the times, history, literature, and *civilite* which is perhaps best translated as 'a civilized manner of behaving'. The latter accomplishments led to the assertion that the pupils of the Religious of Mary Our Lady directed their education towards children who were of a 'higher' clientele than that of the Ursulines who were nearer to the people. In response to this, the biographer of Jeanne de Lestonnac responded that 'nothing determined the admission of one social class in preference to another, since the education given was absolutely free for girls of all conditions'.[25] They charged a fee for boarding, not for tuition.

Jeanne de Lestonnac governed the Congregation until 1622 when, through malicious gossip, she was discredited and replaced as superior. After bearing this trial and subsequent humiliations with heroic patience and confidence in God she was vindicated in 1624. Her last years were given to assisting new foundations and to revising the order's constitutions. She died in 1640 and was buried in Bordeaux.[26]

Luisa de Carvajal (1566-1614)

Apart from the activities of women's groups as indicated above, there were individual women who launched out on their own to carry out mission work. Such a one was the noble Spanish lady, Luisa de Carvajal. She was inspired by Edmund Campion's martyrdom and decided to take up apostolic work in England. She came to England in 1605 and soon had helpers in her dangerous work with Catholics.

With Jesuit influence, Luisa planned a Marian institute with constitutions which, as well as the three vows, included a vow of obedience to the pope. She did not plan a centralised government, nor enclosure for her institute, because this would not have been possible in England at that time. The congregation was called the Society of the Sovereign Virgin Our Lady.

Luisa was quite effective in converting non-Catholics and bolstering the faith of her co-religionists. She commented that being a woman helped her, as the English never suspected a woman could be a missionary.[27] The activities of the group were discovered and Luisa was arrested. The Spanish ambassador intervened and she was released. In 1608 she moved from the Barbican to Spitalfields, outside the walls of London, but in October 1613 she was again taken prisoner, and once again freed at the intervention of the Spanish ambassador. Her death on 1 February 1614 forestalled her deportation from England.[28]

Luisa de Carvajal's initiative was that of an upper class Spanish woman who obviously had friends at the embassy to help her. Nevertheless, her work illustrates the courageous activity of such women. Luisa de Carvajal has been declared Venerable - the first step in the process of canonisation.[29] Peters asserts that it was highly probable that Mary Ward met Luisa.[30]

The Ursulines of Anne de Xainctonge (1567-1621)

The group of Ursulines of Anne de Xainctonge was different from the groups of Ursulines already mentioned. Anne de Xainctonge (1567-1621) began her work of education at Dijon in France where she observed the work of the Jesuits who were not constrained by enclosure. She moved from Dijon to Dole, a town under Spanish rule and attached to the Germanic Empire. There she opened her own school in 1606 to offer free education to girls.

Anne de Xainctonge and her companions took vows of chastity and stability. Following Jesuit advice they undertook to follow the constitutions of the Ursulines under the protection of Our Lady. In this way Anne was able to benefit from the approval granted to the Daughters of St Ursula by Pope Gregory XII. In 1623 the Ursulines of Dole obtained official recognition by a brief of Urban VIII. This recognition was not official approval of them as a group with a religious rule, but as a pious association. Not being officially nuns they avoided enclosure, retaining complete freedom for the fulfilment of their educational mission, and so they were faithful to the original vision of Angela Merici.[31]

In summary form, Waters says of the Ursuline groups that in their long evolutionary development there were three discernible stages since the beginnings in Brescia in the early sixteenth century. The first stage was a loose union whereby the houses in the diocese of Brescia were in some way related to the mother house in Brescia. The second stage was 'the Italian development' so called, by the Ursuline scholar Ledochowska, because communities were organised by bishops after the decrees promulgated by Charles Borromeo at the Fourth Provincial Council of Milan. This expansion did not stem from the original company itself, and produced a number of companies and communities unconnected with one another and non-enclosed.

The third stage was the development in France that occurred mainly through filiation, the establishing of daughter houses, which retain certain links with the mother house.[32] The Ursulines themselves organised this and some became autonomous (such as the group in Dole) because of the peculiar circumstances of a region that afforded them adequate protection from the universal ecclesiastical directives and the spiritual currents of the time that compelled the others to adopt a monastic form of life.[33]

Lucy Perotti (1568-1641)

Lucy Perotti and her associates are another typical example of women taking initiatives in Reformation times to organise themselves at the diocesan level to work for the Church. By 1617 Lucy Perotti and some women companions had established schools for day girls in Cremona, Italy. When they applied for confirmation of their community in Rome they were urged to join an order already approved by the Pope. In spite of this exhortation from Rome, the community preserved its individual identity and submitted to the bishop's authority as a pious association of women taking simple vows.

Cardinal Sfondrato, Bishop of Cremona, had permitted the establishment of Lucy Perotti's group in 1601 and his successor, Bishop Gianbattista, confirmed it. The Roman confirmation was given by the Sacred Congregation for Religious only in 1934. This institute succeeded in escaping enclosure and suppression in Italy through being content to remain under the jurisdiction of the local bishop.[34]

Jane Frances de Chantal (1572-1641)

Francis de Sales (1567-1622) and Jane Frances de Chantal (1572-1641) initially had a broad vision for the Order of the Visitation which they co-founded. Francis de Sales did not wish the order to be enclosed, but that the members would be free to serve in the wider world community through the visitation of people in their homes. The papal brief in 1618, however, established the Visitation as a canonical order which had to be enclosed and the Sisters necessarily gave up their visits to the poor. Soury-Lavergne comments that 'young girls were welcomed as boarders, but this educational experiment was intended mainly for the upper classes. It did nothing to help the spread of education for the masses'.[35]

Alix Le Clerc (1576-1622)

Another significant Catholic woman involved in educational initiatives for girls in the Reformation period was the noblewoman, Alix Le Clerc. With Peter Fourier she became co-foundress of the Canonesses Regular of St Augustine of the Congregation of Our Lady. It had become increasingly clear that the education of girls (especially in the faith) was necessary for the revitalisation and preservation of the Catholic faith in the climate engendered by the Reformation.

Peter Fourier was a parish priest of Lorraine in France and through his studies at the Jesuit University at Pont-a-Mousson in 1585, the year of Mary Ward's birth, he asked to be admitted to the Canons Regular of St Augustine at the abbey of Chaumousey. In 1589 he asked to have care of a neglected parish, and so became parish priest of Mattaincourt, a market town of the Vosges.[36] Peter Fourier became aware that it was necessary for families to be strengthened. He realised that boys of the parish could be educated by clergy, but girls needed women to teach them and that this was a critical area for innovation.

With the encouragement of Peter Fourier, and although having led a sheltered life, Alix Le Clerc and four other women began the work of education at a village of Poussey near Mattaincourt in 1597. They were to take in village children and teach them to read, write and sew, and especially to love and serve God. At first the community was not cloistered and there were no vows and no habit.

In 1598 a rule was drawn up by Fourier for Alix and her community with the following objectives:

The first and most important part of our objective, by which we hope to cause God to be honoured and served by many is to set up free public schools and there to teach girls to read and write, to work with the needle and to learn christian doctrine, striving, to the best of their ability and ours to make them understand the catechism and to initiate them in piety and devotion, to shun every sort of vice and sin and to embrace virtue according to the state, age and capacity of each of them.[37]

However, as papal approval was sought there was a problem because Fourier and Le Clerc wanted to have 'open schools' for day scholars, and 'enclosed schools', or boarding schools, where the girls lived in the convent. This necessitated two different rules, one for Sisters who taught day scholars and one for those who taught boarders.[38]

There were crises about this in 1606 and 1613. Finally in 1617, a papal bull from Pope Pius V incorporated the congregation into a religious congregation with solemn vows and enclosure. This called for costly changes on the part of the founders, Peter Fourier and Alix Le Clerc. In 1628, however, a bull promulgated by Pope Urban VIII re-established the educational objective of the congregation. By this bull the Sisters were permitted to take a special teaching vow, while retaining the monastic lifestyle.[39]

It would seem that Fourier and Alix Le Clerc substantially achieved their object because Fourier understood the Roman mentality. He always placed before Rome only one point at a time - without including too many explanations. He said that the Roman authorities could not at all understand how enclosure affects school authorities. He worked in three steps:

1. Erect the monastery according to the Rule of St Augustine with enclosure according to the first plan.
2. Obtain permission to instruct boarders.
3. Make the principal request - a school for externs.[40]

Francis de Sales had followed the same procedure in connection with the establishment of the Visitation Order with Jane Frances de Chantal.[41] Every one of these initiatives for women wanting to be religious without enclosure resulted in all finally accepting enclosure.

Louise de Marillac (1591-1660)

Another significant Catholic religious woman of the Reformation period was Louise de Marillac, co-foundress with Vincent de Paul of the Daughters of Charity. Louise was the 'illegitimate' daughter of the French nobleman, Louis de Marillac. Louis always acknowledged his daughter and gave her financial support. In 1613 Louise married Antoine Le Gras and they had an only son.[42]

When Louise was widowed in 1625 Vincent de Paul was her spiritual director. Recognising her spiritual depths and ability, he sent her to make an inspection tour of the confraternities (groups to assist the poor) he had established in the French provinces. As a result Louise began training poor country girls in her home in Paris in 1633.

By 1634 Vincent was giving the Daughters of Charity (as they are now called) conferences on the basic rule composed by Louise. Later, noblewomen joined this pious association. Other houses were opened and their works included the care of: abandoned babies, aged people, poor children, lunatics and galley slaves. The plight of the poor in France was very severe and women tended to be the greatest sufferers.

Louise and Vincent also gave spiritual retreats to lay men and women. Although their first apostolate was to the poor because they were the neediest, they did not hesitate to respond to other needs as they appeared.[43] By 1655, twenty-two years after its beginning, the Daughters of Charity had 143 members.

In 1641 the company assumed the work of free school-ing for poor girls in Paris. Monsieur des Roches, Chantre de Notre-Dame de Paris, answered Louise's petition to open these schools. He charged Louise and her companions 'to instruct poor girls, and to raise them in good morals, gram-matical letters and other pious and upright exercises'. Thus were inaugurated the same free schools for the poor of Paris that the poor of the villages had long enjoyed.[44]

Vincent de Paul evaded enclosure for this new founda-tion by not seeking for them the status of a religious order. They remained simply a pious association. The Daughters of Charity renewed their vows each year for a year, and so were not religious in the strict canonical sense. This was the strategy used by Vincent de Paul to avoid enclosure, and yet maintain certain traditional structures of religious life, such as community and spiritual exercises in common.

Jesuit influence

The Jesuit influence in many of the initiatives discussed above has to be acknowledged. Peter Fourier, who estab-lished a new group with Alix Le Clerc, was educated by Jesuits at the University at Pont-a-Moussan. Jeanne de Lestonnac, who established the Company of Mary Our Lady, was impressed by the Jesuit model of educating boys, and Jesuits were sympathetic to Jeanne and her work for girls. Eventually the two Rules of St Benedict and St Ignatius were approved for that congregation. The Ursulines at Dijon in France, under the leadership of Anne de Xainctonge, were also advised by Jesuits. It is noted that Luisa de Carvajal intended to adopt the Jesuit practice of taking a vow of obedience to the pope. No doubt this was indicative of a strong Jesuit influence in her formation.

It is significant that groups mentioned in this chapter began their initiatives within a northern European geographical area. From the map overleaf it can be seen that most of their initial foundations were in the Catholic territories bordering on Calvinist regions. When we consider their efforts to educate women, their counter-attack to the influence of the Reformation is clear.

It is interesting to note that all the foundresses, except Mary Ward, have been canonised, beatified, or, in the case of Luisa de Carvajal, declared 'Venerable'. The papal Bull of Suppression of Mary Ward's Institute has been one of the stumbling blocks in presenting the cause for her canonisation.

The initiatives of these women were a counteraction to the limiting of choices for women. Education for women from childhood was seen by such like-minded women as a necessary step towards the advancement of women in Reformation society, most especially in the development of their Catholic faith. All of these groups depended upon the bonding of friendship between the members, as well as their sharing in the charism of the founders, and this element of friendship in the company of friends was crucial to the survival of Mary Ward's Institute.

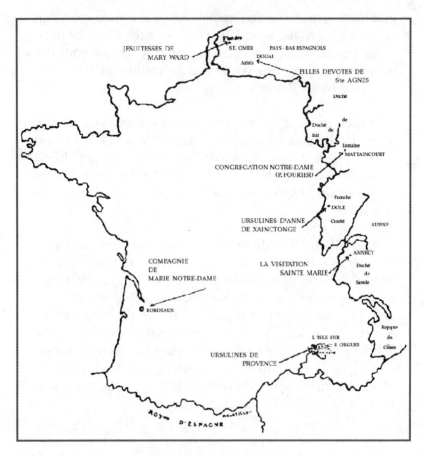

Some significant initiatives in Catholic feminine education between 1592 and 1611. (Adapted from Francoise Soury-Lavergne, *A Pathway in Education*, p 397.)

CHAPTER 5

Mary Ward:
Early attempts to establish
the Institute

Women in the Reformation period, both Protestant and Catholic, were deeply involved in the problems of their time. A number of Catholic women had taken initiatives to provide education for girls at all levels of society. It was noticeable too that there was often a strong Jesuit influence in their initiatives. It is not surprising then that Mary Ward should have followed in their wake.

Further enlightenment

Mary Ward was well accustomed to God's will being made known to her in stages. After a severe attack of measles, which Mary caught from the boarders whom she nursed, there came another time of enlightenment for her in 1611. Mary recounted the details of this vision twice: in a letter to Father John Gerard SJ in 1619, and in a letter to the Nuncio Albergati in 1621. In the latter she wrote:

> ... being alone in some extraordinary repose of mind, I heard distinctly, not by sound of voice, but intellectually understood, these words: 'Take the same of the Society' so understood as that we were to take the same both in matter and manner, that only excepted, which God by diversity of sex hath prohibited.[1]

To the Jesuit, Father John Gerard, Mary wrote with a different emphasis, saying more about her experience and of the inspiration to go to the Father General of the Jesuits:

'Take the same of the society. Father General will never permit it. Go to him.' These are the words whose worth cannot
be valued, nor the good they contain too dearly bought; these
gave sight where there was none, made known what God
would have done, gave strength to suffer what since had happened, assurance of what is wished for in time to come. And
if ever I be thought worthy to do anything more about this
Institute hither I must come to draw.[2]

This inspiration given to Mary Ward, 'Take the same of
the Society', was to be the source of the constitutions she
desired for her Institute - and the reason for some of her
great suffering. The first printed edition of the Jesuit Constitutions in 1558-59 was comprised of four separate trea-
tises left by St Ignatius. They were the 'General Examen',
the authoritative explanations of it entitled 'Declarations
on the Examen', 'The Constitutions of the Society of Jesus',
and the 'Declarations on the Constitutions'.[3]

The collection of the four documents named above however is not the basic rule nor fundamental code of legislation in the Society of Jesus. This supreme authority and dignity belongs to the papal document commonly called the
'Formula of the Institute'. This Formula consists of the bull
of Paul III in 1540, and, in slightly revised form, the bull of
Julius III of 1550. The Formula described the fundamental
structure of the new order and authorised its General to
establish, with advice from his companions, more detailed
statutes or determinations called 'Constitutions'. In modern editions of Ignatius' Constitutions, the Formula is
printed as a kind of preface to them.[4] Wright says that 'its
originality depended not so much on the individual details
as on the overall intent of the "Formula". It was the first
"rule" in which the total orientation of the way of life was
towards the apostolic aims of the Order.'[5]

It is worth noting too, as Wright does, that the Fourth
General Congregation of the Society of Jesus in 1581 pre-

pared a new Latin text, which, since that date, has been the official Latin edition. The Spanish version, first published in 1606, is the definitive source for interpretation of the document. The first complete English version ever published was that of George Ganss SJ, in 1970.[6]

It is important for our understanding to note that the Ignatian Constitutions are a heritage text and no changes have been made to them since the death of St Ignatius. The Society of Jesus updates itself chiefly through the decrees of the general congregations and the writings of the superiors general.[7]

The document which Mary Ward evidently understood to be meant by the words of her revelation was the 'Formula of the Society'. Mary, apparently with the aid of the Jesuits, had access to the English translation to this 'Formula of the Society'. Modelling her Institute on the Jesuits meant that Mary would have the power of a general superior which included the missioning and placement of individuals in the congregation, and the composition of rules with the consultation of the members. It also included the legal independence of the order such as that held by male orders. In addition, every member would be bound to the pope by a fourth vow with regard to their mission.[8]

Enclosure is not envisaged in this Formula and Mary Ward and her companions in St Omer had been living without enclosure for years before 1611. When Mary made known publicly the way her Institute was to be founded it was regarded as a female Jesuit Order. Many offers of plans for the Institute were made. Concerning these initial moves, Peters comments that: 'to be objective about the plans of the Institute that have come down to us, it must be remembered that these were not prepared by Mary Ward and her first members, but by friends of the Institute'.[9] Of all this Mary herself wrote that '... various plans were drawn up by several persons, some of which were approved and greatly commended by the last bishop, Blaise of St Omer, our so great friend, and other divines. These were offered us and as it were pressed upon us; there was no remedy but to refuse them'.[10]

One of the rules presented to Mary was drawn up by her confessor, Father Roger Lee SJ. She rejected it, but Father Lee was called the Institute's founder in reports by Father Robert Sherwood OSB to Pope Gregory XV in 1622; in Matthew Kellison's report to Nuncio Francesco Guidi di Bagno in October 1622; and by Secretary Ingoli's dorsal comment on the petition of the English Agent Rant to Pope Urban VIII in 1624.[11] The reason for this appears to be that it was not usual for a woman to work without the 'support' of a male co-founder, so Father Lee was perceived as the founder because of his association with the Institute at that time.

It should be mentioned at this stage that Father Lee had his critics. Because the Jesuits wished to send priests quickly on to the English mission some men studied a short course in preparation. Father Lee had done this short course of studies in Rome before ordination.[12] This point was brought up later when Mary was accused of having been guided by uneducated Jesuits.

Already there was growing opposition in Rome to Mary's proposed Institute. Because there was uncertainty in Rome about the status of Mary Ward's group of women the then Jesuit General, Claudio Aquaviva, wrote to the members of his Gallo-Belgian province saying that a secular priest should take over the administration of the English women. Later in another letter he said that they were not religious sisters and that the fathers were forbidden to direct the community.[13]

Father Lee was pressed by his order to have nothing more to do with Mary Ward. He was loyal to her, but had difficulty with her aim to take the Jesuit model against the wishes of the Society, as expressed by the General. Nevertheless, he appears to have given conferences to the community. Father General obviously wanted Father Lee away from the scene of Mary Ward's activities and directed him to leave St Omer. However, he died at Dunkirk in 1615 on his way to England. Mary was now released from her vow of obedience to Father Lee.[14]

After Father Roger Lee left St Omer, Bishop Blaes, according to Peters, 'exerted himself on behalf of the Institute, ensuring the right to work as a Pium Institutum for the education of English girls... The Bishop had defended an Institute acceptable to the Jesuits and, in a particularly comprehensive paragraph, had denied any pastoral activity of its members in England.'[15] The last point was to be a further problem for Mary Ward as the Sisters were actually working in England at that time.

Meanwhile the continental work of the Institute had grown and in 1614 Mary and her companions had purchased a third house, the Cistercian Abbey of Revensberg near Watten in Belgium.[16] As the Institute had not yet been approved, the Sisters, in accordance with canon law, took private vows at first for a limited time.[17]

Official Jesuit opposition

In order to appreciate the strong opposition of the Jesuit General to Mary Ward's proposed Institute it is necessary to appreciate the previous history of the Jesuit Order in relation to women seeking to use their Rule and Constitutions.

As a result of the requests that had been made by women to St Ignatius to join the Jesuits, he envisaged the possibility of a female branch of the Society according to the existing fully cloistered 'second orders' of women Dominicans and Franciscans. This would have required Jesuit priests as regular and fixed chaplains and government by the male branch.[18] Such a female branch Ignatius considered would be contrary to his vision for a mobile society - ready to go at any time where the pope would send them.

Ignatius' uncompromising rejection of a female branch of the Society of Jesus was based also on his unhappy experience of such experiments. The most celebrated situation has been described by Ganss, translator and author of the Introduction to *The Constitutions of the Society of Jesus:*

> In 1545 Isabel Roser and two companions, Francisca Cruyllas and Lucretia de Biadene, successfully petitioned Paul III to pronounce religious vows and to place themselves under obedience to Ignatius. After a time, however, distressing experiences ensued, as a result of which Ignatius addressed a petition to the Pope, asking to be freed from obligation of being the regular or steady directors of convents of religious women and of receiving them under obedience to the Society. The Pope approved this in 1547 and confirmed it anew in the bull, 'Licet debitum.' Then Ignatius incorporated his experience and decisions into the compressed legislation of this constitution [588].[19]

Among the 'distressing experiences' which Ignatius had in connection with Isabel Roser and Francisca Cruyllas was the fact that the ladies took up residence in the Jesuit house in Rome. Father Nadal was scandalised because Isabel Roser 'got her food daily from the Fathers' kitchen... and she imposed herself as nurse upon the sick Ignatius'.[20] The end of Ignatius' patience came when Isabel Roser invited two of her nephews to come to Rome. The nephews found it intolerable that their rich aunt had now bequeathed what was left of her property to the Jesuits. Further trouble between the women and the Jesuits finally caused Ignatius to ask Pope Paul III for help and 'Pope Paul III gave oral permission for the women to be released from the vows which he had not long before ordered them to make.'[21]

As a result of this early experience of female Jesuits the Jesuit Constitution Number 588 states:

> Likewise, because the members of this Society ought to be ready at any hour to go to some or other parts of the world where they may be sent by the sovereign pontiff or their own superiors, they ought not to take a curacy of souls, and still less ought they to take charge of religious women or any other women whatever to be their confessors regularly or to direct them. However, nothing prohibits them in passing from hearing the confessions of a whole monastery for special reasons.[22]

Ganss comments that the chief motive of St Ignatius in having this constitution was avoidance of impediment to the mobility of his men rather than an anti-woman stance. Indeed St Ignatius himself was a prolific writer of letters to women which, according to Ganss, 'reveals him as a zealous, interested, prudent, and understanding spiritual director of women whom they highly esteemed. He inaugurated many works in their behalf, received much help from them, and ever remained grateful to them.'[23]

It is recorded that Juana of Austria, the wilful daughter of Charles V, sister of Philip II of Spain (who married Mary Tudor of England), and who was Regent of Spain in Philip's absence, managed to persuade St Ignatius to accept her vows in the Society. According to O'Malley: 'Juana became a Jesuit and remained one until her death in 1573 - a secret known only to herself and a few members of the Society.'[24] No doubt the necessity of retaining royal patronage was a significant factor in pressuring Ignatius into granting this concession.

The Vow Formula used by Juana in 1554 is almost identical with the vows of Mary Ward's Institute today.[25] Because Juana was a nineteen-year-old widow it was still possible that she might marry. Therefore, the vows that Juana was allowed to make were the vows of a scholastic in the

Society of Jesus, according to the provisions laid down in the fifth part of the Constitutions.

Hugo Rahner asserts:

> The peculiarity of this form of vows, newly introduced by Ignatius and only after lengthy opposition, consists in the fact that though they are permanently binding vows of poverty, chastity, and obedience, only the individual who makes them is bound by them, while the Society reserves to itself the freedom to release from them for just causes. This interpretation... relieved the General from the embarrassment in this particular case: he did not have to refuse his royal petitioner, and yet her acceptance could be revoked if necessary.[26]

Juana lived a half-religious, half-courtly, way of life until her death in 1573. Her spiritual director was Francis Borgia, who became General of the Jesuits after Lainez in 1565.[27]

In light of this previous history of the Jesuits in connection with women seeking to live according to their Constitutions, and the official binding direction of Ignatius in this matter, it is not surprising that Mary Ward experienced problems such as the General's withdrawal of Father John Gerard from Liège in 1621 because of his association with her group who were wanting to use the Jesuit Formula.

As Mary Ward saw it, there was a misinterpretation of her intentions with regard to those Constitutions, but the knowledge that she wanted the Jesuit Constitutions was sufficient for some Jesuits to be wary. Even non-Jesuits tended to associate the Sisters with the Jesuits - to the point at times of calling them 'Jesuitesses'. However, Mary Ward never envisaged her Institute being a female branch of the Jesuits.

The Jesuits' concern about Mary Ward's Institute may seem difficult to understand because they appeared to be about the same enterprise - the assistance of English Catholics and the eventual reconversion of England. However, the idea of women taking their Rule, and maybe performing priestly duties, such as preaching and preparing people for the sacraments (without sufficient theological training), was abhorrent to most clerics, and the Jesuits were no exception to this attitude.[28]

As a result of the controversy concerning Mary Ward's proposed Institute during this early period, questions about the Institute's right to exist were put by the Society of Jesus to their noted Flemish moral theologian, Father Leonard Lessius. The report concerning Lessius' response has been copied several times and is found in various archives.[29] Peters notes that there was tension between English Jesuits in Belgium and other Jesuits who had doubts about Mary Ward's initiative.[30] Peters also comments that the Jesuit authorities were not completely hostile to Mary Ward, or they would not have commissioned Lessius to answer the questions.[31] These questions were:

1. Is this Institute allowed and pious?
2. Can the bishop approve it and authorize it?
3. Can the Institute be considered a reliable state for its members?

Lessius gave affirmative answers to all three questions.[32]

Enemies and critics abounded however, and a second report on the Sisters was required by the Jesuits from the Jesuit canonist, Francesco Suarez.[33] Suarez was a Spaniard and in Spain, religious life, especially for women, was very strict, with enclosure for women religious being the norm there.[34]

The same three questions as had been given to Lessius were given to Suarez and, predictably, his answers for all three questions were negative. He said papal approval was necessary and without it there were no valid vows, and without valid vows there was no permanent status.[35] This was the ultimate challenge for Mary Ward.

Work in England - Sister Dorothea

Meanwhile, during the years 1609 to 1615, Mary Ward is known to have made several visits to England. Peters mentions an anonymous author who refers to six Sisters in England doing activities unsuitable for women.[36] Mary and her companions probably had a house in London as it is known that Anne Gage travelled there to take up her post as Superior in 1615.[37]

The work of the Sisters labouring in England is described well in the story known as 'Sister Dorothea's Narrative'. Sister Dorothea was said to be a lay sister, but she was in fact a woman of rank who chose to hide her identity. Her true name was known to Mary Ward, as she was a member of the Institute, but her family name was never recorded.[38]

The autobiographical account of her life and work was written at the command of her Superior, Frances Brooksby, in about 1621.[39] Members of the Institute in England at that time could rarely live in communities, or even in pairs. They worked singly in all classes of society, but were often housed in the country houses of the rich in order to avoid observation. This was later to become one of the accusations against Mary Ward by her English enemies.

Sister Dorothea reported that in the years 1622 and 1623 she laboured in the county of Suffolk and lived at one time in the house of Lady Timperly, pretending to be her kinswoman. She taught children in the houses of their parents, preparing them for the sacraments and obtaining the confidence of the adults.

Sister Dorothea also looked after the sick. She wrote:

> I tend and serve poor people in their sickness. I make salves
> to cure their sores, and endeavour to make peace between
> those at variance. In these works of charity I spend my time,
> not in one place, but in many, where I see there is best means
> of honouring God.[40]

Apart from ministering to the sick, Dorothea had priests
brought to reconcile Catholics through the sacrament of
penance and to convert others. She said:

> Three things I observe happen at the conversion of any.
> 1. That I never gain but one alone, but more.
> 2. One at least ever dieth happily, the rest lives.
> 3. That whenever any are reconciled presently comes upon us
>   persecution much more vehement than at other times.[41]

Unmarried women in seventeenth century England had
few choices in their state of life.[42] The closure of the convents limited the choice for women to become religious.
Sister Dorothea, who was a member of Mary Ward's Institute, although this was unknown to the authorities, exem-
plified a way in which to live a religious life in England at
this time. When she was brought before a magistrate in 1622
she was asked, 'Are you a maid, a widow or a wife?'. Upon
answering that she was a maid, the magistrate was relieved
and replied that she could find 'a good husband (who) will
persuade you to change your religion'. The magistrate dis-
missed her because of her 'much service to the poor - to
give you your due'.[43]

As an incognito member of the Institute, Sister Dorothea
was in a position to be aware of the various opinions concerning Mary Ward and her associates. Of one such conversation she reported:

> Mr. Palmer, the Benedictine, and others being much pleased
> to see my manner of living and the good success that God
> hath given unto my poor endeavours, fell many times into

speech of our Mother and Company, and said they would see Mrs. Mary Ward send some of hers to live and labour in the manner I do, then they should like well of them, etc, but they live in great houses for their own ends only, and by their means to draw the Society thither; others said that it was unfit that religious women should live out of monasteries, retiredness and recollection were fittest for them...[44]

Dorothea also reported that 'My Lady' answered the Benedictine at length saying, in part: 'I wonder much you can so mislike Mrs. Ward and her company; it seems to me that you condemn those whom you know not.' Lady Timperly continued to defend Mary Ward and her Institute using words of the greatest praise. 'They are women of much prayer, great austerities, and exemplar lives.'[45]

The Benedictine priest, Father Palmer, apparently could not leave Sister Dorothea in peace. The conclusion to her narrative recounts another of her encounters with him. Dorothea obviously enjoyed the humour of the situation as she narrates:

Upon April 2, 1622, Mr Palmer again disputed against our Company and in jesting manner asked me if I would be a galloping nun or a preacher etc. I answered I was content with my present state. Indeed, he said, so I might be, for I did more good than any of them had done, yet he should like me much better if I would make the vows of obedience and chastity to my ghostly father.[46]

There was opposition from the English secular clergy to the Jesuits and their mission in England. The association of Mary Ward with the Jesuits drew opposition to her and the women known to be associated with her. There was also the possibility that some of Mary's associates in their youthful enthusiasm, like the young Jesuits, may have been imprudent at times. An apparently trivial example concerned women's costume. Mary Ward's sister, Barbara, was described as being dressed in a bright taffeta gown, with rich petticoats trimmed according to the latest fashion with a starched yellow ruff *à la mode.*[47]

This comment appears to be merely a remark on fashion until we find that Elizabeth I dressed in white, or black and white, which remained her favourite, while her predecessor Queen Mary had worn 'a riot of colour and gold that she (Mary), as a conscientious Catholic sovereign, felt obliged to wear'.[48] According to Johnson this was because: 'where rival clergymen fought with texts, the weapons of women of rank were needle and thread. Elizabeth was an ocular rebuke to the old religion'.[49]

Progress on the continent

At the same time in St Omer the school was flourishing with thirty boarders, and there were thirty members of the Institute itself. It is known that a few years later (1618-1621) classes for the girls of the neighbourhood were held free of charge.

In 1615 Mary Ward asked Father Lee to direct her retreat. Although very ill (he died two months later) he consented to direct her. Towards the end of the Spiritual Exercises Mary received special insight into the nature of perfection within the Institute. This came to be called the 'Vision of the Just Soul'. Mary described what she experienced in a long letter to Father Lee.

According to Orchard this insight can be summarised as 'the fundamental state of soul of one called to serve the Church and give glory to God in Mary Ward's company (which) is characterised by the virtues of freedom, justice and sincerity'.[50] It was another key experience for Mary - one which was part of the founding charism.

It is useful at this stage to summarise the three key revelations which were guiding Mary into her path as foundress:

1. The Glory Vision of 1609 - confirmation of her personal activity in England;[51]

2. The Vision of 1611 ('Take the same of the Society') - the spiritual and constitutional foundation of her community;[52] and,

3. The Vision of the Just Soul in 1615 - the spirituality of the members of her congregation to resemble that of the Society of Jesus, in so far as it is possible for women to live and operate in their sphere of work.[53]

On these three visions rested an entirely new concept for women's orders, which was to transform women's congregations in the centuries to come.[54] The 'Glory Vision' had given confidence to Mary Ward to continue her search for the right form of religious life for her by seeking approval to use the Constitutions of the Society of Jesus adapted to women, not as a female branch of the Jesuits, but an independent female institute. This was an entirely new and daring initiative in the light of the fact that Jesuit authorities would perceive it as involving themselves, and, therefore, in direct opposition to the command of St Ignatius, and, as a result, feel conscience-bound to oppose it.

The Constitutions of the Society of Jesus as such (alone) had never been approved for a congregation of women religious. From this time on Mary spent her energies in working to have her Institute confirmed as an Institute with no enclosure, no habit, nor Office in common, and governed by a Sister Superior General. In essence this meant the founding of an Institute for religious women with the Constitutions of the Society of Jesus adapted for women.

From group to Institute

It is difficult to know precisely when Mary Ward and her group of companions came to be known as an 'Institute'. In the text presented to Pope Paul V for approval in 1615 the group was called 'our Institute'. The letter of reply written by Cardinal Lancellotti to Bishop Blaes refers simply to 'some English virgins' and 'their Institute'.

Later on, in 1621, we know that Mary Ward favoured the name of Jesus, but the group could not publicly adopt any name that might give the impression that it was an official religious order. In general, people called the group by the obvious name of 'English Ladies'. After Mary's death in 1645 there were attempts to establish the group in England. When Frances Bedingfield founded houses in Hammersmith and York in 1686 they were referred to by the Bedingfield family as 'our Institute'.

In October 1990, there was a meeting in Rome of all the Institute branches. It was a congress to discuss the union of these branches. The minutes of the meeting showed that the name of the Institute was discussed.

> It was generally allowed that the earliest name was Institute of Mary, which appears in the earliest formula of the vows, and in an old German print of Mary Ward in which she is styled as Foundress of the Institute of Mary. It was also allowed that Institute of the Blessed Virgin Mary was adopted later, lest Institute of Mary should be taken to signify Institute of Mary Ward.[55]

The eighty-one rules of the Institute were approved by Pope Clement XI in 1703, yet it seems that neither the Institute itself, nor the Roman authorities, gave a formal religious title to the group, although the name 'Institute of Mary' began to appear on internal Institute documents. The rescript from Propaganda establishing the new Irish community in 1821 mentioned 'a celebrated Institute of English nuns'. From then on the use of 'Institute' became more widespread.[56] It is now known as an 'Institute' in official documents and the title is used publicly. The Sisters are known as members of the Institute of the Blessed Virgin Mary with the abbreviation IBVM after their names. Those of the Roman Generalate, such as Sister Immolata Wetter, use the abbreviation IBMV from the Latin words of the title.

What is known for certain is that, following this early period Mary Ward and her associates embarked upon a period of expansion as they concurrently pursued their goal of being recognised fully as religious according to the adapted Jesuit Formula, and papal approval was necessary for this.

CHAPTER 6

Period of Expansion of the Institute (1615-1621)

Seeking papal approval

Hope sprang eternal with Mary Ward and she resolutely set about seeking papal approval for her Institute. It was imperative for the Institute to be confirmed as a religious order if it were to continue its work, take novices into the group, and to have public acceptance within the Church and among the families from whom its members were drawn. Indeed, parents were loath to pay dowries for their daughters to an Institute as yet unrecognised by the Church.[1] In 1615 Mary Ward sent recommendatory letters from Bishop Blaes to Pope Paul V. With them was a 'Petition' for approval of the Institute.[2] They were taken to Rome by the English nobleman, Thomas Sackville.

In this petition to Pope Paul V in 1616, Mary Ward wrote:

> We have in mind a mixed life, such a life as we learn Christ Our Lord and master taught His chosen ones, such a life as His blessed Mother lived and handed down to those of later times, in those times especially when the Church was afflicted as in our country now, so that in this way we may more easily educate maidens and girls of tender years in piety, in the Christian virtues and liberal arts so that they may be able thereafter to undertake more fruitfully the secular and monastic life, according to the vocation of each.[3]

Pope Paul V referred the petition to the Congregation of the Council, which issued 'a commendation' of the Institute. In summary, it said that confirmation was not to be given as they had no need of it since, if the Institute proved fruitful, it could be discussed later on; a letter of recommendation was to be sent to the nuncio and prelates. A plenary indulgence was to be granted to Sisters at the hour of death and on the Feast of the Assumption of Our Lady, but not for the day of entrance as had been requested. The question was also asked as to whether the members of the new Institute instructed English girls only, or accepted others including the local girls.[4] As indicated previously, in answer to this criticism, it was known that they instructed local girls, as well as the English emigrants.

The cardinals of the Congregation of the Council made a decision on 23 March 1616 which, according to Peters, said in effect that 'the Institute, or rather the nameless community of Englishwomen, was placed under the protection and care of the Bishop of St Omer. He could even support them.'[5]

This was actually a momentous step for Mary Ward and her Institute because she had secured from Rome a first testimonial so that it might continue its work with the blessing of the pope and might hope for further favours.[6]

This early request for approbation should have squashed all future accusations against Mary's supposedly high-handed way of proceeding without papal knowledge or approval. But the situation in which Mary was involved was far too complex to admit of such simple logic.

Another problem soon arose because of the circulation of a new 'Relatio'. This was a new plan for the Institute which involved the separation of the members involved in the active apostolate - that is, the community in St Omer and those in England - two groups with connection only through the person of the chief superior. This 'Relatio' appears to have been promoted by the nuncio and Bishop Blaes.[7] Peters suggests that this manuscript was written probably in May or June, 1616, by an English Jesuit.[8]

According to this 'Relatio' the Bishop of St Omer could have care for the Sisters in Flanders, which was in his diocese, but not for those in England because he had no authority in relation to the persecuted Church in England. In consequence, there would have to be two separate communities - one in Flanders and the other in England - with the local Bishop Blaes in Flanders 'protecting' only the community in Flanders. This was contrary to Mary Ward's plan of one Institute under a Superior General. Mary Ward could only decline this plan which was never presented for approbation because, as Peters explains:

> Mary Ward left St. Omer in the interests of an undivided Institute with two equally important spheres of work, active apostolic work among adults, and the teaching and education of English girls; in the interests of an Institute which would be extra-diocesan, independent of bishops, and modelled on the Society of Jesus.[9]

The breadth of Mary Ward's vision was obviously in conflict with the limited jurisdiction of the Bishop of St Omer. Not only was Mary faced with this dilemma, but also with poor health. In 1616 Mary Ward went to Spa to take the waters for gallstones - an illness which was to trouble her for the rest of her life. She was also planning to negotiate for a new foundation in Liège.

Foundation at Liège

In 1616 fifteen English women of Mary Ward's company moved to Liège. This state was then an independent prince-bishopric, which belonged to the nunciature of Cologne in Church matters and was a member of the German states, the Trier group.[10] Despite its borders, the population was mostly French-speaking Walloon and Catholic in religion. Since 1612 Ferdinand, brother of the Elector, Maximilian I of Bavaria, had been prince-bishop of Liège. He had studied at the Jesuit University of Ingolstadt and in Rome. Bishop Ferdinand had little to do with his subjects in Liège, but was a political prop to his brother, Maximilian, who protected the Catholic cause in Bavaria. In Liège government business was carried on by the Privy Council, and a vicar general represented the bishop.[11] The idea of a prince-bishop was certainly new to Englishwomen who came from a country with no Catholic hierarchy at that time.

There were many religious houses in Liège. According to Peters: 'out of a population of 40,000, there was a women's convent for every 3,500 of the inhabitants'.[12] In 1616 Mary Ward rented a property called Mont St Martin. Because of the large number of convents in Liège acceptance from the local people did not come easily nor quickly.

On 2 February 1617 Bishop Blaes of St Omer wrote a letter of recommendation to the Bishop of Liège for the members of the Institute who had moved into his area. In his letter Bishop Blaes made clear that the lifestyle of the Englishwomen in St Omer was exemplary and they were esteemed by the local inhabitants. The pope had entrusted the congregation to Bishop Blaes who expected that his letter of recommendation of the Englishwomen would assist the Bishop of Liège to favour and protect them.[13]

Financial difficulties

However, the Institute was very poor, and they were also vulnerable as was shown when a man infected with the plague broke into the convent. Therefore, the Sisters applied formally to the prince-bishop for protection. The times were indeed violent and women needed the protection of men for their safety. The bishop, through his Privy Council, took the Englishwomen under his protection.[14]

But this did not pay the rent, and after being there for six months the Englishwomen requested the chapter of the Collegiate Church of St Martin for financial help. They were looking for a guarantee of part of the chapter's income as security for the rent payable to the owner of their house, Canon Michel de Merica. In order to avoid possible future litigation the chapter refused to put their property at risk. The Bishop of Liège does not seem to have known of their problems.[15] What is remarkable is that this group of women was essentially conducting its own affairs.

Further Jesuit involvement

The fate of the Institute in Liège was to be inextricably bound up with the affairs of the Jesuits there. The Jesuit house in Liège was a novitiate house and the superior was Father John Gerard, also known as John Tomson. He had taken part in founding the first novitiate for English Jesuits in Louvain, so this was an obvious reason for his appointment to Liège.[16]

We have seen that Mary Ward had written to him about her vision which had instructed her to 'Take the same of the Society'. He became her confessor and spiritual direc-tor, and therefore necessarily an influential person in Mary's life during this period.

Father John Gerard was born in 1564 in Derbyshire, England. He studied at Oxford and was accepted into the English College in Rome. He was ordained a Jesuit in 1588 and returned to England with Father Edward Oldcorne, who was later martyred. John Gerard was imprisoned in the Clink prison in 1597 and was later severely tortured in the Tower of London. His hands were crippled for life as he had been tied up by his wrists. With help from friends he had escaped from the Tower.[17]

But as Peters points out, John Gerard had enemies within his own order. One can surmise that he was a strong, adventurous man and few people can be unreactive about a man who had demonstrated such heroism in his life. Later we find the Jesuit General, Father Mutius Vitelleschi, being somewhat indulgent (for those times) towards Father Gerard, this English Jesuit who had barely escaped martyrdom.[18]

An Englishman, Mr Thomas Sackville, was involved in the business negotiations of both the Jesuits and Mary Ward's Institute. Father Tomson (Gerard) asked Thomas Sackville to buy a farm for the Jesuits in his (Sackville's) name. In 1618 Sackville bought a house and garden to give to the Englishwomen. The problem was that he used the Jesuits' farm (in his name) as surety. Thomas Sackville was not justified in mortgaging the Jesuits' property, but he was supposed to have been expecting a large sum of money from England.[19]

It is interesting to make a further reference to Thomas Sackville. As noted above, he was the Englishman who took the Petition for approval of the Institute to Rome in 1615. He was one of the Earls of Dorset and son of England's Lord Treasurer.[20] Chambers also notes that Thomas Sackville was the founder in pecuniary matters of a 'House of Writers', of the English secular clergy, called the 'College of Arras', established in Paris in 1611, for the purpose of assisting the Catholics of England in their controversy with Protestants.[21] So Thomas Sackville was a great friend of the Jesuits, and also of the English secular clergy.

Mary Ward spoke of Thomas Sackville as a very influential person in the Kingdom of England who was related to, and highly esteemed by, many of the English Ladies and was distinguished for his good life. Sackville lived on the continent from 1610 to 1619 and made a name for himself there by his endowments, which however did not always materialise.[22]

The domestic complication for the English ladies was that Thomas Sackville was related to Jane Browne, one of their first members, and perhaps also to other members of the Institute whose names are no longer known. There were several connections by marriage between families of the gentry and the nobility connected with the Institute.[23]

When Sackville left Liège encumbered with debts, the Englishwomen were left with a debt of 20 000 guilders owing to the Jesuits.[24] The St Omer house had to help with financial aid. The Jesuits were also in debt and Father Burton was sent to replace Father Gerard (Tomson) as Superior of the Jesuit house.

The Sisters however remained at Mont St Martin in Liège. This house behind a protective wall was intended as a novitiate, and also to function as a boarding school for young English women, though some local girls may also have attended it.[25]

Return to England

It was in 1617, when she was in Liège, that Mary began the autobiography of her early years.[26] She crossed to England in the spring or early summer of that year. The debts on the continent were probably a pressing need for Mary's return to England as she sought to obtain financial assistance there. There was no doubt, however, of her great concern for her people and country, and her desire to visit and minister to them.

It is difficult to know exactly what Mary Ward did in England in 1618, but Chambers says she joined in all the labours and dangers of her Sisters there. Chambers reports that 'Mary Ward's house was a shelter for Catholic priests and a centre of operations carried out for the conversion and relief of ignorant and oppressed souls.'[27]

Of course this work did not escape the attention of authorities and the Anglican Bishop of Canterbury, George Abbot, is reported to have said of Mary Ward that 'that woman had done more harm than many priests and he would exchange 6 or 7 Jesuits for her'.[28]

Chambers further relates that the boat on which Mary was subsequently returning to the continent was blown back to the shores of England where she was captured. She was brought before the justices of the Guildhall in London and then imprisoned. It is surmised that it may have been the gatehouse at Westminster in which she was confined.[29]

In connection with this incident Chambers quotes a letter by Father Adam Contzen which says: 'Mrs. Mary herself suffered imprisonment in England; sentence of death was passed upon her for religion, but there was no execution for fear of odium.'[30] Father Dominic Bissel (an early biographer of Mary Ward) commented that she was freed 'by her friends paying down money'.[31]

Problems within the Institute

Mary Ward returned to St Omer and then went on to Liège. Her embryonic Institute was put to the test in 1619. In Liège, Sister Praxedes claimed to have visions about being the true foundress of the Institute. She said she was enlightened concerning the spirit and organisation of the congregation. Mary's response was to pray in order to discover God's will. She did this by making the Spiritual Exercises of St Ignatius with Father John Gerard as director. Orchard reports that during Mary's retreat Sister Praxedes became ill. By the time it was ended she was dead, 'having protested that if she died, all that she had seen or heard was false'.[32]

The English life of Mary Ward describes Sister Praxedes as a simple maid from the Ardennes.[33] There were however worse enemies within the Institute. Another Sister, Mary Alcock, who was the first 'minister' at Liège - a trusted position - was very jealous of Mary Ward and, on leaving the Institute, she supplied information for a scandalous pamphlet about her former superior.[34] Mary Alcock, however, also died soon afterwards, in 1623.[35]

Mary Ward showed no harshness to her enemies within the Institute, but rather used the Ignatian method of discernment by a testing of spirits. Mary was familiar with the Spiritual Exercises of St Ignatius which have rules for the discernment of spirits. Ignatius understood that in the reality of our humanness both good and bad spirits are at work within us. The practice of discernment enables a person to enjoy a certain inner solitude whereby they can test periods of desolation and consolation and judge the movements of the good spirit.[36] Mary certainly used this method at this time of trouble and challenge. She acted humbly, doubting herself 'in a sea of uncertainties' as she wrote to Father John Gerard in April 1619.[37]

Affairs in Liège continued to be very difficult. The financial stress was indicated by the fact that the Sisters had some of their furniture confiscated. A seventy-year-old widow who lived with them also had her bed and other objects removed.[38] However, these goods were restored as a result of a court judgment in their favour.[39] Meantime, Father Tomson (Gerard) was transferred to Madrid.

This seemed hardly the time to begin a new foundation, but the Prince-Bishop, Ferdinand, asked Mary Ward to found a house in Cologne - another of his dioceses. The people of Cologne wanted the Englishwomen there and a house was offered to Mary to begin the new work. For lack of money Mary delayed the Cologne foundation for six months.

Foundations at Cologne and Treves

In 1620 Mary established new houses in both Cologne and Treves. Father Gerard raised money on her behalf for these projects.[40] The house at Treves was founded 'with the approbation of the Archbishop of the city and the Papal Nuncio Albergati'.[41] This is significant in illustrating the esteem with which Mary was held by the Church authorities in that region.

Why did Mary Ward establish two more houses at this time when there were financial difficulties in Liège, as well as community disunity as a result of the Praxedes and Alcock affairs? Apart from expanding the apostolate of the Institute, it would seem that to ensure the progress of the Institute, Mary considered that such moves would strengthen ties with significant authority figures in the Church, such as the Prince-Bishop, Ferdinand, and the Papal Nuncio, Albergati. Mary Ward was necessarily involved in the politics of both Church and state. But it was essentially Roman approval that Mary Ward needed and sought.

CHAPTER 7

Roman Venture

By the time that Mary Ward had established houses in Cologne and Treves in 1618 Pope Pius V had died. Mary's friend, Bishop Blaes of St Omer, also died in that year. Her next plan was to go to Rome to present her plan for her Institute to the new pope and request confirmation for it.[1]

She began her journey from Liège to Rome in 1621. The Infanta Isabella Clara Eugenia advised Mary and her companions to wear pilgrims' clothing as a safeguard against bandits on the way. This dress comprised a large-brimmed felt hat, strong shoes, a long dark dress and a staff. The pilgrim hats worn by Mary Ward and one of her companions on this journey were made of some kind of beaver or felt, high-crowned, with broad brims for protection from the sun, and are still preserved as precious remembrances at the Convent of the Institute of the Blessed Virgin Mary at Altötting, Bavaria.[2]

The journey to Rome took seventy days across Europe which was suffering the trauma of the initial phase of the Thirty Years' War. The group averaged thirty kilometres a day, which was an amazing feat for the women since walking was their only means of travel. Sources differ on the number of persons who made this journey but it appears to have been eight or nine people.[3]

The likely members of this group were: Mary Ward and her sister, Barbara Ward; Margaret Horde, who was Mary's secretary; Winifred Wigmore, who was a close personal companion; Anne Turner, who had medical knowledge; and Susanna Rookwood, who had language gifts. The priest who also accompanied them was Henry Lee, a nephew of Father Roger Lee SJ. In addition, they had Robert Wright as a secular companion. He was a cousin of Mary Ward - possibly a son of Christopher Wright or John Wright, her uncles, both of whom were involved in the Gunpowder Plot to blow up the English House of Lords and the King, James 1, in 1605.[4]

Indeed Robert Wright was to devote his life to the service of Mary Ward and the Institute. He died at a great age in 1683 at Augsburg. Robert is one of the unsung heroes of the whole enterprise of establishing the Institute. He acted as a guardian on the various long journeys carried out by members of the Institute, and as serving-man at other times, and he was assessed as a humble man of virtue.[5]

Attempts to secure papal approval

The travellers arrived in Rome on 24 December 1621. The new pope was Alessandro Ludovisi, who took the name of Gregory XV. He was an old, delicate man and relied on his nephew, Ludovico Ludovisi. Like his uncle, this nephew had been educated by the Jesuits and had studied law at Bologna. He was made a cardinal and ordained soon afterwards at the age of twenty-five. All important papal transactions passed through him.[6]

The Spanish Netherlands was represented at the Holy See by the Spanish nobleman and famous humanist, Juan Baptista Vives. He was not friendly to the Jesuits and may not have helped the Englishwomen if the Infanta had not written him a letter asking him to do so. He was able to obtain an audience for Mary Ward and her associates on 28 December, very soon after their arrival in Rome.

Vives accompanied Mary and her companions to their audience with the pope and spoke in Latin on this occasion on their behalf. In a report to the Infanta about the audience, Vives said: 'people at this court were astonished by the Englishwomen, particularly by their large hats. Even the Pope remarked on these and asked about them pointedly. I told him that this was part of their dress and that they always wore them.'[7] Vives' remarks to the Infanta illustrate his lack of understanding of the position of the women, and his little sympathy for them.

But Mary Ward and her associates also presented a petition to the pope. In this they presented themselves as a Society of Jesus for women and requested recognition as religious. They expressed submission to the pope in obedience, praying for his special protection, so that they might not be subordinate to the jurisdiction of a local bishop. They explained that their work was to help the salvation of their neighbours' souls.[8] The presentation of themselves as a Society of Jesus for women necessarily involved exemption from enclosure.

The Council of Trent had ordered all bishops, under the threat of eternal damnation, to ensure the enclosure of all nuns under their jurisdiction. Bishops had to give professed nuns permission to leave the cloister. The only legitimate excuses for leaving the cloister were fire, leprosy, and contagious disease. Enclosure (clausura) 'protected the honour of religious women; saved them from exposure to the influence of the world... and protected them from the violence of the world'.[9] The Council of Trent had also decreed that female monasteries had to be surrounded by their own walls, and also to be located within cities which had their own walls. This was to give the nuns double protection from outside influence.[10] This kind of clausura was appreciated by Catholic reformers and contemplative communities, but it did not look forward to the active apostolic groups which were then emerging and for which Mary Ward's Institute was to be a precedent.[11]

It soon became apparent that the request for exemption from enclosure posed the greatest difficulty for their obtaining confirmation of the Institute. Indeed, as Peters points out, 'it may be taken as certain that the Englishwomen went to this audience equipped with the "Formula Instituti" of the Society of Jesus altered for their Institute'.[12]

Wright comments that this petition of Mary Ward's outlined their apostolic activity and it was clear, precise, flexible and quite revolutionary for the time. Mary's early perception of the necessity of a sound Catholic education for women in the Church's fight against heresy was here given prominence as the chief means towards the end 'of defence and propagation of the faith'. Mary Ward presented this plan to the Holy See knowing the impossibility of her petition being granted.[13]

The pope transferred Mary Ward's petition to the Congregation of Bishops and Regulars. There were thirty cardinals in this Congregation, but only about ten attended their regular meetings. Mary thought such a meeting would take too long and asked Vives to request that a special congregation of fewer cardinals be formed. However, the question of confirmation remained in the hands of the Congregation of Bishops and Regulars.[14]

The Sisters were dependent on Vives for financial aid, which he gave sparingly, although the Infanta sent money for them. At this stage Vives was almost eighty years old and the affairs of the Englishwomen must have appeared trivial to him. Moreover, he was a Spaniard and in his country women religious were enclosed. Because he was not partial to the Jesuits, he probably lacked sympathy for Mary Ward's project.[15]

The Roman people laughed at the strange women in the quaint costume walking freely through the streets. Ladies of the nobility in Rome were not usually seen on the streets without a companion (male), or wearing a veil covering most of the face, or being driven in a carriage when they went visiting. Grisar is of the opinion that it was good that they were laughed at, because if their actions had been seen as the initiation of a new kind of religious order for women, the authorities would have taken prompt action to suppress them.[16]

Finally on 21 January 1622 the Congregation of Bishops and Regulars met and dealt with Mary Ward's request. Through Vives, Mary learnt that Cardinal Bandini had been appointed Referent for the English Sisters' business.[17]

Cardinal Bandini was born in Florence in 1558 and was made cardinal by Pope Gregory XV, at the age of thirty-eight. However, as Mary Ward discovered he was not entirely reliable. He attempted to be a friend to both the English Sisters and the English secular clergy who, as will be seen, caused Mary a great deal of trouble.[18] His dubious help ended when he died on 1 August 1629.

When Mary Ward's plan for her Institute was being examined by a congregation of cardinals in 1622, Cardinal Bandini, whom Mary then regarded as a friend, suggested that the confirmation of the order could be granted if the English Sisters were prepared to accept the kind of enclosure practised by the Tor de Specchi. They had a type of incomplete enclosure as mentioned above. This was an apparently friendly advance from Cardinal Bandini, but Mary could not be satisfied with such a solution.

At this very time, on 12 March 1622, St Ignatius Loyola, founder of the Society of Jesus, was canonised in Rome. With him were also canonised Teresa of Avila, Philip Neri and Francis Xavier.[19] Mary Ward was in Rome seeking papal approval for her Institute.

Meanwhile the pope had become ill and was granting no audiences. In May, Mary Ward sent him a new 'Petition' asking for confirmation of the Institute in England, Belgium and Germany - all without enclosure. In a spirit of faithfulness to her visions, Mary would not concede any changes to the structure of the Institute, but sought only confirmation for her present foundations.

In a now memorable document written in 1622 on 'Reasons why we may not alter', Mary Ward drew up her apologia for the new Institute. She wrote it on two pages, perhaps as an aide-memoire for a consultation, or as a rough workout of a letter.[20] The following is a summary of the apologia, according to Peters:

1. The Englishwomen had chosen the Institute of the Society of Jesus, which had already been approved by the Church and had proved itself suitable for the apostolate.

2. Social changes and their own experience had caused them to choose this model.

3. A trial period of twelve years in following the Jesuit Rule (the same Rule) had guided the members to their own and their neighbour's salvation.

4. They were called to this Institute above all, and it had been confirmed in them by the exercises prescribed by St. Ignatius. This Institute offers women a place in the Church in working for their own and their neighbour's salvation. It embodies a striving for God's greater glory, which is the personal right of the vocation of anyone called to an Order. As the choice of a partner is free in marriage, so is the choice of an Order free for those called.[21]

School in Rome

There seemed no resolution to Mary Ward's affairs. The congregation was taking a long time to discuss the question of confirmation and the Sisters were in dire financial need. But Mary was not going to give up and so she embarked on the establishment of a house in Rome. The Sisters appealed to their Referent, Cardinal Bandini, for permission to establish a convent in Rome. They heard that the cardinals wanted to know what they would be teaching. They responded that 'reading, writing and needlework of all kinds' would be taught. Bandini required more detail and they added that 'they wished to teach every kind of work, as well as good behaviour and morals fitting the female sex'.[22]

The limited Italian of Mary Ward and her companions would have made even this teaching very difficult. Bandini made no response, but eventually Cardinal Millini granted permission - written in June on the back of their 'Petition'.[23] Possibly Mary Ward did not wish to make a permanent foundation in Rome, but rather to find occupation for her group and earn some income.

The first foundation of the Institute in Rome was made in November 1622 in a building on the corner of Via Monserrato and Vicolo Montoro.[24] It consisted of two storeys over a fairly high ground floor. This rented house was in the vicinity of the English College.[25] The Sisters began a day school. This was an innovation in Rome because, formerly, girls had to live within the convent enclosures in order to be educated. By February 1623 there were 123 pupils coming to the school which proved to be successful. According to the English Vita:

> She obtained to do in Rome as in other places, that was both in their own personal practice and assistance of others, teaching gratis those of our sex both virtues and qualities which produced such effects, as the wicked said, if this went on, the stews (brothels) in Rome would fail; and poor parents felt the pleasing benefit of having their children made fit by qualities to gain their livings honestly, and by virtue made capable to know it was their duty so to do.[26]

Perhaps the founding of these 'trade' schools was among Mary Ward's most innovative tasks. They were established in Rome and later on in Perugia. The account in Chambers gives some idea of this initiative:

> We are so accustomed in the present times to hear of public schools of all kinds for every class, as much for girls as for boys, that Mary Ward's schools in Rome, do not come before us at first sight with all their merits and attendant difficulties. We may be apt to forget that such schools were unknown there for girls, though Scoule Pie had lately been established there for boys by St. Joseph Calasanctius, and were meeting with the greatest encouragement.The merit of being the first on a hitherto untrodden field only added to the difficulties which beset the enterprise in Mary's case.[27]

We know that the parents objected when the Roman school was closed and appealed to the pope's sister-in-law, Constanza Barberini, for it to remain open.

Mary Ward saw the work of this school as assisting the cause of the confirmation of her Institute. Cardinal Millini, the Pope's Vicar of Rome, kept Mary Ward and her companions under surveillance. According to the English biography of Mary Ward: 'Cardinal Millini, then Vicar in Rome, himself told our dear Mother, that he kept not one or two but 24 spies over her, insomuch as there was not what passed in or out that he had not notice of.'[28] No doubt this was an exaggeration, but spies were generally known to operate around Rome, and their watching was accepted, but it could not have been comfortable for the women.

Opposition from English clergy

Mary Ward was aware of the tension between the Jesuits and secular clergy in England, but possibly she was not aware of the full extent of the animosity that this tension generated. As indicated, apart from their own alleged misdemeanours, Mary Ward's Sisters were not in favour with the secular English clergy because of their association with the Jesuits. Letters had been sent from the English secular clergy to the Curia complaining about the Englishwomen.

The archpriest, William Harrison, wrote from England about Mary Ward in 1621. After his death in May 1621, his former assistant, John Bennet, left England to take up office as the Roman Agent of the English secular clergy. Peters notes that John Bennet came from Wales, studied theology in Douai and Spain, and as a secular priest on the English mission was imprisoned in Wisbeach. When appointed to succeed Harrison in Rome he worked for the nomination of a bishop for England. He succeeded in having Dr William Bishop appointed as Vicar Apostolic for England. Bennet returned to England in 1623 and died in the same year. As a fierce opponent of the Jesuits he had opposed Mary Ward and her work.[29]

What William Harrison had written in England concerning Mary Ward and her associates John Bennet now had circulated. It was called the 'Informatio' and Peters' summary of it makes illuminating reading.

The Archpriest gave a range of offences attributed to Mary Ward and her associates in seven points:

1. Up to now it has never been known that women undertook apostolic work. They are not capable of it.

2. Such an Institute, without enclosure, is canonically forbidden. The Englishwomen call themselves 'religiosae' but not 'moniales', and refuse to accept enclosure.

3. They dare to speak on religious topics and give public 'exhortations' even in the presence of priests, whereas women should keep silent in church. (Here Harrison not

only quoted St. Paul's famous passage, 1Cor. 11, 34-35, but also several fathers of the Church, and named passages in Canon Law.)

4. It is not yet possible to prove the danger of heresy. The Archpriest calls to mind the history of the Beguines.

5. The Jesuitesses gad about all over the country, creep into houses of the aristocracy, put on different sorts of dress, consort with men among others and talk with people of ill-repute. Sometimes they travel to and fro between Belgium and England.

6. Not only are they not needed in England by the Church, they are a danger to its reputation.

7. Several of these female Jesuits are held to be of bad repute, frivolous and shameless, and a scandal to the Catholic faith.[30]

Another English priest, Thomas Rant, who succeeded John Bennet in Rome supported the latter's opposition to the Englishwomen. Rant considered their work in England a cause of concern to the Church. He asserted:

The Jesuitesses lead a loose life. They run about all over England and associate with men. They refuse to pray in choir or to follow conventual practices and, on the Continent, they train their pupils for just such a daring way of life by the production of plays. In doing so they are a threat to the women of England and a scandal to catholics. Might the Pope consider the following suggestions?

1. He should either confirm their Institute as an enclosed Order for teaching girls within the enclosure, or

2. Forbid their pastoral activities in England, as their form of life there is fraught with danger, or

3. Suppress their community as it is, so that they cannot admit any new members, deprive devout girls of their goods

and chattels, and rob other Orders of their much-needed candidates.[31]

In a letter to Winifred Wigmore, Mary Ward wrote with a touch of humour: 'M. Rant, the English priest who negotiates here in M. Bennet's place, makes himself hoarse with speaking against the English Gentlewomen and their Institute.'[32]

Opposition of the Benedictines

The Benedictines, Father Robert Sherwood and Father Palmer, were also active opponents as was indicated in their conversations with Sister Dorothea in England. It seems unlikely that these men actually met Mary Ward, as they based many of their accusations on hearsay. The Benedictines had been in England many decades before the Jesuits and had lost much of their property and prestige in the dissolution of the monasteries, so they were not welcoming to the vigorous young men of a 'new' active order like the Jesuits. It was these opponents of Mary's active work for the education of women who were successful in having the order suppressed by papal bull.

A 'smear campaign' against Mary Ward and her associates was conducted by Father Robert Sherwood. He was Procurator of the English Benedictines and felt that they had been superseded in England by the Jesuits. In the name of his congregation, Sherwood asked the pope either to direct these women into an order already established, or to impose enclosure on them, or to dissolve their congregation out of hand, or to forbid them taking part in the dangerous missionary work in England.[33]

At that time Mary Ward was unaware of many of these accusations, so she could not defend her Institute by rebutting them.[34] Another negative report was written in 1622 by Dr Matthew Kellison, President of the English Seminary in Douai. It appears he wrote his report from accusations already made by others and from rumours. He described Mary Ward, the Superior General, however as 'an extraordinarily gifted and graced lady who was now working for the community in Rome'.[35] Again non-enclosure was the controversial point.

Peters sums up the fiery opposition against Mary Ward and her proposed apostolate:

> Some of the secular clergy did indeed dislike the Jesuits and similarly any Jesuit-influenced community of women. The Jesuits defended themselves against the imitation of their Institute by women. Finally both came together on one point: a refusal to co-operate in pastoral work with women, however subordinate these might be. The meeting place of their complaints: Rome.[36]

The refusal to co-operate in pastoral work with women marks a basic point of difference between men and women in Reformation times. From the perspective of men the role of teaching and preaching was the prerogative of men only. As already indicated, it was difficult for Protestant wives to have an active teaching role in the Reformed Churches. Wiesner remarks that for properly constituted religious at this time the only active apostolate for religious women was the instruction of girls, and that only within the convent.[37]

Certainly, as has been seen, communities of women of pious association carried on ministry in the wider Catholic Church, but official religious did not. Protestant theology stressed the priesthood of all believers but repressed it for women in practice. The wives of Protestant clergymen helped their husbands, the sick and the poor, but they were not able to preach publicly.[38] A stereotyping of the function of the sexes seemed to be operating in all the main Christian denominations.

Unfortunately for Mary Ward the struggle over the participation of women in ministry in the Church was being fought
out over her plans for the confirmation of the Institute.

Personal Dealings with the Jesuit General

Mary Ward's dealings with the Jesuit General, Father
Mutius Vitelleschi reflected the prehistory of the Jesuits in
connection with their experience with women desiring to
live by Jesuit constitutions. Father Vitelleschi was born in
Rome in 1563, and was therefore twenty-two years older
than Mary Ward.[39]

When Mary went to Rome in 1621 she was well acquainted with the fact that Father Vitelleschi did not favour women who wanted to follow the Jesuit constitutions. He was opposed to it because it was against No 588
of these very constitutions, in which Ignatius forbade it,
as has already been explained. As Jesuit General he was
responsible for implementing the Jesuit Constitutions, so
Father Vitelleschi was officially against Mary's plans, but personally he was friendly to her in their frequent encounters.

Peters underlines this situation as she explains that:

> ... it must be recognized that Father Vitelleschi was, per-
> sonally, very kindly disposed towards Mary Ward, and it
> transpires that he helped her Institute in as much as this
> continued to be involved in the teaching and education of
> girls, and remained a 'Pium Institutum', but that constitu-
> tionally he opposed a congregation of women 'in the mat-
> ter and manner' of the Society of Jesus.[40]

Later on, with regard to her trials in Vienna and
Munich, Mary Ward received tender support from Father
Vitelleschi. No doubt the sanctity of both found a meeting
place and it would seem that Mary's personality - charm
and integrity - was a strong factor in her favour.[41]

The ambivalent relationship between the Jesuits and the Sisters was further displayed at the time of the death of Mary Ward's sister, Barbara, in January 1623. Barbara Ward was prayed for in the Jesuit church, the Gesu, at the command of Father General Vitelleschi. The fathers in the English College offered Masses for her and she was buried before the altar of Our Lady in that College.[42] What is clear throughout the life of Mary Ward in her efforts to establish her Institute is the ambiguity of the Jesuits in their attitude to her and in their involvement in the venture of establishing her Institute.[43]

Pope Gregory XV died on 8 July 1623, so negotiations for the confirmation of the Institute could not be dealt with until there was a new pope. After a long conclave Maffeo Barberini was elected as Pope Urban VIII. He had been born in Florence in 1568, studied Law in Pisa and held many Church positions, such as Nuncio in Paris, Protector of Scotland and Bishop of Spoleto. Pope Gregory XV had appointed him to the newly constituted Congregation de Propaganda Fide and in this capacity he may have first heard of Mary Ward.[44] The Barberini family was powerful in Italy and the number of the Barberini 'bees' apparent on the architecture in Rome is evidence of their influence in public administration since they were in a position to have the family symbol on so many public buildings. It was Pope Urban VIII who consecrated St Peter's Basilica in 1626.[45]

Urban VIII was a very difficult man. It has been said that he was 'self-assured, could not endure contradiction - disdained to hear another point of view'.[46] His practice of nepotism is well documented, as is also the fact that he was conscience-stricken in his old age.[47] Mary Ward was to experience much suffering through Urban VIII.

CHAPTER 8

Further Expansion of the Institute

Foundations at Naples and Perugia

Despite the frustration she was experiencing in Rome in 1623 Mary Ward established another house in Italy at Naples, which was then a city belonging to the Spanish crown. Indeed, in May 1623, she went on foot to Naples. Father Vitelleschi sent letters of recommendation and the Jesuits helped her generously because the house was very poor. Susanna Rookwood became the superior of this new house in November 1623, but unfortunately she died there in October 1624.[1] Susanna Rookwood was one of the first members of the Institute who travelled to the continent with Mary Ward. Subsequently she worked for a long time in England where she was superior for three years and was imprisoned on five occasions.

Winifred Wigmore, who had accompanied Susanna Rookwood, continued their work in Naples by establishing a school there. Mary Ratcliffe replaced Susanna Rookwood, but in 1625 there was a drastic blow when Pope Urban VIII ordered the suppression of the house. The Institute's school had become very useful to the city, and it was a matter of great regret to the people that it was closed.[2]

In January 1624 Mary Ward opened another house in Perugia. The Bishop of Perugia, Napoleone Comitoli, had invited the Sisters to come to his diocese. The founding Sisters travelled there on foot, covering the 180 kilometres

Houses founded by Mary Ward between 1609 and 1628. (Adapted from Emmanuel Orchard (ed), *Till God Will*, p 4.)
1609: St Omer; 1613: London; 1616: Liège; 1620: Cologne; 1621: Treves and Rome; 1623: Naples; 1625: Perugia; 1627: Munich, Vienna and Pressburg; 1628: Prague.

between Rome and Perugia in six days. By this time Mary was ill again with an attack of gallstones.[3] Girls came to the house of the Sisters in Perugia for lessons, but there were no boarders. The criticisms of the Institute's enemies were known in Perugia and when the bishop died in August 1624, his successor was no friend to the Englishwomen, who finally left Perugia in April 1625.

The foundation of houses in Naples and Perugia seemed madness at this time in light of the opposition to the Institute in Rome. But no doubt Mary reasoned that the establishment of strong houses in Italy would surely assist the confirmation of the Institute. Peters also suggests that these foundations in Italy would have provided living conditions less daunting than those in northern Europe for the young people who had joined her and her Institute.[4] At this time also the establishment of some more prosperous houses may have seemed desirable, since the Sisters were in financial troubles in Liège and conditions in Rome were very austere.

In 1622 Pope Gregory XV had established the Congregation for the Propagation of the Faith. It became known conventionally as *Propaganda*.[5] At first its work was limited to countries which had fallen into heresy - Protestant parts of the Continent, Anglican England and the Islamic Near East. In 1622 Cardinal Farnese was made responsible for England and Ireland. The nuncio in Brussels, geographically close to the British Isles, was appointed as his assistant. Francesco Ingoli was the 'bustling, efficient' secretary of this Congregation. In relation to Mary Ward's Institute the Congregation decided that the women should be compelled to adopt enclosure.[6]

As expected, Mary Ward resisted this direction and in October 1624 she had a private audience with Pope Urban VIII at Mondragone near Frascati, where he was convalescing. She asked the Pope to entrust her business to a special Congregation of Cardinals.

In a letter to Winifred Wigmore, Mary wrote, 'I but begged him very earnestly to trust the matter to God, for we had entrusted it entirely to God and his Holiness'.[7] Mary also requested that they have a chapel (oratory) in their house in Rome. The Pope said he would commission Cardinal Millini (Vicar General of Rome) to see to it. Peters pays tribute to Mary Ward's audacity in speaking thus to the Pope: 'Only a woman who was utterly convinced could have spoken in such a fashion to a pope in the seventeenth century. Only a woman totally given to God would have dared to suggest to this particular pope that he turn to God.'[8] But Peters adds: 'It was her mistake that she took this exterior appearance of benevolence of the Pope as genuine.'[9]

Special Congregation of Cardinals

A special Congregation of Cardinals was set up at the end of 1624 to examine the accusations against Mary Ward's Institute. Again Mary sent a petition for recognition of her Institute to this Congregation. According to Grisar the members of this Special Congregation were:

> Cardinal Millini, who, as Vicar of Rome, had to do officially with the English Sisters coming to Rome; Cardinal Corbelluzio usually named from his titular Church, Santa Suzanna, who was actually a member of the Congregation of Bishops and Regulars, but up to now had not been prominent in the case of the English Sisters; and lastly, the older brother of the Pope, Cardinal Antonio Barberini, who belonged to the Capuchin Order and had been created Cardinal in 1624. He was usually named after his titular Church, Saint Onofrio.[10]

None of these cardinals seemed violently opposed to Mary Ward, but they would have wanted Church reform –

hence enclosure for nuns. Since it appears also that the accusations against the Sisters came from English sources, such as the agent Rant in Rome, it was above all the open pastoral apostolate in England of these Englishwomen which was completely repudiated by this Special Congregation.

On the 11 April 1625 Pope Urban VIII ordered the Congregation of Bishops and Regulars to suppress the Englishwomen's houses in Italy. It is important to note, as Peters does, that reasons of canon law were the decisive factors for the suppression of the Institute, and not its Ignatian charism.[11]

Grisar deduces from meagre evidence that it appears that the General Congregation of Bishops and Regulars was 'not willing to give confirmation to the new Association and had considered it inadvisable to grant it for Italy. Urban VIII, by giving the order, (that is, to suppress the Institute) showed his approval of the decision of the Congregation.'[12]

As well as suffering extreme poverty like the rest of her companions, Mary Ward herself continued to experience very poor health. The trying conditions and difficult weather of Rome did not help attacks of gallstones as she endeavoured to cope with the Pope's decision. With regard to this first suppression Peters notes:

> Once, the well-known and saintly discalced Carmelite, Father Dominicus a Jesu Maria, who had been present as observer at the sessions of the Congregatio de Propaganda Fide, said of Mary Ward and her companions that it was inevitable that they were crushed underfoot. They had to have the same dependence on God as young crows, abandoned by the older ones because they did not have the same feathers.[13]

The two congregations which had been commissioned to deal with Mary Ward's case both condemned her initiatives. The Special Congregation of Cardinals had been set up to examine the accusations made against her. Unknown to Mary many of these accusations were put forward by her own countrymen. As a result of the Special Congregation's deliberations, the Roman school had to be closed, although the Sisters could continue to live in Rome. Winifred Wigmore recorded that the children's parents went in troops to the Cardinal Vicar's palace, and to Donna Constanza (the Pope's sister-in-law) where they hoped their tears and lamentations would bring the Sisters help and relief.[14]

However, the orders for the suppression of the houses which Mary Ward had established in Italy were not carried out until 12 November 1625, when, on the Pope's command, Cardinal Millini sent an order for the suppression of the community in Rome, but not their Institute. As already related, the communities in Rome, Naples and Perugia were to be closed according to instructions, though the English-women might continue to live in the Papal States.[15]

The other houses which were not in Italy were not then suppressed. According to Grisar, the Special Congregation seemed to have ceased to function after that. The General Congregation, too, from the evidence of the Acts, did not deal any further with the question of the English Sisters. The decision regarding the new Institute was left completely to the Congregation of Propaganda which had some of the same Cardinals belonging to it.[16]

Proposed foundation in Sicily

After the closure of the houses in the Papal States, Mary Ward was intending to make a foundation in Sicily. The Sisters had to go somewhere, and Sicily (as well as Naples) was under the Spanish crown. According to Peters, 'for more than a year Mary Ward considered a foundation in Sicily as a possibility for her Institute and its members, and Father Vitelleschi (the Jesuit General) helped her during this time'.[17] But such a foundation was never made because opportunities opened up in the north for the expansion of the Institute.

Although Mary Ward was in poor health and concerned about the Sisters in the other houses of St Omer, Liège and Trier, in November 1626 she left Rome for Munich with a small group. They were welcomed by friends along the way. In Florence the Grand Duchess Christina, mother-in-law of Grand Duchess Maria Magdalena, the sister of the Electress Elisabeth of Bavaria, issued a testimonial letter for Mary Ward.[18]

In Milan, Charles Borromeo's nephew, Cardinal Federigo Borromeo, gave Mary Ward an audience.[19] This was a remarkable occurrence since he had a reputation of being a very austere man.[20] The group reached Munich in January 1627.

Foundation at Munich

Munich was in Bavaria, a country which had remained Catholic. At that time the Jesuit-educated Elector Maximilian I had been ruling there for thirty years. During the initial period of his reign Maximilian had improved the finances of Bavaria. He had joined the counter-reformers and in 1609 became head of the Catholic League. By his first marriage he was brother-in-law to the Emperor Ferdinand II, who gave Maximilian the position of elector.

It is not known why Mary Ward then travelled to the north of Europe and not first to the houses in Flanders. Chambers hazards that Mary's knowledge of the kindness of the Emperor Maximilian to the religious foundations in

Flanders, together with advice from such influential people as the saintly Father Domenica di Gesu, influenced her decision to go to Germany at this time.[21] Maximilian and his wife, the Electress Elisabeth, welcomed Mary Ward and her group. Eventually they gave Mary and her associates the Paradeiser House (this building was named after a previous owner, Christoph Paradeiser, Graf von Neuhaus).[22] The Elector also gave them a subsidy of 2000 guilders annually - a provision for ten people.[23]

Day and boarding schools were opened in Munich in April 1627. To the primary subjects of the three Rs, the languages of classical Latin, Italian and French were added, as well as a variety of types of handwork. This school for girls was the first of its kind in Munich.[24]

The Bishop of Basel, supported by the Electress Elisabeth had planned to bring a foundation of Pruntrut Ursulines from Switzerland to Munich to educate girls. These Ursuline Sisters came from the Ursuline Association of Borgogne, founded by Anne de Xainctogne (1567-1621). As explained previously, these women belonged to a pious association, and therefore, not being nuns, avoided enclosure.[25] The coming of the Englishwomen stopped this plan, but then it was further proposed to unite the Pruntrut Ursulines with Mary Ward's Sisters. Mary wanted the Ursulines to join her Order completely, and this included a full novitiate. The plan was subsequently dropped because the Ursulines did not agree to Mary's proposals for their integration into her Institute.[26]

Some of the Jesuits in Munich were not helpful to the Sisters. Apart from their opposition to the Institute, which may have stemmed from their constitutions forbidding the establishment of female Jesuit congregations, this situation could have simply reflected German resentment of the English. Among the Sisters Mary Ward gave such enemies the cover name of 'Jerusalems'.[27]

Foundation in Vienna

Just six months after her arrival in Munich, Mary Ward was on her way to establish a new foundation in Vienna. Maximilian wrote a letter of recommendation to the Emperor, Ferdinand II. The Emperor and Empress welcomed the Sisters and gave them the use of a state house, Stoss am Himmel, as well as an allowance of six hundred guilders per year from the Emperor and four hundred guilders per year from the Empress. This amount would have supported five Sisters and, by October 1629, there were eleven members.[28]

The population of Vienna was between 70,000 and 100,000.[29] When a school was opened there a year later it had an enrolment of 475 girls.[30] The eleven Sisters were too few for all these pupils but by 1629 there were fewer boarders. The school in Vienna was free for the poor as Mary wrote to Winifred Wigmore: 'Jesus forbid you should make such children as you teach pay one penny for windows, wood, or anything else. For God's love, if you do that work of charity, do it like yourself, not mercenarily, else my dear Winn, follow my poor counsel and let it alone.'[31] This school for poor girls appears to have been a separate school because Mary Ward wrote about it to Winifred Wigmore - exhorting her to do this work with large-heartedness. Teaching in this poor school was done publicly because Chambers notes that Mary wrote 'without disguise of the school of the poor'.[32]

There were troubles within the Church in Vienna as a result of conflict over Church jurisdiction. The diocese of Vienna had been suppressed and Cardinal Melchior Klesl, Bishop of Vienna, had been removed from his diocese.[33] He was away from it for nine years. By January 1628 he again solemnly entered Vienna. As the Emperor Ferdinand had established the Sisters, Cardinal Klesl complained to Rome saying:

In Vienna there are certain women, who call themselves Jesuitesses, take three vows and, without the previous knowledge or permission of the Bishop, have opened a school for girls in the city. They do not wish to be subject to the episcopal court, but only to their superior general and are dependent on the Emperor alone. The Jesuits do not support them. A few days ago their pupils produced a play. The General Superior has gone to Hungary, in order to found a house under the Emperor's protection. As scandals are feared, would Cardinal Bandini possibly send him, the Bishop of Vienna, instructions as to how to handle this matter.[34]

Hungary (Pressburg) foundation

Mary Ward had indeed gone to Hungary. She went to Pressburg, today's Bratislava, which was then a small town on Austria's eastern border, only sixty kilometres from Vienna. The Bishop of Pressburg was Cardinal Pazmany. He obtained advice from the Nuncio, Carlo Carafa, about the Sisters. Carafa was favourable towards them but Pazmany had to get permission from the Protestant city councillors for the Sisters to come to Pressburg. The permission was given, so in March 1628 Cardinal Pazmany brought Mary Ward and four Sisters to Pressburg. Barbara Babthorpe was appointed Superior.[35]

The nature of their educational work in Pressburg (brief though it was) is shown by the following description of their school curriculum:

The main emphasis was on religious teaching, in accordance with the aim of the Institute and the need of the Church. The elementary subjects of reading, writing and arithmetic bear witness to the laborious first steps of girls' education in general. Latin was an option; the beautiful handwork and painting techniques conformed to the educational pattern of women in those days.[36]

Barbara Babthorpe wrote that the school had a good number of pupils, but many did not attend regularly because they were needed at home for the wine harvest. However, according to Peters, 'in spite of this somewhat pessimistic opinion, on 25 April 1628, seventy of the Institute's pupils took part in St. Mark's procession through the streets of the city. A fine achievement for a short time.'[37]

Attempts at a Prague foundation

The next attempt by Mary Ward and her companions at a foundation was in Prague. The Emperor, Ferdinand II, was also King of both Hungary and Bohemia. With the Emperor's patronage Count Michael Aldof von Altham invited Mary to Prague, offering a house and a generous benefice for the support of thirty persons.[38] But Church and state relations in Prague presented problems too complex for Mary Ward to master. Indeed secular rulers and potentates could give material support and privileges, but it was with difficulty that they carried any weight in the sphere of canon law or ecclesial jurisdiction in the Church, especially if political tensions played a role, as it assuredly did during the time of Mary Ward's negotiating for a Prague foundation.[39]

Grisar describes the situation where there were two parties. One stressed Church authority in opposition to the Emperor, while the other sought to support the Emperor's activities in recognition of his services for the Church. The Jesuits belonged to the latter group. Pope Urban VIII championed the greater freedom of the Church, but political reasons made him cautious towards the Emperor. So Mary Ward and her cause floundered in this area of tension.[40]

The Church authorities, responding to Rome's negative assessment of Mary Ward's Institute, opposed the foundation proposed by the secular ruler. Therefore, the foundation at Prague was never destined to last and Mary Ward finally abandoned it.[41] Meanwhile the relentless disapproval in Rome concerning her Institute was hardening still further.

CHAPTER 9

Further Roman Developments

In Rome in March 1628, the Congregation of Propaganda Fide in its eighty-ninth session made three decisions with regard to Mary Ward. Peters gives them as:

> 1. To set up a special congregation, which should enquire how the suppression of the Englishwomen's Institute could be achieved... Their task, the destruction of the Institute of the Jesuitesses, had already been made known to them.
>
> 2. Father General Vitelleschi was to be warned against promoting the Institute.
>
> 3. Cardinal Lorenzo Magalotti should be charged with finding out the connection between the Institute of the Englishwomen and the Belgian 'Angelicae', and the Beguines.[1]

Peters comments that 'the ignorance of the congregation and of their secretary Ingoli is here made abundantly clear'.[2] The houses in the Papal States had already been suppressed, but now the Decree for the Suppression of the Jesuitesses was sent to the Nuncio of Naples and he was to advise the Archbishop, but he did not do this. Propaganda had to write three letters to the Nuncio ordering him to carry out the suppression. Information about why this happened is lacking.[3] However, the Congregation had directed that the four Italian Sisters were to be sent home to their parents and the other four (Englishwomen) were to be accommodated in the town.[4]

Suppression of the Vienna house

Carlo Carafa was Nuncio in Vienna, but a specially commissioned Nuncio-Extraordinary, Pallotto, received the commission from Propaganda Fide to suppress the Institute there. Pallotto was recognized by Cardinal Barberini 'as a master of devious diplomacy'.[5]

As mentioned previously, Cardinal Klesl had been restored to his diocese of Vienna, but in this matter of the suppression of the house of Mary Ward's Institute he was bypassed by the Nuncio. Eventually Cardinal Klesl made an episcopal visitation of the Vienna house to provide himself with reasons for *not* suppressing the foundation. Klesl was able to produce evidence of only the 'possibility' of scandals, but no inadequacy in the Sisters' teaching, nor any questionable conduct.[6]

There was also a report about the Sisters visiting the parents of their pupils and the sick. It is the first time, with the exception of the contact they had with their pupils' mothers in Rome and Perugia, that we hear of the Englishwomen's work in adult education on the continent, although it was known, as recorded earlier, that they worked clandestinely with adults in England.

Although a Decree of Suppression of the Institute had been prepared by Propaganda on 12 January 1629, Cardinal Klesl did not carry it out in Vienna. About this, Peters comments:

> Not even the Emperor had been able to bring pressure to bear on Cardinal Klesl to make him give the slightest appearance of carrying out the Curia's mandate by subordinating himself to the Nuntius and supporting him. He would not do it. His actions supply the answer to the question as to whether Cardinal Klesl saw the suppression of the Institute as a priority for the good of the Church in Vienna.[7]

It appears that this was a typical example of Church politics - Cardinal Klesl had formerly rejected Mary Ward and her Institute because he had not been in control of his see when they came to Vienna. Subsequently he refused to suppress them because the Congregation had informed the Nuncio first instead of himself. Cardinal Klesl died on 18 September 1630.[8] In October of that year the Roman Congregation commissioned the new Nuncio, Ciriaco Ricci, with the suppression of the Englishwomen and it was duly carried out.[9]

Suppression of the Pressburg house

The suppression of the house in Pressburg probably took place in 1629, although there are records in the Hungarian Treasury of allowances paid to the Englishwomen until the end of 1632. Archbishop Pazmany was always supportive of the education of girls as being 'almost more important than that of boys'.[10]

Archbishop Pazmany wrote a letter to Cardinal Millini, Vicar of Rome, who had suppressed the Roman houses. In this letter he said that education was most important in Hungary, where there was greater threat of heresy, than in Italy.[11] His defence of Mary Ward also stated that the education of girls was essential because 'from the mothers we get first principles for later life, and the aroma of what they whisper into tender ears even lingers in later years'.[12]   Although bishops and cardinals supported in theory the ministry of educating girls by religious, they hampered it especially by the insistence on convent enclosure.

As well as defending the education of girls, Pazmany, unlike many bishops and cardinals, wrote in defence of the Institute's way of doing it. He declared that 'the establishment of a truly great Institute for the education and instruction of young girls, as the time demanded, could no longer be achieved by the confined schools of the old Orders'.[13] Nevertheless, the house was suppressed, although there is no exact date when the Sisters left Pressburg.[14]

When Mary Ward was struggling for the continuation of her work in Vienna, Nuncio Pallotto persuaded her to go once again to Rome to plead her cause before the Pope, Urban VIII. This showed Pallotto's duplicity because Mary would have undertaken this journey only if there was some hope of approbation. Pallotto knew that the contrary was the case. Because she was very ill, Mary was not able to leave Munich for Rome until the end of 1628. In May 1629 Mary had another audience with Urban VIII. The Pope was affable and Grisar remarks that 'the thought never occurred to her that Urban VIII had been playing with her'.[15] However, the Decree of the Congregation of 30 November 1629 was directed expressly against the Institute of the English 'Jesuitesses'.[16]

Suppression of houses in the Netherlands

After returning from Rome to Munich Mary Ward went to Vienna to have an audience with the Nuncio, Pallotto, and again Mary was not told that the suppression was inevitable. Mary returned to Munich where she was again very ill. Her visit to Pallotto had not clarified matters for her.

At this crucial time a letter of Mary Ward to all the Sisters, dated 6 April 1630, exhorted them to have courage because the order for suppression of the Institute was 'based on false accusations and the decrees had come from and been written by Cardinal Bentivoglio, an old enemy of our Institute. The orders came without His Holiness's knowledge.'[17]

This letter indicates that Mary knew nothing of what had actually been decided about her Institute (that is, the Decree of Suppression), but she believed that approval was still being considered and that the Pope had offered her hope. She thought that the bad reports had come from enemies. Copies of this letter found their way to Rome as Peters states that:

> ... from the house in Mont St. Martin (Liège), the letter found its way to the translator. It arrived as translated and probably, too, as a much abridged version in Rome, where, inevitably, it was to be the prelude to a new and final movement against the Institute and above all, Mary Ward.[18]

No doubt Mary Ward was naive in her continued hope for approval of the Institute at this time when there was such obvious reluctance of Church authorities to sanction official religious life for women outside the cloister. But as Peters comments, from the perspective of the Curia it was de facto a matter of secondary importance to them to have had bad reports of such a group of women. What was significant to them was that these reports were dangerous in so far as they affected the political balance between Church authorities and the secular princes.[19]

Mary decided to send her close friend, Winifred Wigmore, to visit the houses in Trier, Cologne and Liège. There were unfortunate consequences from these visits because Winifred Wigmore appeared to disobey the papal directive for the suppression of the Institute. She was not told that the Pope and the Congregation of Cardinals had decided to suppress the Order since she believed Mary's assessment of the situation as given to her before leaving Munich. She replied to the Church authorities in defence of Mary Ward and her vision for the Institute.

As Visitor (sent by the Superior General) to these houses, Winifred Wigmore may have been foolish, naive, or simply ignorant of the papal directives, but Grisar asserts that:

... the Institute would have been suppressed even without the Visitation, and the clumsy manner in which Winifred Wigmore carried it out. But the dispatch of the Visitress and her activity are chiefly to be blamed for the suppression by a Papal Bull so severely damaging to the prestige and honour of Mary Ward, and the punishment imposed.[20]

Nuncio Carafa interrogated each Sister in the Liège community and they answered in loyalty to their foundress and with absolute loyalty to their vows. The Nuncio's response was the recommendation to Rome to treat these women with a strong hand - by a papal bull against their Institute.[21] As a result of the interrogations of the individual Sisters, Nuncio Carafa in 1630 wrote to Francesco Ingoli, Secretary of the Congregation of Propaganda Fide, and made three suggestions as to what to do with these women:

1. The Pope should publish a Bull against these 'loglio' - poisonous plants.[22]

2. The General Superior should be imprisoned and punished severely.

3. The houses in Vienna and Munich should be dissolved, as there was no point in closing the communities of the Institute in some cities while allowing them to flourish in others.[23]

The Sisters in the Netherlands were still bound by their vows. Carafa asked Ingoli for faculties to dispense the Englishwomen from their vows. He never received an answer.[24] Like Mary Ward, Winifred Wigmore did not believe that the Decree of Suppression came from the Pope. However, the Roman Congregation of Propaganda told Carafa to imprison Winifred Wigmore. Therefore, on 13 February 1631, the Nuncio, Carafa, and the bishop's official, Rosin Serau, took Winifred Wigmore into the enclosure of the Collegiate Church and placed her in detention. On 19 February 1631, 'in a special session of the Chapter, a message from Carafa was read out in which he made known that by imprisoning

Winifred Wigmore, he had performed an official act within the enclosure of the Collegiate Church at the command of the Holy See'.[25] Winifred was subsequently released when in 1632 Mary Ward asked the Pope for her freedom.

The official account of events in Liège led to the final blow for Mary Ward's Institute. Under the presidency of the Pope the cardinals decided to transfer the matter to the Holy Office. As Peters explains: 'this (office), known until 1908 as "Congregatio Romanae et universalis Inquisitionis", had been re-organised in 1542 by Pope Paul III; it was the Papal authority for the teaching of faith and morals for the Roman Catholic Church, and had great juridic power'.[26] This power was to be used in the framing of the Papal Bull of Suppression. (The Congregation is now the 'Congregation for the Doctrine of the Faith'.)

The house in Liège had long had financial difficulties and many members had returned to their homes. The Nuncio, Pierluigi Carafa, was determined on reform. As Nuncio of Cologne he lived also in Liège. On 30 April 1630 the Decree of Suppression of the Englishwomen's foundation in Liège was promulgated.[27] Winifred Wigmore was not imprisoned until the following year.

Peters asks the question: what was being suppressed? She comments:

> The Englishwomen, after the promulgation of the decree of suppression, were to be regarded as lay people. But had they not been so before, according to canon law? Their Institute had been unable to obtain papal approbation. Moreover, the vows of the now-declared laywomen were not dispensed. Neither the Bishop nor the Nuntius had the right to do so, and Rome was silent on the matter, even after a second request from the Nuntius.[28]

The suppression of the Cologne house followed in May 1630. It was done very harshly and publicly and the Sisters' creditors all clamoured at once for payment - a very sad end to their work there.

The house in Trier was another to be suppressed and this took place in August 1630. Here the Archbishop had problems with the secular authorities while the Nuncio, Carafa, pushed for the suppression to be executed. The religious princes were bound by the Decree and their obedience to the Pope. This explains why the English women's communities could expect less protection in the ecclesiastical territories than in the realms of the secular princes, who could at least save them from eviction.[29]

One group that was often confused with Mary Ward's followers was the Daughters of St Agnes. At that time they were a pious association which followed the Augustinian rule like that of the Ursulines in Paris. They devoted themselves to the education of girls of all classes. In 1626 they received episcopal approval. In the older writings about the town and the bishopric of St Omer, they were often confused with the Englishwomen.[30]

When the College of Propaganda in Rome gave the order for the suppression of Mary Ward's Jesuitesses, authorities in the Netherlands did not know that there were Jesuitesses other than Belgian Jesuitesses. The English or Belgian nationality then became an important issue - as well as that of their being lay associations. Grisar notes that '... they resembled the communities of nuns who had to be suppressed according to the existing Canon law. How could such communities be officially subject to a pastor since they were certainly established as lay institutes?'[31] To be associated with the name 'Jesuitesses' was a cause of suspicion and the Daughters of St Agnes were suppressed for this reason, in mistake for Mary Ward's Institute.[32]

The suppression of the Jesuitesses (Mary Ward's Institute) in St Omer was finally carried out in April 1630. It had taken five years for the negotiations. Nuncio Longonissa ordered the suppression, but Bishop Paunet, who had only become bishop in 1627, had to find the Sisters, and after having located them, their suppression was carried out gently in 1630.

The Institute house in Munich seemed safer than other houses. The Jesuit General, Father Vitelleschi, and the Elector, Maximilian I, supported the women there. At that time there was no nunciature in Munich.[33] Mary Ward remained in the Paradeiser House in Munich in 1630.

Papal Bull of Suppression

As explained previously a papal bull of suppression had been suggested by the Cologne Nuncio, Pierluigi Carafa, after the interrogations of the Sisters in Liège. Pope Urban VIII signed such a bull (*Pastoralis Romani Pontificis*) on 13 January 1631.[34] The document was phrased in 'extraordinarily harsh language'.[35]

It is worth noting here that papal bulls were weighty, written mandates which were termed 'bulls' from the Latin word 'bulla', or seal, because the documents were sealed in the earliest times with the Pope's signet ring, just as the emperors had done, though from the sixth century they had seal boxes in red, or signets stamped in wax - a practice followed by the Holy Roman Emperors.[36]

A summary of the bull states that the Pope's responsibility was to protect the Church from undesirable labourers. It goes on to explain that new religious orders had been prohibited by the Lateran Council and the Council of Lyons. Therefore, the Pope was compelled to suppress Mary Ward's Institute, since without papal approval this congregation could not exist. It was under a woman as general superior - to her vows were made, and the members do not

observe enclosure. The bull most harshly comments that
'... under the guise of promoting the salvation of souls, (they)
have been accustomed to attempt and to employ themselves
at many other works which are most unsuited to their weak
sex and character, to female modesty and particularly to
maidenly reserve'.[37]

Peters observes:

> One can see here how canonical decrees have been inter-
> woven with traditional concepts of the frailty of women. It
> must be pointed out once more that the apostolic activity
> of the members of the Institute, especially in England, was
> sharply condemned, not for any substantial failings but sim-
> ply because they were women, and therefore beings of in-
> ferior intellectual capacity.[38]

The Institute was suppressed by the Pope and the following prohibitions were named: the members' vows were
to be considered as dissolved and the offices such as superior, visitor, general superior were to be considered as suppressed. Communities were suppressed and members were
to leave them. The publication of the bull was to be carried
out by nailing it to certain doors. In Rome the nominated
places were at the Lateran Basilica, St Peter's, the Curial
pulpit, and at the Campo dei Fiore, the place of execution.
This direction was carried out on the 10 May 1631, four
months after the promulgation of the bull. In Bavaria, Vienna and Belgium the bull was nailed up in July, and August, 1631 respectively.[39]

Mary Ward's arrest and imprisonment

Mary Ward was arrested in Munich on 7 February 1631.
About four o'clock on that afternoon, Dean Golla, Dean of
Our Lady's Church in Munich came to Mary Ward in the
Paradeiser House and read her the letter ordering him to
take her prisoner. In fact he had postponed this distasteful

task for two weeks. The accusations against Mary were those of heresy, schism and rebellion against the Church.[40]

Mary Ward was therefore imprisoned in the Poor Clare Convent on the Anger from 7 February till 14 April 1631. Anne Turner, a member of the congregation, was allowed to share the dark, dank, convent cell with Mary Ward to act as her nurse. The room was double locked and bolted and four Poor Clare Sisters were placed on guard outside the door. When Mary became very ill she asked to receive the last sacraments. Dean Golla gave permission for this if she first signed a declaration repenting of her heresy against Holy Church and regretting it. Mary Ward refused to sign such a document.

At the end of March some members of the Institute were allowed to visit Mary. She gave them her own declaration which said, among other things:

> Never have I said or done anything, whether important or insignificant, against His Holiness... or the authority of the Holy Church... and I would not do the slightest thing for a thousand worlds, for a present or future good, that would not be consistent with the real duties of a loyal catholic and an obedient daughter of the Church.[41]

As a dying woman Mary received Communion of the sick and was anointed on 1 April. During her imprisonment Mary Ward carried on a correspondence with the members of the Institute which became known as the 'lemon juice' letters. These letters to and fro were written in lemon juice on scraps of paper sent in to her around food parcels. They could be read only when heated. The English women had not survived the English persecution without learning some ingenious communication skills.

Peters says: 'It is not known why she was released from prison in the first half of April... It is possible that her release was in connection with the publication of the Bull in Rome.'[42] She could have left before Palm Sunday, but chose to remain in prison for that special feast day and so left the Poor Clare convent on Monday, 14 April 1631. Although the relationship between the Electress, Elisabeth, and Mary Ward had become strained due to the troubles of the Institute, the Electress sent a conveyance to take Mary back to the Paradeiser House on her release from prison.

Winifred Wigmore was imprisoned on 14 February 1631 in the Collegiate Church in Liège.[43] She was there until June or July 1632 when Mary Ward begged for her release during the audience with Pope Urban VIII. Winifred returned to England with Mary in 1637 and was present at her death in 1645. Before Mary's death Winifred undertook to return to London on foot to look for letters because Mary was anxious to hear word of the Sisters in Rome and perhaps also from the Roman authorities. There was no correspondence and Winifred returned by 13 January.

In 1650 Winifred Wigmore went to Paris and combined there the roles of novice mistress and headmistress. With Mary Poyntz, Winifred wrote the first biography of Mary Ward, *A Briefe Relation*. Winifred Wigmore died aged seventy-two and was buried at the Bernardine Convent in Paris.[44]

Mary Ward's letters to Winifred Wigmore bear ample testimony to the love and confidence between them. A quote from Mary Ward's letter written from Munich to 'Win' in Naples on 27 May 1627 well illustrates this:

> Now, of our College in Naples and all ours in it, take you charge and care, and according to your usual fidelity do what is to be done, for the greater glory of God, the good of our course and the comfort of her who in this world and the next, if I be worthy, will be mindful of you...[45]

Winifred Wigmore was a steadfast follower of Mary Ward, a strong, religious woman who in her own person bore the burdens of those who are 'founding' people - in this case of an active, non-enclosed religious life for women.

This picture, from No 2 of the *Painted Life* series, shows Mary Ward (centre) with her parents and one of her sisters – perhaps Barbara. The scene takes place after one of Mary's refusals of marriage. The background picture of the Madonna and child emphasise Mary's Marian devotion.

This excerpt from No 10 of the *Painted Life* series shows Mary Ward at prayer in a bedroom.

Mary Ward and her early companions. Left to right: Mary Poyntz, Jane Browne, Catherine Smith, Susanna Rookwood, Winifred Wigmore, Mary Ward. The small inset shows them having a last meal together in England. (*Painted Life*, No 22, left panel)

This picture from the *Painted Life* series (No 22, right panel) shows the pioneer members of the Institute leaving their homeland. Only four of them are represented boarding the ship.

Pilgrim Portrait of Mary Ward at the pilgrim centre, Trier, painted in 1621. (IBMV, Burghausen)

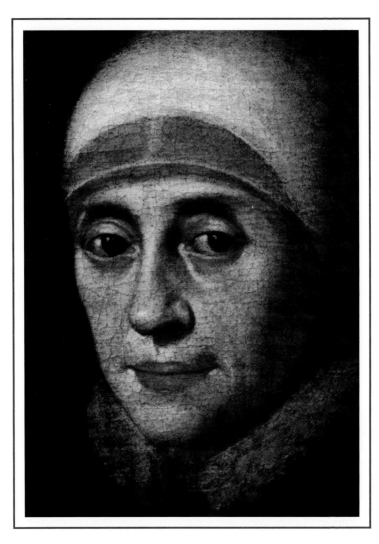

Portrait of Mary Ward (1585-1645), aged between thirty-six and forty. (IBVM, Augsburg)

Winifred Wigmore IBVM (1585-1657), Mary Ward's friend and companion.

St Ignatius Loyola (1491-1556), founder of the Society of Jesus. He is depicted here writing the Constitutions of the Society.

CHAPTER 10

Last Years of Mary Ward and the Aftermath (1631-1645)

Mary Ward's return to Rome

After Mary Ward's imprisonment in the Anger Convent she was informed by an unknown source that she was to go to Rome. Peters comments 'It is not known when she received orders to travel to Rome - only that the fear of it gave her pain.'[1] Indeed the conditions imposed by the Holy Office were stringent. The journey had to be at her own expense, and in the company of a deputy chosen by Dean Golla. The time of the journey was stipulated, too, as her arrival date in Rome had been determined. Also her Institute in Munich had to produce bail, the amount of which was to be decided by Nuncio Carafa.[2]

After her release from prison Mary wrote a petition to the Pope asking for some mitigation of the conditions imposed on her release, and her journey to Rome. The demands of the Holy Office were lifted - apart from the bail.[3]

Being ordered to Rome as a prisoner of the Inquisition caused great suffering to Mary after ten years of fruitless negotiations and appeals to the Pope and the congregations of cardinals. (The Inquisition was a judicial process for gathering evidence against suspected heretics, and prosecuting them when sufficient evidence was amassed. Procedural safeguards were only part of later jurisprudence, so in the Inquisition proceedings the accused was assumed guilty until proven innocent, rather than the reverse.[4]) The journey itself was very difficult for one so weakened by illness and imprisonment, nevertheless she understook it. Mary Ward may have been weak in body; but spiritually, it seemed, she was indefatigable and unbroken.[5]

This was Mary Ward's third trip to Rome and she probably arrived there in early 1632. Soon after arrival Mary had an audience with Pope Urban VIII. According to the early English and Italian biographies Mary Ward is supposed to have said the following often-quoted words: 'I neither am, nor ever have been, a heretic.' Urban VIII is also reputed to have said, 'We believe it, we believe it, we need no other proof. We and all the Cardinals are not only satisfied, but edified at your proceedings; neither must you think it much to have been proved as you have been, for such have been the proceedings of other Popes with other servants of God.' Peters does not give much credit to the sincerity of such words - unless as a kindness from the Pope who was trying to mollify Mary.[6]

At her audience with Urban VIII in 1632 Mary asked three things:

1. That he remove from her and her companions the stigma of heresy.

2. That he order the release of Winifred Wigmore who was still imprisoned in Liège.

3. That as there were still members who wished to live under her direction and under the protection of the Holy See, he give permission for them to come to Rome where once more the authorities could keep them under close surveillance.[7]

The Holy Father acceded on all counts. Mary Ward was acquitted of the charge of heresy on a date unknown.[8] A letter issued from the Holy Office in 1633 attempted to rehabilitate Mary Ward and her companions.[9] In effect the letter from the Holy Office said in part: '... if your Holiness should be questioned, you may affirm that in this holy tribunal, the English ladies who have lived under the Institute of Donna Maria della Guardia (Mary Ward), are not found, nor have ever been found, guilty of any failure which regards the holy and orthodox Catholic faith.'[10]

Mary Ward also asked the Pope's permission to buy a house in Rome. Permission was not given quickly, but a house was certainly obtained with the Pope's knowledge and approval. The house was situated opposite Paul V's Lady Chapel, in the Basilica of Santa Maria Maggiore. It is also recorded that Urban VIII ordered bread and wine to be sent to Mary Ward from the supplies of the papal larder from April 1633 to the beginning of November 1637. On 1 December 1635 Winifred Bedingfield wrote to the Elector of Bavaria that twenty-three members of the Institute were living in Rome.[11]

Each year the Sisters renewed their vows (private ones since the suppression) before the icon of Our Lady, Salus Populi Romani, in the Church of St Mary Major.[12] The Roman house was home to surviving members as there is an extant letter written by Mary Poyntz in England to Barbara Babthorpe in Rome dated 31 January 1645. The letter gives details of Mary Ward's death and burial.[13]

Chambers notes that the house at Rome was not given up until the confirmation of the Institute in 1703:

It continued until that date to be more or less the residence of the successors of Mary Ward in their position as its head or chief Superior. Young English girls were received as boarders there, as well as foreigners, and some of them became members of the Institute from time to time, and were transferred elsewhere.[14]

Return to the north: civil war

On 10 September 1637 Mary Ward and her companions left Rome for England. Mary Ward had begun thinking of a journey to England soon after her release from the Anger prison.[15] Her ill health and the restrictions on her movements made the journey impossible until 1637. No doubt this return to her native land was not only due to homesickness, which she never lost, but also was attributable to her deep desire for the conversion of England.[16]

At this time Catholics in England were experiencing a little relief from persecution under the influence of the Catholic Queen Henrietta Maria from France, wife of Charles I, the son of James I, who had succeeded Elizabeth I. Mary's companions were Mary Poyntz, Winifred Wigmore and Anne Turner. They left Rome with valid passes and explicit permission of the Pope. The journey was long and difficult and because of Mary's ill health (fever and kidney trouble) they remained in Paris until 20 May 1638 and were at Liège at the end of May.

In September 1638, Mary received a letter of recommendation from Cardinal Francesco Barberini, Pope Urban VIII's nephew, to be given to Queen Henrietta Maria of England. Peters comments that the Pope's nephew wrote to the Queen because 'from this carefully phrased recommendation it is more than likely that the Pope and his nephew knew of Mary Ward's plans for her Institute in England, and, moreover, supported them'.[17] This would seem to be an incredible claim, even in the light of ecclesiastical politics, given all the previous condemnation of Mary Ward by papal pronouncements and the extremely harsh Bull of Suppression of the Institute. However, Urban VIII had received Mary Ward on her return to Rome and allowed the Sisters to live there. The situation again highlighted the ambiguity of the positions taken by various male authorities in the Church to Mary Ward.

On 20 May 1639, Mary Ward was again in England - for the last time. Although Queen Henrietta Maria was a Catholic, the Parliament wanted the return of recusancy laws to fine and punish Catholics. Consequently Charles I dissolved Parliament and reigned without it. The King favoured the Anglicans, but was opposed by the Puritans who wanted a democratic parliament. It was politically a very unstable time because the King's attempt to enforce his absolute ecclesial sovereignty on Scotland also met with bitter opposition. These difficulties, and the King's struggle with Parliament in London led eventually to civil war.[18]

Queen Henrietta Maria does not seem to have helped Mary Ward, although she received the letter of recommendation favourably.[19] Mary wanted to establish a school in London. In a letter to Mary Poyntz in Bonn, Mary wrote on 4 February 1639 of her wish that 'we may have common schools in the great city of London, which will never be without a miracle, and all else will be to little purpose, the ungrateful nature of this people considered, but try she must for the greatest good of this poor country.'[20]

The impending civil war and the wide religious differences would have made the establishment of a Catholic school for girls impossible at that time. In 1642 London finally turned against Charles I and he left for the north to raise troops against the rebels. In the north the nobles and the Anglicans supported Charles, while in the south the citizens and Puritans supported Parliament.

Mary Ward and her companions set out for the north. There was danger everywhere, but after four and a half months (they stayed some time at Newby and at Ripley Castle) they reached Hutton Rudby where they were able to rent an old house. It belonged to either the Inglebys or Gascoignes who were strong recusant families and relatives of the Ward family.[21] This house had also belonged to the

Carthusians of Mt Grace before the dissolution of the monasteries. The ruined chapel of Mt Grace was a place of pilgrimage. The companions, and Mary herself, went there to pray for her health.

For greater security, at the beginning of 1643, the group moved to Heworth, a village just outside York. Charles I was then being attacked by the Scots who favoured Parliament. The Battle of Marston Moor near York on 2 July 1644 was decisive when Oliver Cromwell gained the victory over the Cavaliers. York was taken by Cromwell in July 1644 The Sisters had taken refuge in York City, but were eventually able to return to Heworth, where four hundred soldiers had been quartered.

There they celebrated Christmas in 1644, and although Mary's health was extremely poor, she was not then anointed by the priest who was unaware of her extreme illness. As Mary was anxious to hear news of her Sisters on the continent, Winifred Wigmore undertook to go to London for letters and news. She came back to Heworth on 13 January without any news of the other Sisters.[22]

Death of Mary Ward

On 28 December Mary had become bed-ridden and by 15 January 1645, she was in agony. Mary Poyntz wrote later:

> I asked her often where the pain was. She answered, 'from head to foot'... Yet her sweet, serene look never changed... Mary regretted that she had not asked for a priest in time... Then she commended, with greatest feeling, the practice of God's vocation in us, that it be constant, efficacious and affectionate. She said, 'God will assist and help you, where or through whom is no matter. And when God shall enable me to be in place, I will serve you.'[23]

Mary Ward died peacefully on 30 January 1645. At that time the burial of Catholics in England was still difficult. It had been known that the graves of Catholics had been torn up by Protestants. According to Chambers, Mary's companions found 'a little churchyard, where the minister was honest enough to be bribed'.[24] He was of course an Anglican minister. The little church was in the village of Osbaldwick, about a mile or more from Heworth. The tombstone is now erected on a wall inside the church. The inscription on it reads:

> *To love the poor,*
> *persevere in the same,*
> *live die and rise with them*
> *was all the aim of*
> *Mary Ward*
> *who having lived 60 years and 8 days*
> *died 20th* [sic] *January 1645.*[25]

Aftermath: The Second Institute

But Mary's death was not the end of the Institute. In 1635 the Emperor Maximilian I of Bavaria gave permission for the two remaining members of Mary Ward's Institute in Munich to teach as seculars in the Paradeiser House. Maximilian supported them financially.[26]

Living was still difficult in England during the days of the Commonwealth (1649-1660) under Oliver Cromwell. The house at Heworth was required by the owner, and so Mary Poyntz and those with her at Heworth moved to Paris about 1650, where they established a school. They took with them some of their English pupils. Mary Poyntz was the superior and the others were Winifred Wigmore, Frances Bedingfield, Isabella Layton and Catherine Smith. The latter became the headmistress of the boarders. Winifred died in 1657 at the age of seventy-two. During this time the biography of Mary Ward, known as *A Briefe Relation*, originated. The handwriting is that of Winifred Wigmore, while the composition is said to be due to Mary Poyntz.

Mary Poyntz died in Munich in 1667. She had succeeded Barbara Babthorpe as General Superior in Rome. Catherine Dawson of the Roman house succeeded Mary Poyntz as General Superior. In 1693 she presented a petition for confirmation of the Institute to Pope Innocent XII. This was rejected on the grounds of the former Bull of Suppression and the non-enclosure of the members.

In 1669 Frances Bedingfield, who had been present at Mary Ward's death, left Paris to return to England, intending to establish a community of Sisters there. Some Sisters lived together at Heworth at the place where Mary Ward had spent her last days; another group lived at Hammersmith near London.

Eventually, in 1686, Frances Bedingfield was given 450 pounds to buy a house and land just outside the walls of York at Micklegate Bar. The donor was an English Catholic gentleman, Sir Thomas Gasgoigne. His niece, Helena Thwing, entered the Munich house in 1654, and after some years was sent to England to become the superioress of the house at Heworth, where Mary Ward died.[27] From 1699 the Sisters taught local girls in a day school, and they conducted a boarding school for the daughters of the old Catholic families.[28] The political climate was hostile towards Catholics, so their religious activities had to be well hidden.

Francis was known as Mrs Bedingfield (not a religious Sister) and her companions were also known as Mrs Cornwallis etc. Frances herself survived several bouts of imprisonment and lived into old age.

This establishment of the Bar Convent was significant because no convents had existed in England since the dissolution of the monasteries in 1535. The schools at Hammersmith and in Yorkshire were in fact the only convents in England until the French Revolution began to force the emigration of French religious to England in 1792.[29] The Bar Convent is still occupied by Sisters of the Institute.

When Catherine Dawson died in 1696, the first *elected* General Superior was Mary Anna Barbara Babthorpe. She presented a new petition for approval to Pope Clement XI in 1703. This time the office of chief superior was a problem, but eventually the Pope said the oft-quoted words 'Let women be governed by women.' The rules and interior organisation and government, the way of life as practised, the construction of the buildings and other matters, were examined. The religious dress or habit also was inquired into, when a pattern of that in use - being an adaptation of what ladies in the world wore in the middle of the seventeenth century, when in mourning - was sent to Rome and approved. Pope Clement XI in a papal bull of confirmation issued on 13 June 1703 confirmed a summary of eighty-one rules. They were the essence of the constitutions which Mary Ward wanted - the fundamental spirituality according to St Ignatius.[30]

By the Bull of Suppression Pope Urban VIII annulled what is now called the First Institute. In 1703 Pope Clement XI approved the so-called Second Institute. The Sisters to whom approval was granted were lineal descendants and successors of Mary Ward, but they were not legal descendants of the Order which had been suppressed by papal bull in 1631.[31]

There were further complications in 1747 when a dispute arose between the Mendelheim community and the Bishop of Augsburg, who wanted to have the Sisters under his jurisdiction. This led the Sisters to seek a clarification from the Holy See. The result was that Pope Benedict XIV issued a constitution, *Quamvis Iusto*, in 1749.[32] With this constitution, the Pope achieved three objectives:

> First, he established the legitimacy of the community by insisting on the discontinuity between them and the 'suppressed' Jesuitesses. Secondly, the constitution tacitly accepted a religious way of life without enclosure. Thirdly, the role of the superior general over houses in many dioceses was acknowledged and defined in relation to the jurisdiction of the local bishops.[33]

The cost of obtaining this ecclestiastical recognition was the loss of links with Mary Ward and a ban on acknowledging her as foundress. However, this cost would be payment towards a recognition of Mary Ward at a later time. It was a watershed decision for active, non-enclosed groups of women, for as MacGinley asserts:

> ... it was Mary Ward's institute which issued the challenge for new juridical forms in the early 17th century and which, a century later, occasioned the new bridging legislation between an older canonical understanding and a developing social context where public responsibility would be exercised by women in their own right.[34]

In February 1877 Pope Pius IX gave the final approbation to the whole Institute by quoting Clement XI's approval of the Rules in 1703, and acting on the advice of the Cardinals of the Sacred Congregation of the Propagation of the Faith who approved the Petition of the Sisters of the Blessed Virgin Mary for confirmation.[35]

In 1821 the Irish branch of the Institute was established with Mother Teresa Ball. She brought the Mary Ward Constitutions to Ireland from the Bar Convent at York, where she had spent her novitiate and early religious life. The Sisters of the Irish foundation are now called Loreto Sisters.

The first Australian foundation was made from Ireland at Ballarat in 1875. Australia is thus a province of the Irish Generalate. There are two other generalates (provinces, regions and missions): the Roman Generalate and the North American Generalate. In 1909 Pope Pius X officially declared Mary Ward the foundress of the Institute, a title which had been denied her in view of its earlier canonical suppression.[36]

The Papal Bull of Suppression has never been rescinded.[37] However, it was in fact contradicted by the 1703 approval of the Rules, the 1877 approbation of the Institute, and by the 1909 recognition of Mary Ward as foundress of the Institute. It is one view in canon law that the pontiff is not bound by the actions of his predecessors - that he can in fact override them, which appears to have been done in the case of Mary Ward. Another view is that 'Rome' never admits a mistake (a view contradicted by the recent apology about Galileo). According to this view, Rome tries to work its way around a previous law to make the new decision look as though it was saying that all along, but just in different words or a different context.[38]

The Ecumenical Council of Vatican II directed all religious congregations to return to their sources and examine their charism. This involved a re-writing of constitutions, and to prepare for this a process of discernment was initiated in Rome by the Sisters of the Institute of the Blessed Virgin Mary in September 1979. This process involved all members of the Institute at personal, community and provincial levels. Finally all provinces of the Irish Generalate agreed to adopt the Constitutions of the Society of Jesus.

In 1980 these decisions were taken to the General Chapter of the Irish Generalate which unanimously decided:

> That it is advantageous for our purpose that the Institute take the Constitutions of the Society of Jesus, adapted

according to the mind of Mary Ward, together with the modern document, as our fundamental law.[39]

The General Chapter of 1983 finalised the selection of the Constitutions of the Society of Jesus and the incorporation into each part of certain additions necessary for the updating and application of the text to the Institute today. The Constitutions of the Institute are thus the Constitutions of the Society of Jesus, adapted according to the mind of Mary Ward with a modern document incorporated as a supplement. Mary Ward's vision of 1611, 'Take the same of the Society', was now fulfilled!

A central question now emerges from the history of Mary Ward and the establishment of her Institute. What inspired and sustained her throughout her life and enabled her to bequeath in apparent failure such a viable legacy to her companions? Mary's spirituality no doubt provides part of the answer and the following chapter addresses this.

CHAPTER 11

Mary Ward's Spirituality

It would seem that at the heart of Mary Ward's strength of purpose was a strong spirituality, which had been established in her early years and which she conscientiously developed throughout her life. This spirituality was characterised by a deep prayer life and ascetical living, and was nourished by the Gospels, the spirituality of the times, and the English ethos.

Early formation

As already mentioned, Mary was a member of an English recusant family and she had experienced the persecution of Catholics from her earliest years. Priests were hidden in the houses of the laity and Mass was celebrated clandestinely. Priests became well known in the recusant families, and promoted a strong spiritual life among them.

Mary Ward's family were good people: her father's charity to the poor was admired by Mary.[1] Mary Ward's mother, and the women with whom she lived from the age of five, were strong models of the Christian life. Her grandmother, Ursula Wright, and her relatives, Catherine Ardington and Grace Babthorpe, provided her with models of Catholic households given to prayer and asceticism. All of these women had been imprisoned for their Catholic faith.

The English quality of 'common sense' was evident in Mary Ward's approach to life and was a strong facet of her spiritual life. To the new kind of religious life which Mary Ward envisaged she brought 'the resolutenesss of a Yorkshirewoman, her strong faith, an adaptability born of her experience in different families, and a marked awareness of each one's personal responsibility for his or her life'.[2]

Mary Ward's family provided her with a humanist and classical education which enabled her to take advantage of the spiritual classics of the Christian tradition and of the various spiritual works produced in her own times. She studied not only Italian, but also learned Latin well enough to write it fluently and to read the literature of the Church Fathers.[3]

Devotional literature

In her detailed study of the spirituality of Mary Ward, Dr Jeanne Cover points out that the religious literature and devotional works available to the recusant women inspired in them a desire for an intimate following of Christ. To them, as to the Protestant women of the Reformation period, the works of the mystics were available. Among these books were *The Life of Mother Teresa of Jesus* (1611), *The Mirror of Religious Perfection* (1618), Francis de Sales' *Treatise of the Love of God* (1630) and others. The desire for perfection (wholeness) was also inculcated in *The Imitation of Christ* by Thomas à Kempis and in the writings of St Teresa of Avila.[4]

According to Orchard there is evidence that Mary Ward's prayer was influenced by *The Spiritual Combat*. About this book Mary wrote that it was 'the best master and instructor that I have had in spiritual exercises for many years'. *The Spiritual Combat* by Lorenzo Scupoli (a sixteenth century Theatine priest) was a manual of rules and spiritual exercises for those seeking perfection. The first English edition was prepared by John Gerard SJ and secretly printed in 1598.[5]

Jesuit influence

Because many of the priests who came to the Catholic houses for Mass were Jesuits they had a strong influence on the spirituality of Mary Ward. Her spiritual director in England, Father Holtby SJ, eventually supported her when she discerned that she would be a religious, rather than marry Edmund Neville, who lay claim to being Earl of Westmoreland. Father Roger Lee SJ gave her the Spiritual Exercises of St Ignatius during the early years in the Netherlands. The English Jesuit, John Gerard, directed her in subsequent years, so that Mary Ward's spirituality was strongly based on the Ignatian charism, which included the process of the discernment of spirits.

The Spiritual Exercises of St Ignatius were made by Mary Ward annually and many of her biographical writings in retreat notes reflect the movements of the Spirit in her life during these retreats. According to Gilles' summary, the Exercises emphasise three elements:

1. Disposition towards God;

2. Purgation from one's consciousness of that which is not of God;

3. A process for discerning God's will for one's life.

The Exercises are divided into 'weeks' (not of seven days) during which the 'exercitant' (one who performs the Exercises) seeks specific graces from God.[6] It was hoped that the outcome of the Exercises would be a profound conversion of intellect, will and imagination. Such a conversion should lead the retreatant to surrender all that is false and illusory in human nature and to centre her or his thoughts, feeling and imagination on Christ's love, and so to become more truly human.[7] In these Exercises contemplation was linked to the greater glory of God in the service of others, and Mary Ward prayed continually to know the will of God.

Wright has written that:

> ... the Constitutions of the Society of Jesus incorporated the psychology and the spirituality of the Spiritual Exercises. Both works are designed to produce people who could re- new the Church from within. In the strictly centralized and disciplined group the members were trained in spiritual discernment, and personal responsibility. The Society itself was organized in order to be able to respond flexibly to the needs of individuals and the challenges of the apostolate.[8]

Mary Ward epitomised this deeply lived spiritual life which was to be the essence of the charism of the Institute - a strong, enriching heritage.

Threefold charism through mystical experiences

With this strong Jesuit influence as a basis Mary Ward adapted her prayer and spiritual life according to the inspi- rations of the Holy Spirit to whom she was attentively at- tuned. Her understanding of the will of God for her was made clear in three key experiences.

The gradual unfolding of the kind of religious life to which Mary Ward was called took place over several years. In 1609 when Mary had left the Poor Clares and returned to England she devoted her time to whatever assistance she could give to English women. In the 'Glory Vision' it was made clear to her that she was not to be a Carmelite, but some other assured good thing more to the glory of God. In her autobiography she wrote that 'I remained for a good space without feeling or hearing anything but the sound "Glory, glory, glory".'[9] The Jesuits refer everything to the greater glory of God and this spirit was then being made clear to Mary Ward.

The inspiration in 1611 to 'Take the Same of the Society' gave a fundamental orientation to the religious practices of Mary Ward's spirituality. Her prayer and penance continued and in 1615 the 'Vision of the Just Soul' showed her again the kind of spirituality to which the group was being called. Mary Ward described this state:

> As a clear and perfect estate to be had in this life and such an one as is altogether needful for those that should well discharge the duties of this Institute. The felicity of this estate was a singular freedom from all that could make one adhere to earthly things, with an entire application and apt disposition to all good works... the freedom that such soul should have had to refer all to God.[10]

These three occasions encompassed the threefold charism which directed and sustained Mary Ward's spiritual life, and hence her external activities.

As Dr Cover shows, the three aspects of freedom, justice and sincerity as indicated in the 'Just Soul Vision', were enriched and deepened in Mary Ward's own spiritual life. Her concept of freedom had a three-fold dimension: freedom from attachment to earthly values and things; freedom for any kind of good works; and freedom to refer all to God.[11]

Justice and sincerity were very difficult concepts to Mary Ward as she notes in her meditation on All Souls Day in 1615: 'I found a questioning in myself why this state of justice and virtue of sincerity should appear unto me so especially requisite as a ground of all those other virtues necessary to be exercised by those of this Institute...'[12] As has been seen in the account of Mary's life, she lived the answer to her questioning concerning having right relations with God, herself and other human beings, and in a faithful response to the liberality of God's graces, with the ensuing freedom to refer all to God and to find all in God.[13] The positive personal response of the popes, and significant other authority figures to Mary Ward, and her continual respect for duly authorised Church authority, witnessed clearly to this.

Dr Cover observes that Mary Ward's approach in her spirituality was holistic. As we can observe in her speech with her Sisters, princes and popes, she was not able to practise any of the mental reservation, or equivocation, which had sometimes been used by English recusants. She had a breadth of vision in justice, freedom and sincerity which 'gave a radically new orientation to her spirituality and found concrete expression in her response to the needs of the Church and the society of her age'.[14]

During her annual retreats Mary Ward regularly made the Spiritual Exercises, and some of her retreat notes are extant. A collection of these reflections form a type of spiritual diary in which Mary Ward wrote of her experiences of God in her meditations and contemplations. Her disarming self-disclosures reveal a person who was aware of the movements of her heart and was therefore able to discern the movements of the Spirit in her life. Thus she revealed the spirituality and depth of her prayer as a 'just person' - one who was wholly God's.

In 1619 Mary Ward wrote of her retreat meditation on the comparison of Christ with an earthly king: 'God was present, I had freedom to speak; the most of this hour was spent in speaking to him with love, and hope: and in harkening to what he would, with desire to do his will.' Later on she wrote of her dryness in prayer: 'Settling myself to prayer, I knew not where to find God.'[15]

The daily spiritual practices of Mary Ward and her Sisters were attendance at Mass, where possible, meditation for an hour and an examination of their lives twice a day - before dinner and at night.[16] They also practised prayers and devotions to angels and saints. When Mary was living with the Babthorpe family at an early age she was scrupulous about her devotions and wrote of the grace she received to deal with the problem of scrupulosity:

> God gave me courage to reason in this manner with myself: these things are not of obligation but of devotion; and God is not pleased with such acts made thus with constraint. To acquire my own quiet, therefore, I will do these things with love and freedom, or leave them alone.[17]

An example of Mary Ward's prayer, which is recorded, reveals her familiarity with God as she begins to pray, saying, 'O Parent of parents and Friend of all friends'. Her trust in Providence is expressed in the words: 'What I want I will find in Him.'[18] After Mary Ward's imprisonment in the Anger prison in 1631 she wrote to the Roman Congregation of the Holy Office. In this letter she declared that she would not act in any way which might be unbecoming in carrying out her duty as a true and obedient servant of Holy Church.[19] Clearly her balanced freedom of spirit, which was characteristic of her spiritual life, existed in harmony with a strong expression of fidelity to the authority of the Church.

Inner freedom

Mary Ward grew in inner freedom as her spirituality deepened and she did not accept that women were inferior to men. This is clear from the text of a speech of hers which is called 'The Verity Speech' because it concludes with the words, 'Love verity and truth.' This speech was made in response to a priest who was the Father Minister of the English Seminary in St Omer. He was present when Thomas Sackville was praising the Sisters and their work and remarked that their first fervour would wear off because 'they are but women'. Mary vehemently replied that fervour would not grow cold because 'we are but women... There is no such difference between men and women that women may not do great things.'

Mary Ward foresaw a future for their kind of religious life for women and expressed it clearly in the Verity Speech when she said that 'women in time to come may do much'.[20] Even the words of the Papal Bull of Suppression 'to root out speedily the brambles growing up in the field of the Church militant'[21] could not dismay Mary Ward as she lived out the spirituality of the 'Just Soul'.

The will of God as Mary Ward discerned it in her life led her to an inner freedom which could be described as the fruit of Mary's Ignatian way. With equanimity Mary was able to converse with popes, nuncios, bishops, noblemen and noblewomen, as well as children and women of doubtful repute. This freedom and integrity were attained slowly and painfully. Mary's English nationality was not the least of her attributes to assist this growth. 'Gifted with that truly English quality often described as "common sense", Mary managed to survive, both in health and in sickness.'[22]

She experienced frequent illness, misunderstanding, ridicule, betrayal, suppression of the Institute by papal bull, imprisonment and surveillance from the Inquisition. This was the woman who was able to say on her deathbed in January 1645, to a few companions, 'O fie, fie! What? Still look sad? Come, let us rather sing and praise God joyfully for all his loving-kindness!'[23]

Devotion to the Blessed Virgin Mary

Mary Ward was an Englishwoman who inherited the English national ethos within the culture of Reformation times.

Not the least of these in English Catholicism was an intense awareness of, and devotion to, the Blessed Virgin Mary. Even the Reformation monarch, Queen Elizabeth I, adopted the title of the Virgin Queen - subsuming to herself the English Catholic devotion to the Blessed Virgin Mary.[24]

Devotions to the Blessed Virgin Mary had a long history in England as well as on the continent. The Reformation historian, Eamon Duffy writes:

> Devotions to Mary proliferated in late medieval England as elsewhere in Christian Europe, and indeed Englishmen were encouraged to think of their country in a special way as 'Mary's Dowry', a notion propagated, for example, by the custodians of the shrine at Walsingham. Her cult came second only to that of Christ himself, and towered above that of all other saints.[25]

It is not unexpected that Mary Ward's orientation to Ignatian spirituality was also characterised by a great love of the Blessed Virgin Mary. This was evident from her childhood as she wrote: 'I had great confidence in the power and help of Our Blessed Lady.'[26] When Mary and her two sisters were in grave danger in the fire at her home in 1595 she attributed their escape to the intercession of Our Blessed Lady to whom they prayed.

Mary Ward's love of Our Blessed Lady was well known to her companions. *A Briefe Relation*, the life of Mary Ward written by Mary Poyntz and Winifred Wigmore, says 'her devotion to our Blessed Lady was very great and tenderly deare, confidently in all occasions she made her recourse to her'.[27] This Marian orientation has been preserved in the Institute - indicated publicly in the name, 'Institute of the Blessed Virgin Mary'.

When we ask what were the driving forces behind Mary Ward's remarkable endeavours, the source of her apparently never flagging determination to establish the Institute, and the basis of her courage, we are forced to conclude that she was a person who was naturally, through education, and mystically, through grace, empowered to be wholly God's. As Mary wrote of herself: 'I had a short imperfect sight of the excellent state of a soul wholly God's, that such only truly live, are strong and apt for all such good works as are in this world to be done.' She concluded this reflection by asking: 'What is there in me that causes so great an unlikeness betwixt such a soul and mine?'[28]

As this indicates, Mary was deeply humble - grounded in the 'humus' of existence and hence she was equipped to survive the cruel politics of the human dimension of the Church. Her spirituality nurtured her growth as a woman, holy, strong and generous - faithful to God and the Church - a woman of extraordinary integrity.

CHAPTER 12

Some Cultural Aspects of the Reformation Period

Saints

The Reformation period challenged people by testing their faith commitment, and many responded by a holy life which was later publicly recognised and honoured by the Church. These Saints were of all ages, men and women, from all kinds of occupations and varying social status, and they performed different ministries.

The Council of Trent was called to reform abuses in the Church and to define Catholic dogma.[1] Among the abuses was laxity in the lives of many religious and clergy. Aiding the reform of religious orders before the Council were saints in Spain and Italy such as the Carmelites, Teresa of Avila, John of the Cross and Mary Magdalen de Pazzi. Their writings told of deep, mystical, contemplative prayer-lives devoted to the love of God and the reform of the Church.

During the Council of Trent and its aftermath were those saints who founded new religious orders, such as Jeanne de Lestonnac, Francis de Sales, Jane Frances de Chantal, Louise de Marillac and Vincent de Paul, who were contemporaries of Mary Ward. Outstanding holiness was also found among the Jesuit saints such as Peter Canisius, Robert Bellarmine, John Berchmans and Aloysius Gonzaga.

The Jesuit, St Robert Bellarmine, taught in the Collegio Romano which had been established by St Ignatius for the education of Jesuits in Rome, but which was later opened up to non-Jesuit seminary students. He had taught the Flemish Jesuit, Leonard Lessius, who was asked to examine Mary Ward's Institute in 1615. Lessius had affirmed the Institute's right to exist. St Robert Bellarmine was made a cardinal and later became Bishop of Capua. When appointed to the Congregation of the Holy Office by Pope Paul V, St Robert Bellarmine had the onerous task of admonishing Galileo for holding to the theory of Copernicus. When St Robert died in Rome in 1621 he was buried in the Church of St Ignatius, having been of considerable help to the Roman Congregations in solving the many questions which arose in this Reformation period.

The great German preacher, the Capuchin, St Fidelis of Sigmaringen was guardian at Feldkirch in the Tyrol mountains from 1619 to 1622. It was in Feldkirch on Christmas Eve 1626 that Mary Ward prayed for the conversion of the King of England, Charles I.[2] St Fidelis was ordered by the Congregation for the Propagation of the Faith to preach in Switzerland. There he was pursued by heretics and was martyred in 1622 and later canonised as a saint of the Reformation period.

Again there were saints of the New World such as Martin de Porres and Rose of Lima. St Rose belonged to the Third Order of St Dominic and devoted her life to caring for babies, destitute children and old, sick people. She is patron of Peru, all the Americas, the Indies and the Philippines.

The only officially recognised martyr in post-Reformation Scotland was St John Ogilvie, who was martyred in 1615. He had been educated as a Calvinist, was converted to Catholicism, and became a Jesuit priest in 1613. After being betrayed, he was imprisoned, tortured and finally hanged in Glasgow. He was beatified in 1622.

Another saint, St Philip Neri, who formed the group of Oratory priests, cared for the poor and the sick in Italy. The Oratory priests gave afternoon talks in Rome and the musician, Palestrina, was one of their followers. The Counter-Reformation Cardinal, St Charles Borromeo, called Philip Neri the apostle of Rome. The English convert, John Henry Newman, belonged to the Oratory and founded the first English-speaking house of the Oratory in Birmingham in the nineteenth century.

Special mention must be made of the martyrs of the British Isles of this time. Forty of them were canonised in 1970 - long after their deaths. This group of martyrs comprised seven laymen and women, thirteen secular priests and twenty religious. Among these forty people the following illustrate the breadth and variety of calling among these martyrs. There was the Jesuit priest, Edmund Campion, scholar and fellow of St John's College, Oxford; Cuthbert Mayne, who was a convert minister, and who became the protomartyr of the continental seminaries; John Houghton, a Carthusian monk, who was Prior of the London Charterhouse; the Welsh schoolmaster, Richard Gwynn; and the Jesuit Brother, Nicholas Owen, who was famous for building the priests' hiding places in the homes of Catholics. He died from torture in the Tower of London in 1606.[3]

Edmund Campion (1540-1581) died as a martyr at the age of forty-one. He was born in London and, under the patronage of Queen Elizabeth I, he became an eloquent Oxford scholar and was ordained in the Church of England. But he had doubts about the Protestant position, eventually entering the Roman College in 1571, and he later became a Jesuit. He returned to England disguised as a jewel merchant and travelled the country assisting Catholics. Eventually he was captured, brutally tortured by the vicious Richard Topcliffe, then hung, drawn and quartered. Queen Elizabeth's chief minister, Sir William Cecil, had described

Edmund Campion as 'one of the diamonds of England'. The irony of being thus described before martyrdom is that this 'diamond' now sparkles in English history.[4]

Another of the noble English martyrs was Philip Howard (1557-1595). He was the Earl of Arundel and Surrey. For some time he led a wayward life, neglecting religion, wife and duties. He eventually reformed his life and, together with his wife, was reconciled to the Catholic Church. However, he was imprisoned in the Tower of London in 1585, the year of Mary Ward's birth. He was condemned to death in 1589, but the sentence was suspended and he died in the Tower in 1595.[5] Long imprisonment before trial and execution was the lot of these heroic martyrs.

Perhaps the most artistically gifted of the English martyrs was the Jesuit poet, Robert Southwell. He was born in Norfolk in 1561 and entered the Society of Jesus in Rome when he was seventeen. Robert Southwell had numerous Copley cousins and could claim kinship with Sir John Coke, Francis Bacon and William Cecil - all actors in the drama of his brief years in England.[6] Southwell was sent on the English mission in 1586 where he was betrayed in 1592 and spent three years in prison before he was tried, tortured and eventually hanged, drawn and quartered as a priest at Tyburn in 1595.[7]

Robert Southwell was probably acquainted with the young William Shakespeare who was well known to Southwell's Copely cousins. Robert Southwell wrote in language like Shakespeare's - young, harmonious, freshly forged, and filled with fire.[8] One of his early poems, 'A Childe My Choyce' is still well known, especially its first lines:

> I praise him most, I love him best, all praise and love is his
> While him I love, in him I live, and cannot live amiss.[9]

But there were many more martyrs of the period. Some eighty-five men of England, Scotland and Wales were put

to death for their Catholic faith during the religious con-
flicts of the sixteenth and seventeenth centuries and these
were honoured by being declared Blessed in November
1987. The first of these to be martyred was William Carter,
a London printer, who was executed at Tyburn in 1584.
Among this group also there were thirty Yorkshiremen.
Sixty-three of the martyrs were priests and twenty-two were
laymen, and they spanned all walks of life from gentry to
servant. Some of them were in their early twenties; the oldest was eighty, Father Nicholas Postgate, who was hanged,
drawn and quartered at York in 1678.[10]

On the continent, a great saint of the Catholic Reformation was St Charles Borromeo (1538-1584). His uncle, Pope
Pius IV, made Charles Borromeo Cardinal-Archbishop of
Milan where he began Church reform programs. He brought
to the Council of Trent an educated mind and a holy life
which were essential for Catholic reform at the highest levels of the hierarchy. He was a key participant in the final
sessions of the Council, helped to draft a Catholic catechism
which served as a basis of Catholic education for four centuries, and spent his spare time as bishop serving the poor
and the sick. St Charles motivated clerical reform by his
saintly example and 'did more than anyone to motivate
Council delegates truly to attend to ecclesiastical reform'.[11]

The changes and turmoil of Reformation times resulted
in conflict among nations and their people, but the lives of
great saints reflected the heroism, generosity and creativ-
ity of Catholics. Among them were many who were eventually canonised by the Catholic Church for their example
and holiness of life.

The arts

As well as the Reformation times giving rise to sanctity,
they were also years when a flourishing of the arts took
place. Nowhere was this more evident than in Italy.

Art

In 1590 the last stone was put in place in the structural building of St Peter's Basilica in Rome.¹² In 1642 Bernini completed the baldacchino over the high altar in St Peter's.¹³
This talented artist also painted scenery for opera, and did
wonderful sculpture, such as a famous statue of David. This
sculpture, dating from 1623, was a marble life-size figure of
the boy David as he was about to sling the stone at the
giant, Goliath. It is now in the Galleria Borghese in Rome.

Bernini also made the figure of Charity which was placed
on Pope Urban VIII's tomb.¹⁴ Urban VIII died in 1644, the
year before Mary Ward's death. Because Mary was in
England at that time she would never have seen this figure
of Charity, which would have been poignant for her in view
of her dealings with Urban VIII, because it was he who
signed the Bull of Suppression of the Institute in 1631.

Gifted artists in Italy were religious people as we find
that 'Guercino spent much of his mornings in prayer;
Bernini frequently went into retreats and practised the Spiritual Exercises of St Ignatius; Rubens attended Mass every
morning before beginning work.'¹⁵

Another artist, Caravaggio, is credited with being the
greatest painter of the period. He experimented with the
kind of lighting which later became fashionable in 'high-
brow' films of the 1920s, and gained thereby a new dra-
matic impact.¹⁶ There were also other great European artists such as Rembrandt, Frans Hals, Rubens, Van Dyck and
El Greco.

Because the English Reformation caused the destruction
of much religious art in the monasteries, churches and ca-
thedrals there were few great English artists of this time.
England then became known as the country of the word,
rather than that of the image. Shakespeare indeed painted

the scenery in the theatre by the words that he wrote in his plays.

Queen Elizabeth I had several portraits painted of herself in which she instructed the painters to see that she remained at the age of thirty-five. These magnificent paintings, such as the Ditchley Portrait, the Ermine Portrait, the Sieve Portrait and the Rainbow Portrait, became the new 'religious' art as they were highly decorative, fantastical and honouring the virgin Queen Elizabeth, who regarded herself as the new Virgin Mary.[17]

Between 1570 and 1600 miniatures became popular as court art in England. The subjects, usually members of noble families, were well painted with brushes of fine squirrel hair, and were decorated lavishly with borders and colourful frames. However, miniatures were usually kept as private art and these pieces were exclusive to the nobility, and were therefore expensive heritage art works.

Again the development of architecture in England at this time was concerned more with the production of the finest country houses and halls, rather than in ecclesiastical structures.[18] For reasons of hygiene (the court residences were not cleaned while people lived in them, but after they moved on) the court travelled around the country, and therefore needed some large places to stay. This trend in building was also a consequence of the suppression of the monasteries which Henry VIII had ordered in 1536. No new monasteries were then built and the desecration of religious art also occurred as a result of the Reformation.

Music

At this time, opera developed in Italy. The Florentine musician, Vincenzo Galilei, the father of the scientist, Galileo Galilei, was among those who created musical drama, and in effect, invented opera.[19] St Charles Borromeo, conforming to the liturgical principles of the Council of Trent, entrusted Giovanni Palestrina with purifying the music at St Peter's. Palestrina was appointed choirmaster and there were few objections to the sensuous beauty of the sounds created by him.[20] Palestrina composed over one hundred ordinaries of the Mass and these, together with beautiful motets, were often sung by unaccompanied choirs. His music became the model for many generations of Roman composers.

Martin Luther loved music and the musical tradition he bequeathed to his Church has been one of its greatest glories. He added congregational singing to Lutheran services: people in the university cities spoke and understood Latin. By contrast, John Calvin allowed the singing of the psalms, but banned musical instruments from church services.[21]

Because of the political nature of the Reformation in England music at this time was predominantly secular with the development of chamber music, both for voices and for instruments.[22] Some composers, including Thomas Tallis, Orlando Gibbons, William Byrd and John Bull, remained Catholics despite the laws, and they wrote for the Roman ritual, but such compositions were not publicly performed, although Queen Elizabeth I had them performed in the royal chapel.

Among their achievements Gibbons, Bull and Byrd produced the initial book of keyboard music in England. The first music was published in England in 1575. Before their suppression the monasteries had employed many full-time musicians. Queen Elizabeth supported chapelmasters who organised large choirs and formal music for the royal chapel, so that it was said that Queen Elizabeth saved English music from Puritan destruction. Women, not boys, often sang the higher parts. In private houses madrigals were sung in parlours and they were described as love in counterpoint.[23]

Literature

Literary expression benefited from advances in printing and publishing. Poetry and prose were written prolifically at this period. Publishing and bookselling were combined into the one trade. There were 250 publishers in Elizabethan England and most did their own printing.[24]

Publishers were dependent on patronage and patronage was essential also for the theatre in England. Theatres were built in London in 1576. In Germany between 1594 and 1612 theatre building was borrowed from the style of the Globe Theatre in England. In these theatres the public mingled with the upper classes.[25] In Elizabethan England this was the great Shakespearian age. William Shakespeare was the great dramatist whose work 'straddled the sixteenth and seventeenth centuries and cut through any restraints which the classical or medieval tradition had put upon the theatre'.[26]

In Spain there were dramatists including Pedro Calderon and Lope de Vega, and Miguel de Cervantes produced the famed prose work, *Don Quixote*. Essay writing became popular through such essayists as Sir Francis Bacon (1561-1626). Great poetry was produced in works such as that by John Milton, John Donne, Edmund Spenser, Richard Crashaw. It was created also, of course, in Shakespeare's sonnets.

Science

Scientific discoveries were burgeoning at this time. Some examples were those of William Harvey, the English physician, who discovered the true nature of the circulation of the blood and the function of the heart as a pump. The talented Francis Bacon wrote about scientific method and developed a plan to organise the sciences.

Blaise Pascal was the French founder of the modern theory of probabilities. The Italian, Galileo Galilei, developed the theory of the planets revolving around the sun, while the Belgian, Gerhard Mercator, developed the science of mapping. The German, Johannes Kepler, was the great mathematician whose work was to aid the later discoveries of Isaac Newton.

The Reformation period was therefore a time of great disturbance in political and religious debates. However, it was also the age of many great saints and the cultural and scientific achievements of such people as 'Shakespeare and Cervantes, Caravaggio and Rubens, of Gabrielli and Monteverdi, and not least, of Kepler and Galileo'.[27] It was this period also which was to encourage and nurture new educational enterprises which would fire the imaginations of many women innovators, not the least of whom was the English woman, Mary Ward.

CHAPTER 13

Educational Aspects of the Reformation Period

Jesuit education

'The Jesuit educational venture originated with concern for the training of younger members of the Society, whose education the first companions hoped would be at least the equivalent of their own.'[1] An important historical event in Jesuit education was the request by Leonor Osorio (wife of the Sicilian Viceroy of Spain) for the Jesuits to found a college at Messina in Sicily. With the prompting of the Viceroy, Leonor's husband, the officials of the city of Messina formally asked St Ignatius:

> ... on 19 December 1547 to send five Jesuit scholastics to study there and five teachers for classes in theology, cases of conscience, 'arts', rhetoric and grammar - all disciplines except law and medicine. The officials promised they would supply food, clothing and lodging for the Jesuits according to their need, so that the instruction could be given free of charge.[2]

By March 1548, Ignatius had chosen four priests and six scholastics from the best talent available to him in Rome. He was also concerned to make the group as international as possible. Never before in the history of the Jesuits had so much talent, nor a group of this size, been 'sent' for any other ministry. It was a very important enterprise as Pope Paul III encouraged the Jesuits in this international grouping of religious men at Messina, and further requested them 'to combat the errors of the Lutherans'.[3]

The latter request for this school was an interesting one because the Pope had also requested that the Jesuits be sent to the Council of Trent. Jesuit Fathers Lainez and Salmeron were commissioned as theologians for the first session of the Council from 1545 to 1547. At later sessions of the Council of Trent the Jesuits, Peter Canisius and Claude Jay, made important contributions on both doctrinal and reform issues.[4] Thus in the early stages of Jesuit history they not only established the college, but they were also able to provide a certain amount of training for their own members with adequate funding for such a venture. That the Jesuits were in demand in these areas was very pleasing to the founder, St Ignatius.[5]

Other Jesuit schools, similar to that in Messina, were opened in Europe and thus the founding of the college in Messina became a springboard for this type of Jesuit ministry. Part IV of the Constitutions of the Society of Jesus, which were drawn up by St Ignatius, dealt thoroughly with the Jesuits' ministry of education. The chapter is headed 'The Instruction of those who are retained in the Society, in learning and in other means of helping their fellowmen'.[6] It is claimed that Part IV of the Constitutions can itself be called a classic treatise on Christian education, and that its influence on the theory and practice in this field is still functioning effectively today.[7]

Successive drafts of a plan of studies were written from the Constitutions in Part IV and this plan is now called the *Ratio Studiorum*. The more concerted versions published by committees in 1586, 1591 and 1592 culminated in the text promulgated by the then Jesuit General, Claudio Aquaviva, in 1599. This was the definitive *Ratio Studiorum* which governed practice in Jesuit schools until the suppression of the Society in 1773.[8]

Through these drafts Ignatius and the Jesuits set up the first extensive school system in history, i.e., an organization of individual schools in close contact with one another, deliberately reviewing and evaluating classroom and administrative experience, and sharing and exchanging teachers on a large scale according to needs... The *Ratio* is, however, more a treatment of curricular organization and pedagogical procedure than of educational theory... One great merit of the *Ratio* of 1599 is that it produced a unity of procedure throughout the far-flung Jesuit schools in Europe and the Americas. That procedural unity was greater than would be desirable or possible today; but it was a significant advantage and achievement amid the educational disorganization of the 1500's and 1600's. The setting up of such a widespread system is what made the Jesuits' educational work the success which is described in histories of education.[9]

However, the Jesuit schools and colleges were not always successful, nor free from crises. It was alleged that they were opening too many schools too quickly. This meant that there were too few Jesuits for the number of schools, as well as for other commitments, and the quality of instruction sometimes suffered.

As early as 1548 the school rules in Messina forebade students bearing arms to enter school buildings.[10] Problems of discipline for unruly boys were compounded by the fact that, according to St Ignatius, Jesuits were never to administer corporal punishment. Ignatius believed that physical punishment diminished respect between teacher and pupil. His solution for correcting the unruly was to hire a 'corrector' to administer punishment, but some schools were too poor to do this. However, the first General Congregation of the Society in 1558 mitigated Ignatius' prohibition against corporal punishment by allowing the General to dispense from it when necessary.[11]

As a precedent for Mary Ward, among other aspects of Jesuit education, there was emphasis on theatre, which included music and dance (as well as ballet), which was usually an integral part of the performances.[12] Among those who received their first education in theatre as students in Jesuit schools were future dramatists such as Lope de Vega, Calderon, Andreas Grypius, Jacob Bidermann, Corneille and Molière.[13]

Despite the failures and less desirable features found in any innovation such as the Jesuit school system, O'Malley summarises the Jesuit achievements in the following ten characteristics which he assesses as contributing to the Jesuits' initial success and to a new, international style:

First, the schools charged no tuition fees.

Second, at least in principle they welcomed students from every social class.

Third, especially the schools of 'humane letters' conformed to the emerging consensus of the age in curriculum, the importance of character formation, and similar matters.

Fourth, the Jesuits postulated compatibility between an education in 'humane letters' on the one hand and in Aristotelian philosophy/science and Thomistic theology on the other.

Fifth, they implemented division into classes (each with its own teacher), ordered progression from class to class according to clear curriculum goals, and similar provisions. In these methods the Jesuits implemented the ways in which they had been taught in the University of Paris, and which came to be called the 'Paris Mode'.

Sixth, they insisted on the active appropriation of both ideas and skills that consisted not only in written compositions and oral repetitions in the classroom, but also in plays, disputations, and other 'spectacles' open to the public.

Seventh, they sponsored a clear, coherent, and basically simple religious program, adaptable to students of different ages and backgrounds - a program that in principle sought to move the student beyond pious practices to an inner appropriation of ethical and religious values.

Eighth, through their Marian Congregations they gave further articulation to their religious program by adopting and adapting one of the most popular institutions of the day, the confraternity. Confraternities were religious associations of lay persons devoted to specific practices or works of charity, usually under the direction and spiritual assistance of clergy.

Ninth, they were on the way to creating an international network of schools, the largest by far under a single aegis the world had ever seen, in which information was effectively shared about what worked and what did not.

Finally, most difficult to calculate, the 'teaching under the teaching' was different coming from this group of men. The Jesuits were on the whole better educated and motivated than most pre-university schoolmasters anywhere in Europe. Further, they tried to influence their students more by their example than by their words. They repeatedly inculcated in one another the importance of loving their students, of knowing them as individuals, of enjoying a respectful *familiaritas* with them.[14]

Feminine educational endeavours

The situation for the education of girls was very different from that of boys - as we have seen in a previous chapter. The invention of the printing press in 1450 enabled works of religion to be published and the Reformers required their people to have literacy skills for reading the Bible and the writings of the Reformers. In response to this, active,

uncloistered women's orders began to arise and this movement was particularly evident in France as we have shown.

Rapley maintains that the Jesuit background is discernible everywhere.[15] We have seen the Jesuit influence in the
founding charism of these orders as they translated the spirit
of the Jesuits to the active apostolate of teaching, drawing
on the principles of the *Ratio Studiorum*, which were then
known to these women teachers.[16]

These groups of teachers were also inventive in their teaching methods. Peter Fourier (co-founder with Alix Le Clerc of
the Canonesses Regular of St Augustine of the Congregation
of Our Lady) is credited with the invention of the blackboard.
They also used large printed cards which were valuable for
beginners, and the other learning tool which made simulta-
neous instruction possible was the cheap reading book, purchased for pupils by their parents or, if they were poor, provided by the school.[17] No doubt Mary Ward's Sisters used
whatever teaching resources they could obtain but, most assuredly, poverty often restricted their endeavours.

Mary Ward's aims with regard to education are given in
her Memorial Petition to Pope Paul V in 1616. She wrote that:

> ... we have in mind the mixed kind of life, such a life as we
> learn Christ our Lord and Master taught his chosen ones...
> so that in this way we may more easily teach maidens and
> girls of tender years, in piety, in the Christian virtues and
> liberal arts so that they may be able thereafter to undertake
> more fruitfully the secular and monastic life, according to
> the vocation of each.[18]

In the Verity speeches given to her Sisters in St Omer in
1617 Mary Ward was adamant that 'there is no such difference between men and women' when it was stated that their
fervour would decay because they were but women.[19] Mary
affirmed the capacity of girls and women to receive educa-

tion because 'women may be perfect as well as men, if they love verity and seek true knowledge'.[20]

In the process of founding the Institute of the Blessed Virgin Mary, Mary Ward had embraced the inspiration 'to take the same of the Society' and this therefore necessarily involved an adaptation for girls of the *Ratio Studiorum*.

Institute schools

Mary Ward established Institute schools on the continent despite difficulties financially and in searching for suitable properties, as well as differences in language and culture. Day and boarding schools were established in the Netherlands, and also in Munich.[21] In the Vienna school in Austria there were 475 girls.[22]

The day school in Rome had 123 pupils, as well as students in a trade school. There was also another such trade school in Perugia.[23] These schools were called 'trade' schools because, as the mothers expressed it:

> ... the girls who had been growing up without any education, had now found a place where they could learn what was useful, and had been brought round to living a christian and morally good life. It is interesting to see from letters of this period the dangers of street-life in Rome; and the anxiety of mothers to safe-guard their daughters.[24]

One of the earliest lives of Mary Ward contained the following reference to these activities of teaching girls such skills for life: 'Poor parents felt the pleasing benefit of having their children made fit by qualities to gain their livings honestly, and by virtue made capable to know it was their duty so to do.'[25]

Mary Ward was not only responsible for the first school for girls in Rome,[26] but also, following the example of the

Jesuits, the Sisters accepted no payment for their teaching.[27] It is noted that like many pioneers, Mary Ward was usually short of money. Education in her common schools was free; only boarders paid fees for their boarding upkeep. Mary was therefore dependent on charity and on the dowry money of members. These were unreliable sources of income especially when it became obvious to the parents of candidates for the Institute that it was not going to gain the approval of the Holy See.[28] When orders for the suppression of the houses were being given there were ten such houses with three hundred Sisters in them.[29] Many of the younger members had been educated in the Mary Ward schools and then joined the group which was growing numerically at this time.

The curriculum in these schools embraced all areas of knowledge with religion being given a special emphasis. Girls returning to England or living in countries affected by the Protestant Reformation required a strong religious formation. Mary Ward was careful about procuring priests to teach catechism and prepare children for the sacraments, but she was still reported to Rome for her Sisters teaching theology and taking on tasks reserved for clerics.[30]

It was in the memorial to Pope Gregory XV by the English clergy in 1622 that the Sisters were referred to as 'Galloping Girls' because 'they ride hither and yon'.[31] This was certainly true of their educational endeavours in England. Mobility was a necessity, as we have seen that the teacher, Sister Dorothea, moved from house to house in the English countryside because the Reformation in that country made it dangerous for Catholics to be caught teaching about religion.

Language teaching was always a specialty in Mary Ward's schools. The girls were taught 'Latin, German, French, English and Italian and this not as a smattering only, but so as to be able to speak, read and write in each language, and also to study good authors in each'.[32] In order for such language teaching to take place Mary was mindful of the formation of the Sisters. In a letter to Winifred Wigmore in Naples written from Vienna in October 1627, Mary said:

> I would have Cecilia and Catherina begin out of hand to learn the rudiments of Latin; fear not their loss of virtue by that means, for this must and will be so common to all as there will be no cause for complacency. I would not have their other work hindered, but what time can otherwise be found beside their prayer, let it be bestowed upon their Latin.[33]

When the teachers were accomplished in teaching languages Mary Ward was quick to praise both the Sisters and their students as the following letter to Winifred Bedingfield in Munich on 16 July 1627 shows:

> My dear Mother, *Pax Christi!* These are indeed chiefly to congratulate the unexpected progress of your Latin schools. You cannot easily believe the content I took in the themes of those two towardly girls. You will work much to your own happiness by advancing them apace in that learning, and God will concur with you because his honour and service so require. All such as are capable invite them to it, and for such as desire to be one of us, no talent is so much to be regarded in them as the Latin tongue. The Latin hand Maria wrote her theme in is here by the fathers much commended, though I think it is far short of what it will be. I fear those subtle wenches have some help at home to make their themes, but you will look to them for that.[34]

Thus classical education was considered essential in Mary Ward's educational philosophy. As already noted, this was different from the education given to Protestant women, as Warnicke points out.[35] The Jesuits subscribed to the humanist tradition of the Renaissance, which O'Malley says had the basic premise that religious and moral inspiration could be found even in pagan authors... Although the Jesuits were not uncritical in their engagement with secular culture, they tended in general to be welcoming of it.[36]

In view of the Jesuit emphasis on drama and theatre, it was not surprising that Mary Ward's schools included drama in their curriculum. The plays (presumably with religious themes) by the Spanish writer, Calderon, were performed by students in the schools. These activities were condemned by Father Robert Sherwood OSB in a document known as 'Sherwood's Petition' which he sent to Rome in 1622 saying that the Sisters 'allow pupils to act plays and to speak in public'.[37] As Provincial of the English Benedictines, Sherwood had written on behalf of his order, because many Benedictines felt they were being overshadowed by the Jesuits working in England.[38] As a 'Jesuitess', Mary Ward also experienced this antipathy.

It must be stated again that these schools for girls were not the first schools for girls. We have already noted the educational pursuits of the Daughters of St Agnes (1601 in St Omer), the Ursuline foundations, and the schools established by Jeanne de Lestonnac and others in France. However, Beales claims that 'Mary Ward's foundations were remarkable rather for the extent to which they provided *elementary* education, and for the *furore* caused inside the Church by the revolutionary character of her apostolate.'[39]

What gave Mary Ward's schools the reputation for excellence among parents and all but the most biased and envious authorities? It is asserted that it was the quality of teaching demanded by the foundress and given generously by all the members, the challenge to every pupil to realise her fullest potential as a Catholic woman, and the context of free, loving partnership between nuns and students.[40] All this aligns clearly with the characteristics of Jesuit education already delineated by John O'Malley in his book, *The First Jesuits*, which is quoted above. The cultural and educational influences of the Reformation period were evident in all this work, but Mary Ward's enterprises were among those which provided for the education of girls in a new, comprehensive way.

CHAPTER 14

An Incomparable Woman

How can we assess Mary Ward as a woman of the Reformation period through her life and work, within the context of the political, social and religious setting of her times? We must not forget that there were Protestant women, as well as Catholics, who were active in their churches. These were women comparable with Mary, in having similar social status and commitment to religion, who also struggled for the betterment of women. An overview of their achievements has been given in previous chapters, and it is important to consider Mary's initiatives in the context of the lives of her contemporaries.

Religious changes

The Reformation period was a time of radical change. In England, Catholics were assailed by the developing theology of Protestantism and by the clarification of Catholic theology following the Council of Trent. The establishment of the Anglican Church in England led to challenges for Catholics, as they were required to attend Anglican services, were fined if they did not attend, and were also fined for conducting Catholic ones. The recusant movement (made up of those who refused to follow Anglicanism), especially in the north of England, was indicative of the attempts by Catholics to maintain their faith.

Mary Ward, along with her companions such as Winifred Wigmore and Mary Poyntz, ardently supported the recusant movement and devoted their lives to promoting it - just as Protestant women, such as Catherine von Bora, Katherine Zell and Argula von Grumbach, identified strongly with the Lutheran and Calvinist reform movements, but suffered persecution from their own authorities.

In this time of great turmoil there was a depth of spirituality well documented in the mystical experiences of both Catholic and Protestant women, as many of them wrote of these experiences for the edification and guidance of others. Teresa of Avila is the best known Catholic woman mystic of the Reformation period. Mary Ward herself was sustained by her deep spiritual life and significant mystical experiences.

Changes in theological doctrines, along with the associated social, economic and political changes, contributed in the Reformation period to the great upheaval which affected various institutions. Most notably, from the perspective of women, these changes impinged significantly on the institutions of the Church, the family and education.

As a result of the disruption of the Reformation, initially both Protestant and Catholic women became actively involved in their respective religious movements. Thus Mary Ward founded a Poor Clare convent for English women on the continent and spent over thirty years attempting to organise an active religious Institute for women, based on the Jesuit Constitutions, which were relevant to the changed circumstances of her times. Similarly, at the beginning of the Reformation, Protestant women were given scope for various initiatives, such as preaching, in the case of Katherine Zell, and engaging in theological polemics, in the case of Argula von Grumbach.

Such activities of Protestant women, and the high profile of women in various Protestant sects, could not be accommodated by their male religious leaders, as their groups settled down to respectability. Similarly Mary Ward's efforts to establish her Institute were thwarted by the institutional Church, as it attempted to enforce strictly the enclosure for women's religious orders, because of the legislation of the Council of Trent.

Nevertheless, the turbulence of the Reformation period increased the scope of activities, especially for Catholic women. It must be recognised that had Mary Ward lived in the preceding period, when enclosed religious life was available to her in her homeland, it is highly probable that she would have simply entered religious life in England, and remained there. However, as a contrast, her life became one of mobility and political activity in both Church and state across Europe.

It is relevant to note, too, that in England some of the Sisters of Mary Ward's Institute, such as Sister Dorothea, worked alone, while others moved from house to house working with adults and children in pastoral ministry, usually in association with priests, a practice to which the English secular clergy objected. This was a particular point of condemnation in the subsequent Bull of Suppression.

The family

The institution of the family was considerably affected by the Reformation. For English recusant Catholics, the Reformation led to a loosening of immediate family ties because education in the Catholic faith, and formal ministry in the Church, often necessitated children and young adults being sent abroad.

In the Protestant tradition the family was strengthened as a unit, because women's activities were confined to the home. It was only the women in the smaller sects, such as the Quakers, who managed to obtain leadership positions in their groups, and which enabled them to operate outside their homes. After the death of her first husband, Judge Fell, Margaret Fell met and married the English leader of the Quakers, George Fox. It was from this position as wife of the leader of this sect that Margaret dispensed the Quakers' 'organizational philanthrophy towards its own members'.[1] But Margaret Fell (Fox) also led the first Women's Petition of 1669 which was a supplement to the general Quaker protest against tithes.

Education

Education was another development important in the lives of women which was affected by the Reformation. Because of the doctrinal differences between Protestants and Catholics both denominations concentrated on education to win people to 'the true faith'. Protestant emphasis on the reading of the Bible necessitated literacy for both men and women. Education was an important factor in Mary Ward's life, and of great interest to her, especially in relation to her participation in the Catholic Church's Counter-Reformation efforts.

As Warnicke shows through her meticulous research, Mary Ward's own education was not typical of Protestant Reformation England. As a result of its over-reaction to Roman Catholic excesses, education in Protestant England moved away from the humanist tradition, and so Protestant women peers of Mary Ward did not receive education in Latin. The recusant Catholic women of the upper classes, however, still received tuition in Latin. Mary Ward valued Latin and gave it a central place in the curriculum of her schools. After all, Latin was the language of the Church, medicine, and the law.

In an effort to counter the educational activities of the Protestants, the Catholic Church, through the initiative of local bishops and priests, and local women, usually of the upper classes, organised both boarding and day schools for girls. Mary Ward became part of this movement, and was sustained in her difficulties by her mystical experiences, which revealed God's will for her.

Like the French Catholic foundresses of religious groups of this time, such as Jeanne de Lestonnac and Alix Le Clerc, Mary Ward was deeply influenced by the Jesuits, both in the organisation of her religious Institute and in her educational endeavours. Indeed the Jesuits typified the institutional changes in religious life of this time, because they had adopted structures to promote unity within the group, and mobility for apostolic effectiveness. While the Church approved of this for religious men, it was cautious about permitting it for formally recognised religious women.

Nevertheless, the Church authorities operated pragmatically concerning pious women's groups engaged in educational endeavours, because they were aware that education was effective in the work of the Counter-Reformation. Such women as Anne de Xainctongne and Lucy Perotti followed the cautious path acceptable to Rome at this time and, foregoing the formal title 'religious', maintained their status as a pious association under the authority of the local bishop. Other foundresses were aided by Jesuit advisers to deal with Rome in such a way as to achieve certain adaptations of the enclosure for educational purposes, while maintaining the status of religious.

Although Mary Ward received much support and advice from churchmen such as Bishop Blaes of St Omer, and various Jesuit sympathisers, and indeed the popes, she steadfastly refused to compromise and follow the strategies of the French or Italian associations of pious women. In this she was not typical of her peers within the Catholic Church, but more akin to Quaker women, such as the English woman,

Margaret Fell (Fox), who ignored formal authority and were obedient to the Spirit as they perceived it.[2]

However, it must be emphasised that, while Mary Ward refused to adopt the various modifications to her plans for her Institute, which were suggested by Church authorities, she was unequivocally obedient, in a spirit of faith, to those authorities. This was despite her awareness of the human politics that were involved in the various decisions that these same Church authorities were making concerning her Institute.

It could be argued that Mary Ward was unrealistic with regard to her demands, and she could have achieved all she really wanted by following the tactics of Jeanne de Lestonnac and Alix Le Clerc. On the other hand, she could well be said to belong to that group of individuals who challenge their age and, while appearing to be failures themselves, actually push the age forward in its thinking. Such people sowed the seed which in time germinated.

Relationship with men

Both Catholic and Protestant women in the Reformation period were supportive of men, and were supported by them, as well as finding men to be their chief opponents. Mary Ward was typical of her period in this respect. Among the Church hierarchy she had both friends and enemies. Bishop Blaes and the Nuncio Albergati helped her at the beginning of her work in St Omer. Cardinal Millini, as Vicar General of Rome, looked after Mary and her Sisters, but also suppressed their house. The three popes with whom Mary had dealings treated her with respect. Pope Urban VIII received her after her release from prison to return to Rome, and the abrogation of the heresy charge against her, although he had signed the Bull of Suppression against her Institute.

Mary Ward's personality no doubt made her an easy conversationalist. Of this gift Winifred Wigmore said: 'Her presence and conversation were most winning. Her voice in speaking was very grateful and in song melodious. In her demeanour and carriage, an angelic modesty was united to a refined ease and dignity of manner, that made even Princes find great satisfaction, yea, profit in conversing with her.'[3]

The Jesuit Generals, although opposing her plans to use the Jesuit Constitutions, still tried to help her as far as they could. As MacGinley points out: 'the wonder was that it took so long for the final ruling to be made by Rome against Mary Ward, in light of the fact of the legislation of the Council of Trent enforcing enclosure for women religious and the endorsement of this by Pius V in *Circa Pastoralis*'.[4]

In her personal dealings with churchmen Mary Ward was treated with respect, but in the Bull of Suppression, which paralleled the treatment given to the Protestant woman, Argula von Grumbach, she experienced the full force of the misogyny of the age. Indeed from Prague the Nuncio Carafa had warned the authorities in Rome about Mary Ward and her companions saying that 'their sex is inconstant and inclined to error'.[5] The English secular clergy had made it abundantly clear to Rome that they were convinced of this. As in previous ages, if a woman in the Reformation period showed sterling qualities, she was likened to a man. It is reported that those who opposed Mary Ward in Rome spoke of her as being 'a woman with the daring of a man'.[6]

Among the words which Mary Ward addressed to her Sisters we find: 'The true children of this Company shall accustom themselves to act not out of fear, but solely from love, because they are called by God to a vocation of love.'[7] As an illustration of Mary's own fearlessness, and her work for the restoration of the faith in England, it is related that the Anglican Archbishop of Canterbury remarked that she was more dangerous than six Jesuits.[8] This bishop, George Abbott (1562-1633), Archbishop of Canterbury from 1611, was known as a great opponent of Catholicism.[9]

Relationship with the state

The relationship between Church and state was very much affected by the Reformation, as well as contributing much to its cause. In Protestant countries the state increasingly controlled the Church, while in Catholic countries the state assumed a greater independence.

Mary Ward, being part of the persecuted Church in England, gained a freedom of action, both from the rejection of the Catholic Church by the Protestant state, and also the lack of a locally recognised Catholic hierarchy. However, after the suppression of the Institute, she gained from the support of the secular government in Munich. Indeed, the survival of her Institute in Munich was aided by the support of the Emperor, Maximilian of Bavaria.[10]

Social status

Social status for women in the Reformation period was very important, especially if they were to influence mainstream Protestant or Catholic religious doctrines and practices. From her position as queen, Elizabeth I in England was able to publish the Thirty-Nine Articles of Faith in 1566. Likewise, the Calvinist position was defended by the noblewomen, Marguerite of Navarre and her daughter, Jeanne d'Albret.

Mary Ward and her early companions all came from the upper class. Having this status meant that they had the

personal resources and connections to be involved significantly in the Counter-Reformation activities of the Church,
and to take initiatives to promote them. Mary also accepted
the advantages of assistance from women of high status, such
as the Infanta Isabella Clara Eugenia, to further her cause.

Ongoing leadership and initiatives

We often ask, 'What did Mary Ward bring to this new way
of life for women religious?' When her family consented to
her leaving home she brought with her the special English-
ness: 'the resoluteness of a Yorkshirewoman, her strong
faith, an adaptability born of her experience in different
families and a marked awareness of each one's personal
responsibility for his or her life'.[11]

Like the other Catholic foundresses during the Reformation, Mary Ward gathered around her a group of loyal
followers who continued the spirit of her work after her
death, and who worked effectively to develop her original
concept of the Institute. In Munich Mary's Institute found
enduring support. From here branch houses were established, and in 1693 the superioress general, Catherine
Dawson, petitioned the Holy See to approve a formulation
of eighty-one rules which defined the purpose, spirit and
mode of operation of the Institute. Approval was granted
in 1703 by the brief *Inscrutabili*. It was on this occasion, too,
that the Pope, Clement XI, said 'let women be governed by
women'. As MacGinley comments: 'Clement was careful
to indicate that the English Ladies were not religious and
that, despite their centralised government, they were still
under the jurisdiction of the local bishop.' MacGinley adds:
'However, a significant papal concession and level of recognition were obtained.'[12]

Mary Ward's sufferings on behalf of the Institute were
certainly an example of the grain of wheat falling into the

204 ❖ A DANGEROUS INNOVATOR

earth and dying (*Jn* 12:24). A further germination of the seed sown by her was evident in 1747 when a dispute developed between the Mendleheim community (in the Augsburg diocese), a branch house from Munich, and the Bishop of Augsburg, who wanted to bring the houses in his diocese completely under his control.[13] The Sisters appealed to the Pope, Benedict XIV, and the Pope personally wrote the Apostolic Constitution, *Quamvis Iusto*, which was issued in 1749. MacGinley points out that:

> It occupies a crucial position in the development of canonical legislation for institutes of women, constituting as it does the first detailed legislation which attempted to formulate a mode of operation for simple-vow institutes with a superioress-general in their relationship with the hierarchy of the Church.[14]

Dr Rosa MacGinley explains that although responding to a specific situation, it soon became:

> ... in the absence of common Church law for institutes of simple vows, a norm for the recognition of their existence and a precedent for at least tacit approval of centralised government... Institutes of simple vows hence entered the official legislation of the Church but with many anomalies still to be resolved.[15]

Indeed, as a result of her detailed study of the canonical evolution of the congregations of women religious with simple vows, MacGinley observes that it was Mary Ward's Institute which issued the challenge for new juridical forms in the seventeenth century and which, a century later, occasioned the bridging legislation between an older canonical understanding and a newly developing context in which public responsibility was being exercised by women in their own right.[16]

The far-sighted vision of Mary Ward is indicated by the fact that official recognition of the Institute of the Blessed

Virgin Mary (the final formal title of the English Ladies) was accorded in 1877, at a time when older institutes of simple vows, as well as newer foundations, were seeking papal approbation, as a result of the practical problems caused by their transnational, as well as transdiocesan, activities.[17]

The final recognition of Mary Ward's Institute is remarkable in the light of the irrevocable expression of the Bull of Suppression: 'Let no one whomsoever be permitted to render void this document of Our suppression, extinction, subjection, removal, destruction, annulment, release, exhortation, of our wishes and orders, or rashly attempt to contradict it.'[18]

While the Dutchman, Father Jacques van Ginneken SJ, founder of the Grail movement, was critical of Mary Ward for modelling her Institute too fully on the Jesuits, he conceded in the light of history that 'a condemnation like that of Mary Ward proves after all to be the way to a revival of the same initiative in later days'.[19] Ginneken also makes the comment that 'we may certainly consider Mary Ward as the pioneer of the lay apostolate by women in the Catholic Church, for which she fought so heroically'.

Pope Pius XII shared Ginneken's appreciation of Mary Ward as indicated in an address he gave to a worldwide assembly of the Catholic apostolate of the laity in Rome in 1951. The Pope applauded the increased participation of the laity in Catholic action and commented that 'it behoves us to recall Mary Ward that incomparable woman, who at the direst and most sanguinary epoch, Catholic England gave to the Church'.[20] Thus in hindsight it can be seen that the work in the Church by lay Catholic women was no small contribution to the reforms of the Catholic Reformation.

Again in the twentieth century Pope John Paul II has included the name of Mary Ward with other 'perfect' women such as Monica, mother of Augustine; Olga of Kiev; Matilda of Tuscany; Hedwig of Silesia; Jadwiga of Cracaw; Elizabeth of Thuringia; Birgitta of Sweden; Joan of Arc; Rose of Lima and Elizabeth Ann Seton. In his Apostolic Letter, *On the Dignity and Vocation of Women*, the Pope said, 'In every age and in every country we find many "perfect" women (cf *Prov* 31:10) who, despite persecution, difficulties and discrimination, have shared in the Church's mission.'[21] This is high praise indeed, and acknowledgment of Mary Ward's contribution as a woman in the Church of the Reformation period.

Conclusion

What was Mary Ward like? From Winifred Wigmore's biography we know that Mary sat twice for the painting of a portrait.[22] The oil painting shown in this book is a print from one of these paintings, which is now held by the IBMV in Augsburg. The date of the picture and the artist are unknown.

Winifred Wigmore's remarks about Mary Ward's general appearance give us a pen picture of a comely woman: 'She was rather tall, but her figure was symmetrical. Her complexion was delicately beautiful, her countenance and aspect most agreeable, mingled with what I know not which was attractive. It was a general saying, "She became whatsoever she wore or did."'[23] Allowing for the fact that these were words from a great friend and companion, we must acknowledge that Mary was an attractive person, a fact which was born out by the number of women who wished to follow her ideals by becoming members of the fledging Institute.

In the last analysis, Mary Ward was essentially a woman of her times. As a talented, deeply religious woman she, like numerous other Catholic and Protestant women, was permitted by the disruption of the Reformation, to take initiatives in the wider sphere beyond the home or convent. Like so many of this period she suffered greatly in pursuing her vision, which was broader than that which could be tolerated by the Church authorities of the time.

Sustained by her mystical faith, and her faithful, talented companions, Mary Ward survived the suppression of her Institute in a spirit of obedience to the Church. Trusting that there would be a future for the Institute, she exhorted her companions: 'Work with great tranquillity, joy and magnanimity, for what is not done in one year can be done in another... We must wait God Almighty's time and leisure, for we must follow, not go before Him.'[24]

Not only were Mary's companions urged to continue the spirit of the Institute, but also Mary Ward herself promised to assist them when she said on her death bed: 'God will assist you; it is no matter the who, but the what; and when God shall enable me to be in place I will serve you.'[25] These are the words of a generous, faith-filled woman of service - a service which showed that the will of God was achieved through her efforts.

Indeed, Mary Ward experienced and witnessed to what Mary Wollstonecraft was to declare over a century later, when she was suffering harsh criticism following the publication of *A Vindication of the Rights of Women*: 'Those who are bold enough to advance before the age they live in and throw off by the force of their minds the prejudice which the maturing reason of the world will in time disavow must learn to brave censure.'[26]

Mary Ward certainly bore censure bravely! When the works of the Institute were condemned in the harshest manner possible by a papal bull of suppression, Mary Ward accepted it all, not only serenely, but with great good humour. In the lemon juice letters from the Anger prison in Munich in February 1631 she wrote to her Sisters 'from my palace, not my prison, for truly so I find it'.[27] Her conduct was the epitome of the words she gave her Sisters: 'In our calling, a cheerful mind, a good understanding, and a great desire after virtue are necessary, but of all three a cheerful mind is the most so.'[28]

In 1634 Mary wrote from Rome to Winn Bedingfield in Munich in words which characterised her whole life: 'Be wholly God's, and keep to your utmost all that he has given yourself or left to your charge...'[29] While enduring the harshest of conditions during the time she spent in the Anger prison, Mary Ward wrote in words which are part of her legacy: '*Vale*, be merry and doubt not our dear Master.'[30] This is the epitaph of an incomparable woman.

Mary Ward: Time line

1585   Mary was born on 23 January in Yorkshire, England. Her parents were Ursula Wright and Marmaduke Ward.

1585-1590   Mary lived with her parents at Mulwith until she was five years old.

1590-1594   Until she was nearly ten years old Mary lived with her grandparents, Robert and Ursula Wright, at Ploughland Hall, East Riding, Yorkshire. Her grandmother taught her Latin and Mary read the Fathers of the Church. When her grandfather died Mary returned to her parents.

1595-1597   Mary lived with her family. She had three younger sisters and two younger brothers. When Mulwith was burnt in 1595 the family moved to Newby.

1597-1598   The family moved to Northumberland and Mary lived with Mrs Ardington of Harewell. She made her first Communion there on 8 September 1598.

1599-1606   Mary lived with relatives, the Babthorpe family, at Osgodby. With her cousins Mary was educated by tutors and learnt Latin, French, Italian and German. In 1605 Edmund Neville became a suitor for Mary's hand in marriage. She refused him and declared her desire to be a religious.

1606 Mary travelled from England to Calais and then to St Omer. Mary became an extern Sister in a Convent of Poor Clares (Franciscans).

1607 Mary left the Poor Clares.

1607-1608 Mary established a convent for English Poor Clares at Gravelines, in the province of Flanders.

1609 Mary understood that she was not called to be a Poor Clare and left the convent she had founded.

    Mary returned to London and visited Catholics in hiding and in prison. She received the 'Glory Vision' by which she understood that she was not to be a Carmelite but was called to another vocation 'to the glory of God'.

1610 Mary returned to St Omer with some companions. They began to teach English girls who went there seeking refuge from the persecution of Catholics in England.

1611 Mary had a vision of the spiritual foundation of her Institute. The words she understood were: 'Take the same of the Society' (that is, of the Society of Jesus, the Jesuits).

1609-1615 Mary and companions lived at St Omer. She made several visits to England and procured a house in London. In October 1615 she had the illumination called 'The Vision of the Just Soul'.

1615 Mary sent recommendatory letters from Bishop Blaes, Bishop of St Omer, to Pope Paul V. The Pope praised their work, commanded Bishop

Blaes to have care of them, and promised the possibility of her Institute being confirmed.

1616   Mary went to take the healing waters at Spa and to investigate the founding of a house at Liège.

1617   Foundation of the house in Liège. Bishop Blaes sent a pastoral letter in praise of them. Mary went again to England and returned to establish the novitiate at Liège.

1618   Mary made another visit to England and was captured and condemned to death without trial. Fine money was paid by friends and Mary was released.

1619   Mary returned to St Omer and Liège. Sister Praxedes and Mary Alcock disputed her leadership. Both soon died.

1620-1621   Mary founded houses at Cologne and Treves.

1621   Mary and four sisters made their first journey to Rome, arriving on Christmas eve. Mary had an audience with Pope Gregory XV, seeking approbation for her Institute.

1622-1623   The founding of a school in Rome and the death of Mary's sister, Barbara Ward.

1623   The opening of a school in Naples.

1625   Another house was opened in Perugia. In August the Roman school was forced to close, but the nuns were allowed to stay.

1626-1627   Mary made foundations in Northern Europe at Munich, Vienna and Pressburg.

1628-1630   Another journey to Rome where Mary pleaded for approbation of the Institute from the next Pope, Urban VIII.

1630   The northern houses of Liège, Cologne and Treves were suppressed and the schools closed.

1631   On 13 January the Bull of Suppression came out and all houses were disbanded, but Sisters could stay in the Paradeiser House in Munich. From there Mary was taken and imprisoned in the Anger convent as a 'heretic'. She was in prison from 7 February till 14 April.

1631   When freed by order of Pope Urban VIII, although she was very ill, Mary travelled again to Rome to plead her innocence.

1632   Mary was acquitted of heresy.

1632-1637   Mary lived in a house near St Mary Major's in Rome.

1637   Mary left Rome again to travel to England. It was a long journey because of the war (the 'Thirty Years War') in Europe.

1639   Mary arrived in London and worked with Catholics there. They were unable to open a school at that time.

1642   Because of the war between the King, Charles I, and the Parliament, the Sisters were forced to travel north into Yorkshire.

1644   The siege of the city of York forced them to move inside the city. They later returned to the countryside at Heworth.

1645   On 30 January Mary Ward died peacefully surrounded by faithful companions. She was buried in the small cemetery (Anglican) of the church of Osbaldwick near Heworth. On her tombstone they chiselled the inscription:

To love the poor,

persevere in the same,

live die and rise with them

was all the aim of

Mary Ward

who having lived 60 years and 8 days

died 20th [sic] January 1645

Afterword: 'Galloping Girls'

The story of Mary Ward would not be complete without some fuller reference to her early companions. There were many who joined the Institute group before its suppression in 1631 and Chambers reported that there were between two hundred and three hundred women in ten houses when the Institute was suppressed by papal bull in January 1631.[1]

However, special mention must be made of seven of Mary Ward's first companions - high-born, heroic English women who bore the burdens of being founding members of a new kind of religious life for women. Not only did they establish houses throughout Europe in Mary's lifetime, but they also endured the suppression of the First Institute, and then developed the Second Institute according to the plan of Mary Ward.

Chambers notes that the lives of these 'gentlewomen' were closely interwoven with that of Mary Ward and had a most important influence upon her vocation. They were led by her example to serve God in a religious state, under her direction.[2]

In 1609 Mary Ward travelled by boat from England to the Netherlands where it was possible to practise publicly as a Catholic, in contrast to life in England where it was necessary to lead a clandestine life as a Catholic. Those who travelled with her, or joined her soon afterwards, were young women, six were in their twenties - Jane Browne was the oldest at twenty-eight years. Barbara Babthorpe and Mary Poyntz were seventeen and sixteen years old respectively.

We know that Mary Poyntz and Mary Ward herself had received offers of marriage, which they declined. Susanna Rookwood had been in English prisons five times and the others were members of recusant families. Fines were imposed continuously on such families for non-attendance at Anglican services, so it is a possibility that these women had decided to forgo marriage and devote themselves to a spiritual life, although the life of a nun was not then available to them in England.

Many women in Reformation times were married at a very young age, and those who could, brought a dowry with them. Contrary to this practice of early marriage, Mary Ward's first companions chose a celibate, active, religious life which meant exile from England and an uncertain future in the education of women and girls.

The following sketches present brief stories of these seven friends and companions of Mary Ward - all 'galloping girls'.

Winifred Wigmore (1585-1657)

Winifred Wigmore was one of twelve children, six of whom entered religious life.[3] She was gifted with languages and could speak and write five.[4] Winifred probably grew to know Mary Ward among the groups of English recusant Catholics, and she was one of those who went to St Omer in 1609.

As a friend and compatriot of Mary Ward's (they were the same age) Winifred was with those who made the foundations in Liège, Cologne and Treves from 1619 to 1620. She accompanied Mary Ward on her first journey to Rome in 1621 and was Mary's stalwart support when her sister, Barbara, died there in 1623. In that same year she assisted Mary in the foundation at Naples, and on the unexpected death of Susanna Rookwood, she was again in charge there.

Two years later Mary Ward celebrated her forty-first birthday with Win in Naples and asked her to go to the new foundation in Munich. The journey on foot via Rome, where she stayed, ended in Munich in 1629.

Around this time the Roman authorities threatened the suppression of the entire Institute and Mary sent Winifred Wigmore to encourage the Institute members in the Netherlands. Winifred and her companion, Mary Wivel, covered their more than one thousand kilometre journey on foot.[5] As an official Visitor, Winifred vehemently defended Mary Ward against the ecclesiastical authorities, but the enemies of the English Ladies had power, and the Bull of Suppression was promulgated in January 1631. In February Winifred was imprisoned in Liège, and remained there until Mary appealed for her release to Pope Urban VIII in 1632.[6]

Winifred returned to Rome and lived there for the next five years. She was among those who accompanied Mary Ward on their return to England where they arrived in London in 1639, yet because of the Civil War, they did not stay there, but moved north to Heworth in Yorkshire in 1642. When Mary lay dying in 1645, Winifred undertook to go to London to seek letters giving news of the other Sisters. Unfortunately there were no letters, but Winifred returned before Mary died.

After Mary Ward's death the Sisters remained in Yorkshire for five years, but then moved to Paris in 1650. Win was over sixty-five years old, but she became headmistress and novice mistress of a new group of students and novices. The specific reasons for this move to Paris are difficult to find, although Chambers described the circumstances as follows: 'The troubles in England and the establishment of the Commonwealth only added to the distresses of Catholics, and the need of a house of refuge abroad, like that which had formerly belonged to the English Ladies at St Omer, for the reception of the children entrusted to them, became more pressing.'[7]

The Sisters had previously stayed in Paris because of Mary Ward's ill-health on their return journey to England, so they knew the city. There appeared to be less religious persecution then because, in 1650, France was being ruled by Cardinal Mazarin, the young king's Prime Minister. Louis XIV, the 'Sun King', was later to assume a leadership which was to make France the dominant power in Europe with little religious toleration of Protestants. Later in 1661 and 1685 there were cruel persecutions of the Huguenots.

France had a population of eighteen to nineteen million, with Paris having 500,000 people - smaller than the population of London.[8] Corruption in the Catholic Church was also rife and the conflict between Jansenists and Jesuits came to a head in the next century.[9] Paris was then a suitable place for the companions of Mary Ward to gather and regroup as the Second Institute.

Among the works written about Mary Ward after her death is *A Briefe Relation* which Win wrote with Mary Poyntz. Winifred died at the age of seventy-two years in April 1657 and was buried in the convent cemetery of the Bernardine nuns in Paris.

Win was Mary's confidante and friend and knew well the extent of Mary's deepest sorrows and fears for the Institute. A fitting tribute to Winifred Wigmore can be found in the letters which Mary wrote on numerous occasions. Though different in style from today, Mary shows her deep friendship: 'My dear Win, my love to you is not little',[10] and again, 'Double the happiness to yourself, which you wish to me.'[11] Winifred Wigmore can surely be described as a valiant woman who supported Mary Ward's endeavours, and, despite their apparent failure and condemnation, maintained the spirit of the 'galloping girls'.

Mary Poyntz (1593-1667)

Here lies buried Mary Poyntz of Iron Acton

Of the noble race of the English Earls of Derby.

When hardly sixteen years of age

She, out of love of God and her neighbour

Left her parents, her native country and the whole world,

And chose to live to God alone, her Spouse.

Always a virgin, not to say a martyr,

She began to live a life of glorious exile

On account of her forbidden Faith.

This she led until her 73rd year.

This inscription (in Latin) was engraved on the stone erected over the grave of Mary Poyntz. She died on 30 September 1667 and was buried in the Chapel of St John in the Augsburg Cathedral. The burial stone could have been seen until the beginning of the nineteenth century when the chapel was pulled down.[12] Despite the flowery language of the seventeenth century, the tribute to Mary Poyntz is unmistakable.

Mary Poyntz was Winifred Wigmore's cousin because her mother was a Wigmore. The family home, The Court, Iron Acton, became known because Sir Walter Raleigh smoked tobacco there in 1580 - the first English house in which tobacco was smoked.[13]

Mary Poyntz refused the offer of marriage by an English gentleman and joined Mary Ward in St Omer when she was sixteen years old and Mary Ward was twenty-four. However, Mother Immolata Wetter believes that she was ten years younger and was therefore with Mary Ward as a pupil in St Omer at the age of five.[14] Whatever the truth of Mary Poyntz's age, Mary Ward was careful to educate this beautiful girl in the spirit of this new Institute.

In 1621 she accompanied Mary Ward to Rome where her brother, John Poyntz, was in the English College, prior to his going on the English Jesuit mission in 1624.[15] When Mary Ward opened the school in Rome, Mary Poyntz was one of the teachers - a difficult task for an Englishwoman in an Italian city.

In 1627 Mary Poyntz was appointed the first superior of the newly opened house in Munich, and she held this role when Mary Ward was imprisoned there in 1631 after the Bull of Suppression. There were then forty nuns in the community and Mary Poyntz was among those Sisters who wrote the lemon juice letters to Mary Ward in the Anger prison. Such letters required heat in order to be read, so that this clandestine correspondence was in the spirit of the English recusants who learned ways of communication during the persecution.

On Mary Ward's release from prison, Mary Poyntz was among those who accompanied her on the journey to Rome, and in October 1633 Mary Poyntz assisted the move of the group to a new house near St Mary Major's Basilica.[16]

In September 1637 the group began a return journey to England, arriving there two years later, in 1639, as Mary Ward's ill-health was the cause of the long delay. After Mary Ward's death in 1645 the Sisters remained in Heworth, Yorkshire, but when the owners required the house, the Sisters were desperate for the finance to enable them to return to Paris. Providentially at this time Mary Poyntz's cousin, the

Marquess of Worcester, left her a gift of five hundred pistoles. The deed of gift from the Marquess is dated 5 January 1650.[17]

Mary Poyntz governed the Paris house for two years and wrote *A Briefe Relation* (the life and work of Mary Ward) with Winifred Wigmore during this time. Mary was elected the Superior General after Barbara Babthorpe, and during this period she consolidated the work of the existing houses, while the mother house remained in Rome until 1711.

In 1662 Mary Poyntz founded the house in Augsburg which became a crucial step towards the confirmation of the Rules in 1703. The newly-appointed Prince-Bishop Johann Christoph von Freiberg decreed that the English Ladies accept the formal status of religious so they could benefit from the financial support which he was able to offer through endowments he received. As formal religious their vows were received by the superioress of the community, rather than by the bishop who was the ecclesiastical superior. The Prince-Bishop then issued a decree of support and recognition in 1680.[18]

However, Mary Poyntz had died in Munich in 1667 and was not to know the future of the Institute in Augsburg. She was given the memorial tribute inscribed on the burial stone. What a great founding companion Mary Poyntz had been in her life of 'glorious exile'!

Barbara Ward (1592-1623)

The first mention of Mary Ward's sister, Barbara, seems to be in regard to her presence with Mary and another sister (perhaps Elizabeth) during the fire in their family home at Mulwith in 1595. Barbara remained close to Mary in this great danger - a symbolic gesture Barbara lived out in subsequent years in the Institute.

Barbara Ward's name was entered in the baptismal register of the Church of Saints Peter and Wilfrid, Ripon, Yorkshire, on 21 November 1592.[19] It could be assumed that this was the year of her birth, but in an England where Catholics were persecuted, this may not have been the case, as baptism could have been given at a later stage in the child's life.

Barbara went to St Omer to join Mary and her companions probably after 1609. She would have been involved there with the others in the education of women and girls.

Barbara Ward was a bright, young person who dared to challenge the English authorities. In the libellous pamphlet, known as 'Godfather's Information', which attacked Mary Ward, the accusation is made that Mary 'allowed her sister Barbara to be dressed in a way that was downright immoral and sent her with a similarly dressed companion into a hostelry in order - so she said - to win souls'.[20] This reference no doubt refers to the description which Chambers quotes about Barbara Ward being 'dressed in a bright taffeta gown and rich petticoats, trimmed of the newest fashion, and a deep yellow ruff'.[21]

Dressing in the fashion of the times obviously enabled the Sisters to be less liable to recognition by the authorities. Peters also makes a very interesting comment on the work they were doing while disguised. They sought out 'fallen' girls in England and they did not always find them in respectable surroundings.[22]

As well as being stylish with regard to dress, Barbara Ward was also a bright, witty, travelling companion. On the arduous journey to Rome in 1621 Barbara is described as one who 'proved a most valuable and efficient fellow-traveller'.[23]

But it was also in Rome that Barbara Ward became ill, and after much suffering, she died there in 1623. The illness began in June 1622. Chambers described the sickness as an epidemic which affected all the household. This complaint, which was supposed to be a kind of smallpox, from which the rest were soon free, laid a withering hand on Barbara's health.[24] We can imagine the suffering of the English women in the stifling Roman summer.

Barbara Ward died on 25 January 1623 and was buried in the English College in Rome - an example of the encouragement and support of the Jesuits there. Mary Ward had been with her frequently during this last illness and Barbara's death was a big blow to her, as well as a great loss for the fledgling Institute. Mary Ward said of her sister 'that in Barbara were summed up all that could be desired in a sister, in a friend and in a subject'.[25]

Barbara's life of fun, courage and holiness was a support to all. An early chronicler, Sister Margaret Hord, described Barbara Ward as 'one of a profound judgment, singular wit, and great resolutions in any business whatsoever, though never so full of impossibilities, and her invincible courage so great, that her voice, presence, and countenance were sufficient to have animated the most fearful or tepidist heart in the world'.[26]

Barbara Ward's death was the first of those who were founding members of the Institute, a remarkable first member, and her early death was a great sorrow for the others. But the spirit of the Ward family would be upheld by the heroic life of Barbara's elder sister, Mary Ward.

Catherine Smith (1583-1655)

Catherine (alternatively, 'Catharine') Smith appears to have been two years older than Mary Ward, but much of her history is unknown. Chambers says that 'it is a matter of conjecture alone that Catherine Smith may have belonged to the Carrington family, the Smiths of Ashby Folvile, Leicestershire, pious and loyal Catholics, who both suffered for their faith and later on fought for Charles I'.[27]

The Smiths had intermarried with the Nevilles of Holt, Leicestershire. The Nevilles were relatives of Mary Ward's, so it is assumed that Catherine Smith met her at one of the family gatherings.

Catherine went with the first companions to St Omer in 1609. In 1614 she returned to England with Mary Ward and was also in the house in Liège during the suppression of the Institute. Catherine was one of the eleven Sisters in the community when the Bull of Suppression was read out to them on 30 April 1630. The General Vicar granted them a period of forty days - till 9 June - to order their affairs and leave the house.[28]

Catherine then went to Munich, travelling on to Rome with Mary Ward, after Mary's release from prison. She also travelled with the first companions on their return to England in 1639. Catherine was present at Mary Ward's death and eventually went to Paris with the others in 1650.

Catherine died on 29 April 1655 and was probably buried in the convent of the Bernardine nuns in Paris.[29] The old French obituary at Nymphenburg said that Catherine Smith was 'endowed with immoveable courage even in hunger, thirst and necessity'.[30] Further tributes are hardly necessary for this brave lady!

Joanna (Jane) Browne (1581-1630)

Jane Browne's father, Sir George Browne, was named in a recusant list in 1583, in which he was accused of keeping a

priest in the habit of a serving man in his house in Shefford.[31]
The dangerous times for Catholics in England called forth
the greatest heroism and the Brownes were not slow to
respond.

Joanna, or Jane, Browne was a cousin of the Babthorpe
and Rookwood families because her mother belonged to
the Tyrwhitt family and was a sister of Mrs Ambrose
Rookwood and Lady Grace Babthorpe. Jane probably met
Mary Ward at one of their homes.

Jane Browne went to St Omer with the first companions
in 1609. She was the eldest of the group at the age of twenty-
eight years. In 1614 Jane returned to England to see her father, Sir George Browne, who was ill, and who, it seems,
died in 1616.[32]

In 1623 Jane Browne was in Naples where she held the
office of Procuratrix (one who manages the temporal concerns in the house).[33] The Naples house was suppressed in
1625, and because Jane's health was then failing, Mary Ward
had her brought to Munich where it was thought that a
change to the northern air might restore her.[34]

Jane failed to respond to the change of air and it is believed that she died in 1630 after a long and painful illness.
Chambers cannot give any date for her death.[35] Jane Browne
'was buried in the cloister of the Franciscan Fathers, the
English Virgins having hitherto had no vault of their own'.[36]
Because there are scant records about her, little is known
about her life, but the fact that she is now numbered among
the founding members of the IBVM is an admirable testimony to her faithful service for the greater glory of God.

Susanna Rookwood (1583-1624)

Susanna's brother, Ambrose Rookwood, was hanged for
his part in the plot to blow up the King, James I, and the

Houses of Parliament. This was to have taken place on 5 November (now known as 'Guy Fawkes' Day'), 1605. Among the conspirators were Mary Ward's uncles, John and Christopher Wright, and her uncle-in-law, Thomas Percy, all of whom were killed in their encounter with the sheriffs at Holbeach.[37]

Susanna Rookwood's parents were Robert Rookwood and Dorothy Drury, Robert's second wife. Susanna's name may have been Cordell, but was changed to Susanna as a caution after exposure of the Gunpowder Plot.[38] Susanna was the name of her married half-sister, but in one of her letters Mary Ward referred to her as 'Doll Rookwood'.[39]

At the time of Ambrose Rookwood's death in 1605 the Rookwoods were living at Coldham Hall, Suffolk. Mary Ward was known to have been there in 1609,[40] and Susanna crossed to St Omer in that same year when she was twenty-six years of age.

Later when some of the Sisters worked in England, Susanna Rookwood was appointed Superior of the group in 1614.[41] It was reported in the French account of the early members that Susanna Rookwood:

> ... was five times in prison for her religion, where she encouraged and refreshed the other prisoners both by spiritual and temporal means. At last she was thrown into a horrible dungeon, or rather hole, where she had to defend herself with a stick from the mice, rats and other vermin which infested it.[42]

In 1621 Susanna Rookwood was again on the continent as the Assistant Superior in Liège and in the next year she fulfilled this same office for the group in Rome.[43] Peters surmises that Susanna was among the first group travelling to Rome because 'perhaps like Winifred Wigmore, she was linguistically gifted'.[44]

Susanna seems to have excelled in the role as leader of a community because Mary Ward installed her as the Superior of the new community in Naples in 1623. Naples belonged to the Spanish crown, so it was 'abroad'.[45] Among the many difficulties experienced by this community were the blazing summer heat and their extreme poverty.

Mary Ward wrote her last letter to Susanna Rookwood in 1624 telling her of the good health of her brother, Robert Rookwood, in Perugia. There was no allusion then to any want of health on Susanna's part.[46] However, her last illness and death followed soon aftwards, but according to Chambers there is no account of these events.[47]

Winifred Wigmore's letter to Mary Ward telling of her superior's death is not extant.[48] Win had written in detail about Susanna Rookwood's death because Mary Ward wrote to Win on 23 July 1624 as follows: 'what you did concerning your happily deceased Superior pleased me so much, I could wish for nothing otherwise. Your signifying those particulars to me (led to) the better knowledge of the good estate of her happy soul, whom the enemy of all good had no power to hurt, and which I verily believe is now with God.'[49]

Susanna had died in May 1624. The Bavarian archives have a lead panel which was intended for Susanna Rookwood's grave, but which was replaced by a more durable pewter tablet put into the grave with the corpse. These are the concluding words on the panel: 'At last, having lived a most holy life in that city (Naples) and having left behind her a great example of sanctity and prudence, she happily fell asleep in the Lord on May 25, 1624.'[50]

Susanna Rookwood was one of the first English members of the Institute. She died at the age of forty-one years, after having lived as a religious for fifteen years. Susanna

Rookwood's death followed that of Barbara Ward. This was another sadness for the other Sisters, but both the deceased were strong, courageous foundation members, who left a living legacy of happy religious women. With sadness for the loss of these companions, there would also have been a sense of celebration for those lives so loyally and generously lived.

Barbara Babthorpe (1592-1654)

If we are to know children by their parents, then we certainly know how Barbara Babthorpe learned to lead such an heroic life. Her father was Sir Ralph Babthorpe, son of Sir William Babthorpe and Barbara Constable. In 1581 Sir Ralph married Grace Birnaud, who was an heiress, though only fifteen years old at that time.[51] Lady Grace was the grand-daughter of Sir William Ingleby, to whom Mary Ward was related on her mother's side.

The Babthorpes had seven children, and two sons, Ralph and Thomas, became Jesuits. Thomas was Rector of the English College in Rome from 1650 to 1653 - a time when Barbara was also in the eternal city. Another son, Robert, became a Benedictine. The eldest son, William, sold their manor at Osgodby in England and entered the service of the King of Spain, but in 1635 he was killed at Ardres in France. He had numerous children and grandchildren, 'many of whom were greatly gifted'.[52] Barbara's two sisters married - Catherine to George Palmes, and Elizabeth married John Constable.[53]

The Babthorpe family were very old landed gentry and were very rich - holding several estates.[54] Their strong stand as recusants is aptly described as follows:

> Sir Ralph and his wife were harassed mercilessly because of their Catholicism. A great part of their estate was confis-

cated and their own lives pushed to the limit with imprisonment. For a short time Sir Ralph bent under such pressures and attended Anglican services, but through his wife's influence he later returned to the Catholic Church. Lady Grace was imprisoned in 1592 under that formidable president of the North, Lord Huntington, for two years at Sheriff Hutton Castle near York. She spent a total of five years of her life in prison. When the family went into exile in Flanders in 1617, they were ruined financially and lived in very modest circumstances.[55]

Sir Ralph died suddenly in Louvain in 1617 whilst making the Spiritual Exercises of St Ignatius.[56] Some years later, Lady Grace, then only fifty years old, entered St Monica's Benedictine Convent in Louvain. She was clothed and professed at the same time as her grand-daughter, Frances. Her son, Ralph, then a Jesuit, preached at both ceremonies. Frances' mother, wife of William Babthorpe, and Lady Grace's daughter-in-law, were also present at the profession of her mother-in-law and her eldest daughter.[57] Lady Grace Babthorpe died there in 1635 - ten years before the death of Mary Ward.

Mary Ward spent six years (1599-1606) of her early life with the Babthorpe family at Osgodby. It was run as a religious household and priests were frequently sheltered there. Barbara, who was the seventh child, was only eight years old when Mary Ward came to live with them. Mary was then fifteen years old.[58]

Barbara was attracted to the young Mary Ward and both would have heard stories about religious life in England, told to them by Margaret Garret, a family retainer, who may have been a nun. Monasteries and nunneries had been suppressed, so the young women would have had no model of religious life in England at that time.

The old manuscript of the Benedictines in Louvain, while referring to Lady Babthorpe's profession says: 'Her daughter, Barbara, had been at St Benedict's at Brussels, but could not go forward for a defect in her throat', which prevented her perhaps from being able to sing, and so from being a choir nun, because choir nuns sang the Divine Office.[59]

However, according to tradition, Barbara Babthorpe travelled to St Omer with the other companions in 1609.[60] Barbara would have been seventeen at this time. In 1612 she was appointed Superior and Novice Mistress when not more than twenty years of age.[61] Mary Ward was then in St Omer but had became ill with an attack of measles.

In 1621 Barbara Babthorpe was Provincial of the Netherland houses and the next year she went to Rome to help in the establishment of the house there. In 1627 she was sent to Munich where four of her nieces later entered the Institute.[62]

Barbara Babthorpe also spent some time in Pressburg at Cardinal Pazmany's request, where she was again Superior. The papal Bull of Suppression was proclaimed in Pressburg in August 1631, and Barbara returned to Munich at Mary Ward's request.[63]

Six years later Barbara was Superior of the group in Rome and remained there when some of the Sisters returned to England with Mary Ward. During this time Barbara's brother, Father Thomas Babthorpe SJ, was Rector of the English College.

On 20 May 1639 the Englishwomen trod on English soil - it was the first time in twenty years for Mary Ward.[64] One can imagine that Barbara would have wished to be with them in her native country.

In her last illness in 1645 Mary Ward named Barbara Babthorpe to succeed her: 'Mary named to her companions her wish that Barbara Babthorpe should be Vicaress over them when she was no longer with them, until they themselves should choose who was to govern them in her place.'[65]

In 1653, after eight years in office, Barbara asked that another Sister should succeed her as Superior General, so that she could live the rest of her life under obedience. The Sisters acceded to her request and Mary Poyntz was elected to succeed her as the next Superior General.

The Sisters had not even left Rome when they were summoned to Barbara Babthorpe's deathbed. She died quietly on 23 April 1654, and was buried in the English College (then staffed by Jesuits). Barbara Ward had been buried there in 1623 and both Sisters are now venerated in the English College.

A Latin inscription, written on parchment and put into a well-sealed metal box, was put into Barbara Babthorpe's coffin. It read:

Jesus, Mary, St Barbara

Barbara Babthorpe, daughter of Sir Ralph Babthorpe, of Babthorpe Hall, County York, after having ruled her Institute and all its members with much-praised wisdom, piety and goodness towards all, died aged 62 years and 8 months on April 23rd, 1654, going to receive the reward of her perpetual virginity which the world could not give. Her mortal remains were laid to rest in the Lady Chapel of the English College to await immortal happiness.[66]

The office of the Superior General was also filled by two great-nieces of Barbara. Mary Anna Babthorpe governed from 1698 until 1711. This was during the time when the Summary of Eighty-one Rules was confirmed in 1703 by Pope Clement XI. Agnes Babthorpe succeeded her and governed from 1711 till her death in 1720.

The example of the heroic lives of Sir Ralph and Lady Babthorpe bore ample fruit in the dedicated work of their children, especially evident in the life of their daughter, Barbara Babthorpe - another galloping girl.

Appendix 1

Some Significant People in Mary Ward's Lifetime (1585-1645)

Saints

Teresa of Avila (Spanish)	1515-1582
Philip Neri (Italian)	1515-1595
Peter Canisius SJ (Dutch)	1521-1597
Edmund Campion SJ (English)	1540-1581
John of the Cross (Spanish)	1542-1591
Robert Bellarmine SJ (Italian)	1542-1621
Camillus de Lellis (Italian)	1550-1614
Jeanne de Lestonnac (French)	1556-1640
Mary Magdalen de Pazzi (Italian)	1566-1607
Francis de Sales (French)	1567-1622
Aloysius Gonzaga SJ (Italian)	1569-1591
Jane Frances de Chantal (French)	1572-1641
Vincent de Paul (French)	1576-1660
John Ogilvie (Scottish)	1579-1615
Martin de Porres (Peruvian)	1579-1639
Rose of Lima (Peruvian)	1586-1617
Louise de Marillac (French)	1591-1660
John Berchmans SJ (Flemish)	1599-1621

Popes (duration of reign)

Sixtus V	1585-1590
Urban VII (12 days)	1590
Gregory XIV (10 months)	1590
Innocent XIV	1590-1592
Clement VIII	1592-1605

Leo XI	1605
Paul V	1605-1621
Gregory XV	1621-1623
Urban VIII	1623-1644
Innocent X	1644-1655

Sovereigns (duration of reign)

England		*Scotland*	
Elizabeth I	1558-1603	James VI	1567-1608
James I	1603-1625		
Charles I	1625-1649		

Spain		*France*	
Philip II	1556-1598	Henry III	1574-1589
Philip III	1598-1621	Henry IV	1589-1610
Philip IV	1621-1665	Louis XIII	1610-1643
		Louis XIV	1643-1715

Artists

Domenico El Greco	1541-1614
Guido Reni	1565-1642
Michelangelo da Caravaggio	1571-1610
Peter Paul Rubens	1575-1640
Frans Hals	1581-1666
Nicolas Poussin	1594-1665
Gian Lorenzo Bernini	1598-1680
Anthony Van Dyck	1599-1641
Rembrandt van Rijn	1606-1669

Musicians

Giovanni Palestrina	1525-1594
Giovanni Gabrieli	1557-1612

| Claudio Monteverdi | 1567-1643 |
| Domenico Mazzochi | 1592-1665 |

English Musicians

Thomas Tallis	1505-1585
William Byrd	1542-1623
Thomas Morley	1557-1603
John Bull	1562-1628
Orlando Gibbons	1583-1625

Writers

Miguel de Cervantes	1547-1616
Edmund Spenser	1552-1599
Sir Philip Sidney	1554-1586
Christopher Marlowe	1564-1593
William Shakespeare	1564-1616
Ben Jonson	1574-1637
University Wits	1580-1600
Robert Herrick	1591-1674
Pedro Calderon	1600-1681
John Milton	1608-1674
Richard Crashaw	1616-1649
John Milton	1608-1674
John Dryden	1631-1700

Scientists

Gerhard Mercator	1512-1592
Francis Bacon	1561-1626
Galileo Galilei	1564-1642
Johannes Kepler	1571-1630
William Harvey	1578-1657
Blaise Pascal	1623-1662

Appendix 2

Significant Events from the Late Fifteenth to the Late Seventeenth Centuries

1492   First voyage of Christopher Columbus.

1500-1558   Charles V created the Holy Roman Empire and was proclaimed Holy Roman Emperor.

1506   Pope Julius II laid the foundation stone of St Peter's in Rome.

1508   Michelangelo painted the ceiling of the Sistine Chapel in Rome.

1517   Martin Luther's Ninety-five Theses promulgated in Wittenberg.

1519   Sikhism (a combination of Hunduism and Islam) founded.

1520   Martin Luther excommunicated.

1521   Pope gave Henry VIII the title, 'Defender of the Faith'.

1540   St Ignatius succeeded - Jesuits formally established by papal bull;

              Council of Trent commenced.

1543   Copernicus published his theory of a sun-centred universe.

1551-1594   Palestrina (composer to papal chapel) in Rome.

1556   Thomas Cramner burnt to death during reign of Mary Tudor.

1557	First Index of Prohibited Books.
1558-1603	Reign of Elizabeth I of England.
1560	Reformed Church established in Scotland by John Knox.
1568	Mercator published a map of the world.
1570	The potato was introduced into Europe from South America.
1571	The Battle of Lepanto.
1572	St Teresa of Avila - mystical experiences.
1579	Jesuits at the Mogul court in India.
1582	Gregorian reform of the calendar.
1585	Decimals introduced into mathematical calculations.
1588	Defeat of the Spanish Armada by the English Navy.
1598	Edict of Nantes gave political tolerance to French Protestants.
1601	Matteo Ricci SJ travelled to Peking.
1607	First English settlement on the American mainland.
1608	Telescope invented by Hans Lippershey.
1610	The violin made its orchestral appearance.
1611	King James Bible (Authorized Version) published.
1614	Prohibition of Christian worship in Japan.
1616	Deaths of Shakespeare and Cervantes.
1618	Beginning of the Thirty Years' War.
1620	The *Mayflower* sailed from England and Holland to America;

Francis Bacon published *Novum Organum* - scientific theory.

1622	Creation of the Congregation for the Propagation of the Faith.
1626	First Church in Tibet.
1632-1643	Taj Mahal built in India as a mausoleum for Shah's wife.
1633	Galileo condemned by the Inquisition.
1642	Beginning of the English Civil War.
1647	Englishman, George Fox, began the Quakers (Society of Friends).
1648	Peace of Westphalia ended the Thirty Years' War.
1649	King Charles I beheaded in England.
1658	Death of Oliver Cromwell.
1660	Restoration of Charles II and the Anglican Church.
1665	Great Plague in Europe.
1688	'Glorious Revolution'- Catholic King James II fled England.
1692	Imperial Decree in China allowed Christian worship.

Appendix 3

The Verity Speech
St Omer, November 1617

This Verity Speech of Mary Ward illustrates her thinking with regard to the status and spiritual capacity of women. On an occasion when the layman Thomas Sackville was commending the Sisters, a Father Minister who was present said: 'It is true whilst they are in their first fervour, but fervour will decay, and when all is said and done, they are but women.' The 'Verity Speech' was delivered by Mary Ward to her associates in response to this. Mary Ward addressed her sisters in the following words:

> I would know what you all think he meant by this speech of his, 'but women', and what 'fervour' is. Fervour is a will to do good, that is, a preventing grace of God, and gift given gratis by God, which we could not merit. It is true that fervour doth many times grow cold, but what is the cause? Is it because we are women? No, but because we are imperfect women. There is no such difference between men and women. Therefore it is not because we are women, but as I have said before, because we are imperfect women, love not verity, but seek after lies. 'Veritas Domini mane in aeternum' - the verity of the Lord remaineth forever. It is not 'veritas hominis', verity of men, nor verity of women, but 'veritas domini', and this verity women may have as well as men. If we fail it is for want of this verity, and not because we are women... Divers religious, both men and women, have lost their fervour, because they have been unmindful of this preventing truth, which is a gift of God, and a sign of predestination, as you have often heard, I am sure I have, of those that are wiser than I.

Fervour is not placed in feelings, but in a will to do well, which women may have as well as men. There is no such difference between men and women that women may not do great things, as we have seen by example of many saints who have done great things. And I hope in God it will be seen that women in time to come will do much... would to God that all men understood this verity, that women if they will be perfect, and if they would not make us believe we can do nothing, and that we are but women, we might do great matters. What can it profit you, to tell you you are but women, weak and able to do nothing, and that fervour will decay? I say what doth it profit you, but bring you to dejection and without hope of perfection. All are not of this opinion. This is all I have to say at this time, that you love verity and truth.

Appendix 4

Bull of Suppression of the Institute
(January 1631)

The pastoral solicitude of the Roman Pontiff, to whom the care of the vineyard of the Lord of Sabbaoth is known to be entrusted by the ineffable providence of the Father on high, has as its particular aim that workers do not rashly and precipitately betake themselves to the field of the Lord, scatter what has been sown, root up what has been planted, introduce cockle and spread false growths over it.

1. Although it has been strictly forbidden by the orthodox decrees of the General Councils of the Lateran and of Lyons for anyone to presume to assume authority to found a new religious order, and likewise, groups of women in fact established by the salutary orders of John XXII and 2. Clement V, Roman Pontiffs and men of happy and holy memory, nevertheless as we have learned with grave trouble of mind, in some parts of Italy and beyond the Alps, certain women or virgins, having taken the title of Jesuitesses, live together for some years without any particular approval of the Apostolic See on the pretext of leading a customary religious life, have worn distinctive dress, have raised buildings as colleges, have created houses of Probation and in these have appointed a Superior and of their pretended Congregation one with the title of Mother General, endowed with seemingly good faculties and in whose hands they pronounce vows of poverty, chastity and obedience with the appearance of solemn vows; free from the laws of enclosure, they wander about at will and, under the guise of promoting the salvation of souls, have been accustomed to attempt and to

employ themselves at many other works which are most unsuited to their weak sex and character, to female modesty and particularly to maidenly reserve - works which men of eminence in the science of sacred letters, of experience of affairs and of innocence of life undertake with much difficulty and only with great caution.

3. Anxious to root out speedily the brambles growing up in the field of the Church militant and in view of the grave dangers already described and the scandals arising from them, we gave orders to our Venerable Brother Aloysius, bishop of Tricary and Nuncio of the Apostolic See in Lower Germany, to try to recall the aforementioned women or virgins, who had already been seriously warned by our Apostolic selves, from a rash undertaking to saner counsels. Because these, in truth, neglecting the fear of God and respect for Us and the Apostolic See, have not only arrogantly and obstinately disobeyed our paternal and salutary warnings to the grave disadvantage of their own souls and the disgust of all good people, but they are not ashamed, even daily, to attempt similar things and to utter many 4. things contrary to sound teaching, we have decreed that such great temerity must be repressed by sharper censure and that the poisonous growths in the Church of God must be torn up from the roots lest they spread themselves further. And, therefore, after mature consideration with our Venerable Brothers, Cardinals of the Holy Roman Church, specially deputed by the same See as general Inquisitors against heretical depravity; with their unanimous advice and consent and following the decrees of the aforementioned Councils and in the footsteps of our same Predecessors, we decree and declare with apostolic authority and by the contents of this present document, that the pretended Congregation of women or virgins called Jesuitesses and their Sect and state was and is from its very beginning null and void and of no authority and importance. And because indeed they have made progress, with the same authority we totally and com-

pletely suppress and extinguish them, subject them to perpetual abolition and remove them entirely from the Holy
Church of God; we destroy and annul them, and we wish
and command all the Christian faithful to regard and repute them as suppressed, extinct, rooted out, destroyed and
abolished; and we do not wish such women and virgins to
be bound and obliged in any way to the observance of the
aforementioned vows. Furthermore, we likewise decree and
declare that those called Visitators, Rectresses and Mother
General and any other such Officials of this Congregation
or sect, whatever their titles be, are and will be deprived of
their offices and duties, which are in fact usurped, and we
deprive and remove them utterly from the same offices and
duties in so far as is necessary; and we absolve and totally
free all and each of these women and virgins who might
think themselves obliged to the obedience of a vow or any
other bond, promise or on the pretext of any other reason
whatsoever, from this and from any bond and promise, even
if it is valid and sworn.

5. In virtue of holy obedience and under penalty of major
excommunication to be incurred ipso facto and from which
they can be absolved, except at the point of death, only by
Ourselves or the Roman Pontiff for the time being existing,
we order and command the women or virgins and their so-
called Superiors, as previously designated or by any other
name, to dwell separately and apart outside the colleges or
houses where they have hitherto lived; not to come together
at the same time to consult about or to treat of any spiritual
or temporal matter or to deal with it in any way; to lay aside
at once the habit which they have put on and which they
display, and not to wear it further; a fortiori, not to admit to
it or receive other women or virgins, nor give advice, help
or favour, directly or indirectly or in any other way, to any
of them in regard to these matters; not to act as religious or
members of a pretended Congregation or sect of this kind.
We also declare that the women and virgins, although they

in fact pronounce vows, (and this is public knowledge), but in such a state of mind that they would not have done so in a situation which has been condemned by the Apostolic See - inasmuch as the tacit condition of their vows was not fulfilled - are completely free and released from the obligation of such vows. Those, however, who wished unconditionally to take vows, since their vows are simple, will be able to live honourably in the world, but apart from the rest of this condemned state and pretended Congregation or Sect, and abstaining from everything forbidden above, under obedience to the Ordinary, with the use but not the ownership of property and with the permission, which we compassionately grant them, to dispose of it in life and in death for pious purposes only and to dispose also of what comes to them from someone who had died intestate in favour of those who would have succeeded them if they had not taken a vow of poverty. And if it should happen that any of the aforementioned women or virgins wish to transfer to the married state, we permit them to contract Matrimony provided the other conditions are fulfilled, and we impart to them the Apostolic blessing together with, in so far as is necessary, the relaxation of all vows, as they are called, which they have in fact pronounced. Since, indeed, according to the Apostle, those who marry do well but those who do not marry do better, we advise the same women and virgins by the bowels of the Mercy of Christ and with all the love of paternal charity, we carefully exhort them in the Lord, that, being mindful of the desire by which they showed they were led to lead a regular life, they should take on themselves the yoke of the Lord, and denying themselves and worldly yearnings, enter as soon as possible some order of nuns which has been approved by the same Holy See; and in it let them vow their vows to the God of Jacob with faithful and holy promises, and let them give edification with innocent hands and pure hearts in the assiduous performance of spiritual works, showing themselves to the more Illustrious portion of the Flock of Christ and, about to meet the heavenly Spouse, let them prudently make ready their lamps, inflamed with the fire of divine love.

6. We decree that this present document, with all and everything contained in it, is never to be charged with the blemish of dishonesty, fraud or nullity of invalidity - even on the grounds that such women and virgins of this pretended Congregation or Sect, or any others with an interest, in the foregoing or in any one of them, shall in no wise agree with it; or that they were or were not summoned and listened to; or still less that the reasons adduced and accepted for its issue will be sufficiently proven to be otherwise - or not proven at all - or on the grounds of the defect of Our intention; or of any other defect however great, unthought of or substantial; or because in the foregoing or in any of the formalities thereof, something was not observed or fulfilled which should have been observed and fulfilled; or of any other count in right or law or statute or custom arising from these - or even on the grounds of enormous great and total breach of law or of any other title, even in one contained in the Code of Law; or on any other occasion or for any cause, however just, reasonable and privileged, even such as should have been expressed for the validity of the foregoing; or because nothing else of this nature - in regard to our wishes and to other matters treated or related above - appears anywhere else or can be otherwise proven,

(We decree) - that this present document is never to be censured, impugned, invalidated, withdrawn, brought again into question or back to court again,

- that in opposition to it no remedy such as full restoration to a former state, freedom of speech, return to process and terms of law nor any other remedy of law, fact, privilege or justice, may be adopted or in any other way granted, or further their interests, in or out of court,

- and that this present document is not subject to withdrawals of favour of like or unlike nature, suspensions, limitations or other contrary dispositions made in any way according to circumstances, but is always exempt from such, valid in perpetuity, firm and efficacious now and in the future, has and enjoys its full effects, and to be inviolably observed by all and everyone to whom it refers or will refer in any way in the future;

- and that all judges, ordinary or delegate, even the Auditors of lawsuits in the Apostolic Palace, Cardinals of the Holy Roman Church and even legates a latere and Nuncios and others, no matter what offices of authority and power they discharge, in whatever suit or importunity, must in this matter and everywhere so give judgement and determine; and that all power and authority to judge and interpret otherwise is withdrawn from each and all of them; and that the action of anyone who tries on whatever authority, knowingly or unknowingly, to act contrariwise is null and void.

7. Wherefore, by this apostolic document we command our Venerable Brothers and dearly beloved sons, both the Nuncios of the Apostolic See and the Patriarchs, Primates, Archbishops, Bishops and other local Ordinaries, wherever they be, as soon as this present letter of Ours comes in any way to their knowledge or to that of any one of them, solemnly to publish it and have it made known, faithfully to fulfil everything contained in it and to take care that it is executed through themselves or through another or others as they shall judge expedient in the Lord; restraining any who contradict, rebel and disobey the foregoing by sentences, censures and ecclesiastical penalties and other suitable remedies in law and fact without possibility of appeal, recourse or remonstrance, even, if need be, with the help of the secular arm. Notwithstanding, as far as may be necessary, what was said by Pope Boniface VIII, Our Predecessor of revered

memory, about one issue and what was said in the General Council about two, and the actions of any other persons whomsoever to the contrary.

8. That this present document and everything contained in it may be brought to the knowledge of all and lest anyone may be able to pretend ignorance of it, we likewise will and order that the same document be fastened to and made public at the door of the Lateran Church, the Basilica of the Prince of the Apostles, the apostolic Chancery and also in a prominent position in the Florine Campus; the notices to be removed after two months, computed from the day of publication; and let the document thus published and displayed influence and curtail all and everyone concerned as though it had been intimated and made known to each of them personally.

9. And the same credence is to be given to printed transcripts of this document, provided they are protected by the seal of any person of ecclesiastical dignity and signed by the hand of a public Notary, as would be given to the document itself, were it exhibited or displayed.

10. Let no one whomsoever be permitted to render void this document of Our suppression, extinction, subjection, removal, destruction, annulment, release, exhortation, of our wishes and orders, or rashly attempt to contradict it. If, however, anyone presumes to make this venture, he should know that he will incur the displeasure of Almighty God and of the Blessed Apostles, Peter and Paul.

Given at St. Peter's, Rome, on the ides (13th) of January in the Year of the Incarnation of the Lord 1631, and the eighth of Our Pontificate.

*   *   *

In the name of God. Amen.

On the 21st. May of the year of Our Lord 1631, on the fourteenth declaration, and in the eighth year of the Pontificate of Our Most Holy Father and Lord in Christ, Urban VIII, by Divine providence Pope, the above mentioned Apostolic letter was published and affixed and, as is customary, copies were sent to the Basilicas of the Churches of St. John Lateran, the Prince of the Apostles, Rome, and to the Apostolic Chancery and the Florian Campus, by me Augustinus de Bolis, Roman Courier of our Most Holy Lord the Pope.

Mathias Spada
Master of Couriers

Appendix 5

Declaration of Mary Ward from the Anger Prison, Munich, to the Roman Congregation, Holy Office, 27 March 1631[1]

If, with no other aim or interest in mind than to direct and devote my efforts entirely to the better service of the Holy Church and the Apostolic See, I have in any way, through my unworthy labour, met with Your Holiness's displeasure, I most humbly ask for your forgiveness, lying prostrated at Your Holy feet, and beg you in the name of God's mercy, to pardon with fatherly love for all things in which, unaware, I might have offended you.

I have been publicly accused and declared a heretic, schismatic, obstinate and rebellious by the Holy Church. I have been arrested as such and incarcerated and driven to the point of death by the ailments that the nine weeks of imprisonment to which I have already been subjected have caused me. I have endured the denial of the Holy Sacraments between the 7th February (the day of my arrest) and the 28th February, the day on which I was given my viaticum, followed two days later by the holy oils of extreme unction.

The infamy of being marked out in every place as guilty of such wickedness, and of being thrown into the jaws of death by order of the Holy Church for having supposedly committed such atrocities, has resulted in great suffering being inflicted upon all the members of our company. Our ladies have been mocked by the heretics for having abandoned their fatherland and families; they have been despised by their closest relations; their annual income has been unjustly seized so that in four of our colleges it has been necessary to ask for alms.

In addition to this, I have already chosen to sacrifice my property and own poor life in particular to make amends. Furthermore, I shall offer this reparation when and where it may be demanded of me. But praying for God's mercy and the benignity of Your Holiness and trusting that these matters will take a turn for the better, I humbly offer an explanation of the conditions imposed on my coming to Rome by the Cardinal of the Sacred Congregation of the Holy Office, in the copy of the letter sent to me herewith by Doctor Giacomo Golla (who came to arrest me).

They are as follows: They want me to come to Rome. I am to arrive in Rome at my own expense, accompanied by a Commissary chosen by the above mentioned Doctor. I am to arrive in Rome at the time fixed by him, otherwise I risk being left penniless. I am also obliged to put down a payment as a deposit for the above amount, a sum which is to be assessed by Monsignor Caraffa, the Apostolic Nuncio in Cologne. If it is necessary that I meet all the requirements imposed on me, it will be difficult, if not impossible, for me to get there, particularly in view of the manner and condition in which these matters have so far been conducted.

I have never, to my knowledge, said or done anything against His Holiness (whose wishes I have offered to obey in the past and offer to obey totally in the present) nor have I ever undermined the authority of the Holy Church; on the contrary, for 26 years, with great respect for both His Holiness and the Holy Church and in the most honourable way possible, I have put my frail efforts and my industry to their service and this, I hope by the mercy of God and His benignity will be accounted for at the right time and place. Nor would I, for any thing in the world, or for any gains at the present time or in the future act in any way which might be unbecoming in carrying out my duty as a true and obedient servant of the Holy Church.

If, despite being authorised to serve the Church by the greatest Pontiffs and Sacred Congregation of Cardinals, I have in their eyes, wished or attempted to serve the Holy Church with anything other than my full ability, let it be known by those responsible for a decision in such matters, that I, in all sincerity, have not in any way been reluctant to serve as a true Christian, nor have I been opposed to serving with the obedience due to His Holiness or to the Holy Church.

I am, and always will be, ready to admit my guilt, ask forgiveness for the offences given and sacrifice my poor, short life in atonement for such sin, together with the public dishonour already suffered and likewise imposed on me.

Appendix 6

Notes on the Sources about the Life of Mary Ward

The available sources about Mary Ward's life require some exposition. Although Mary lived merely three hundred and fifty years ago, in the early modern period, the political, social and religious instability of England and Europe during her lifetime is a significant reason that many relevant and invaluable documents relating to her have not survived. Documents also perished because of the lack of methods of preservation. The fact that many Church documents have not yet been catalogued, or released, and so are inaccessible to researchers, is a significant factor also in the difficulty of obtaining original sources.

Nevertheless, it is now possible to gain access in English to a considerable number of valuable primary documents relating to Mary Ward. Of special significance are Mary's autobiographical notes covering the period of her life up to 1595. These were written between 1617 and 1619 at the request and direction of Father Roger Lee SJ, her spiritual director for eight years. During the period 1624 to 1626 Mary Ward dictated a fuller autobiography in Italian (later translated) which dealt with the years from 1599 to 1609. Also available are her spiritual reflections and retreat notes from some of the years from 1612 to 1636. There are extant plans of the Institute presented to the Popes Paul V, Gregory XV and Urban VIII and other communications of Mary to Church officials.

There are copies, too, of letters to her companions, as well as to her spiritual directors, the Jesuit Fathers Roger

Lee - who was a friend and adviser in the early days in St
Omer - and John Gerard - who supported and guided her
especially when he was Superior in Liège. Among her letters are those written by Mary to the Sisters when she was
in prison in the Anger Convent in Munich. These are the
'lemon juice' letters - so called because they were written in
lemon juice on scraps of paper. They required heat in order
to be rendered legible. It was a technique Mary had learnt
from the persecuted Catholics in England. The bulk of this
material has been collated by Mother Immolata Wetter
IBMV of the Roman Generalate and duplicated in her
Letters of Instruction.

Emmanuel Orchard IBVM has edited an excellent book
called *Till God Will.* It contains a selection of Mary Ward's
writings which are arranged chronologically. Sr Orchard
has prefixed the extracts, giving their context, and has also
included comprehensive notes.

The earliest biographical work of substance concerning
Mary Ward was written by two of her companions, Mary
Poyntz and Winifred Wigmore. This work, called *A Briefe
Relation,* was written in Paris between 1645 (Mary Ward's
death) and 1657 (when Winifred Wigmore died). The oldest copy is at the Loreto Convent, Manchester. The handwriting of the manuscript is that of Winifred Wigmore,
while the composition and facts are said to be due to Mary
Poyntz. These two women were Mary Ward's closest friends
and wrote this account in order to record her story - especially for those of the Institute who had not known Mary
Ward personally. Much of this biography is incorporated
in a late nineteenth century work which is usually referred
to as Chambers' work.[1]

Other unpublished handwritten biographical sketches
of Mary Ward include one written in Italian in 1622 by Vincent Pageti, Secretary of Cardinal Borghese and Apostolic

Notary, and presented to Elisabeth, Electress of Bavaria. A second sketch was produced in Latin about 1628 by Dominic Bissel, Canon Regular of the Holy Cross in Augsburg. A third sketch, written in German in 1689 by Tobias Lohner SJ, includes Mary Ward's addresses to her companions, the originals of which have not survived. The eighteenth century saw two published works, those of Corbinian Khamm OSB in 1717, and in 1733, that of Marco Fridl, parish priest of Suabia.[2]

In addition, a series of fifty large oil paintings depicting aspects of Mary Ward's life and spirituality is to be found in Augsburg at the convent of the Institute founded by Mary Poyntz, one of Mary Ward's first companions. This series is referred to as *The Painted Life*. As copies of some paintings of this resource are used as illustrations in this book it is appropriate to outline its history.

The Painted Life was put together by Mary Ward's early companions. They were members of an as yet unrecognised Institute, but women who were aware of the importance of documenting in this way the history of their foundress. The paintings appear to have been executed by five different painters through the initiative of two close friends of Mary Ward, namely, Mary Poyntz and Barbara Babthorpe.[3]

According to experts, their origin was before 1670. The paintings have had a chequered history. A notable time was during the Second World War when *The Painted Life* was hidden in a castle belonging to the notable Fugger family. When the school at Augsburg was reopened in 1946 the paintings were hung again. After being renewed they now hang in the Mary Ward School Hall in Augsburg.[4]

The artistic quality of the paintings is not outstanding. Many of them have several scenes - indicative of seventeenth century painting. The inscriptions are in early German Gothic script and were added later. Evidence for this is in the positioning of the inscriptions which do not appear to have been included in the original paintings because the artists did not leave room for them. The likely author of the inscriptions is Father Tobias Lohner SJ, mentioned for his 1689 sketch. Therefore, since Lohner died in 1697, the inscriptions were most likely added in the last decades of the seventeenth century.[5]

In the introduction to Volume One of Chambers' Life of Mary Ward, Father Coleridge says of *The Painted Life*:

> ... the tenuous position of the Institute at that time made it necessary to withhold any likenesses of those from whom Mary had received either favours or sufferings. Therefore the series of the Painted Life was selective in its historical context of persons who had played a large part in Mary Ward's life.[6]

The final point to make about *The Painted Life* is that it was a way of depicting Mary Ward's interior strength and her spiritual life, which are integral to this study.

Since 1882 three authoritative biographies of Mary Ward have been published. The first of these, in two volumes, was published between 1882 and 1885, and is entitled *The Life of Mary Ward*. It was written by Mary Catharine Elizabeth Chambers IBVM, who had been one of the first members of the Anglican Sisterhood of Mercy founded by Miss Priscilla Sellon. Chambers left this sisterhood in 1876 and became a Catholic. Her good friends, Father JH Newman and Father Coleridge SJ, encouraged her in the choice of a Catholic religious order. She entered the IBVM in 1879 at the age of fifty-six. After profession her life was devoted to writing the life of Mary Ward in order to rehabilitate the foundress. Mary Catharine Elizabeth Chambers died in 1886, soon after completing the two-volume work.[7] *The Life of Mary Ward* was edited by Henry James Coleridge SJ and published by Burns and Oates, London.

In the introduction to Volume Two of Chambers' *Life of Mary Ward*, Father Coleridge laments the difficulty of access to many documents of importance to the work. However, he claims that it was better to complete the work without the long delay which accessing them would have necessitated:

> ... if it had been possible to wait for the full elucidation of many points of the history which must now be left in some obscurity... The work before the reader is the life of Mary Ward rather than the history of her Institute, and in this respect it may perhaps claim sufficient completeness.[8]

Despite Coleridge's misgivings, this life of Mary Ward is very valuable as it made careful use of relevant documents from archives and libraries in England and Europe and from the records held by the Institute of the Blessed Virgin Mary in England, Germany and Rome. These two volumes also provide excerpts from Mary Ward's letters. This large work (over one thousand pages) has proved to be a very useful resource for this writing.

Father Joseph Grisar SJ, a German Jesuit historian, while professor of Church history at the Gregorian University in Rome, located 1169 sources concerning Mary Ward. They ranged from a few lines to more than fifty pages. These sources are held in libraries and archives in Belgium, Germany, England, France, Italy, Austria, Switzerland, Czechoslovakia and Hungary and were written in English, Italian, Latin, French, German and Spanish. The fruits of Grisar's examination of these works, covering the period up to 1631, are contained in his work entitled, *Mary Ward's Institute Before Roman Congregations (1616-1630)*. This was translated into English and made available by the IBVM General Congregation in 1992.

An invaluable general reference for an in-depth study of Mary Ward is the scholarly, comprehensive work of Dr Henriette Peters' IBVM, *Mary Ward: A world in contemplation*. This study was first published in German in 1991. The English edition was translated by Sister Helen Butterworth of the English province of the Institute and published in 1994. It includes newly discovered documents held in libraries and archives in Liège. Peters' interpretation of Mary Ward is balanced and based on a scholarly awareness of the historical and cultural context of the documents that form the basis of her work. As she explained in her foreword:

> There are three reasons why the documents are difficult to understand and interpret: the baroque style, sometimes inclined to overstatement; the reticence of the members of the Institute - in their then politically dangerous situation - to mention names of people or places, added to which was their use of aliases; finally, the fact that the letters and papers are in six different languages. [9]

Although details of Mary Ward's life are stated clearly and useful interpretations are suggested in this book, the wider history of the period specifically highlighting women's history, was beyond the scope of Dr Peters' work. She died in 1997, (and the translator, Sr Helen Butterworth, has also died), but her work remains as a great tribute to her scholarship and tenacity in pursuing resources. We can resonate with Dr Peters' tribute to Mary Ward in the foreword: 'It was only in the terrible struggle for this Institute, reviled by her opponents as either ridiculous or totally unsuitable, that the shy young girl from Yorkshire developed into a great woman who bears comparison with the saints.'[10]

Notes

Mary Ward in Historical Context

1 Anthony Gilles, *The People of Anguish*, St Anthony Messenger Press, Cincinatti, 1987, ch 5, with acknowledgment of the work of Will Durant, *The Story of Civilization*, Simon and Schuster, New York, 1961, Vol 6, p 278, and Hubert Jedin (ed), *History of the Church*, Seabury Press, New York, 1980, Vol 5, p 18.

2 Owen Chadwick, *The Reformation*, Penguin Books, Middlesex, 1964, p 73.

3 Gilles, p 66.

4 John Scarisbrick, *The Reformation and the English People*, Basil Blackwell, Oxford, 1984, p vii.

5 Ironically, Henry VIII (1509-1547) had the title, 'Defender of the Faith'conferred on him by Pope Leo X for his theological response against Luther's revolt. In this work Henry wrote: 'The whole Church is subject not only to Christ, but to Christ's only Vicar, the Pope of Rome.' (Gilles, p 84.)

6 Gilles, p 86.

7 Durant, *The Story of Civilization*, Part VI, p 558.

8 Chadwick, p 106.

9 David Knowles, *Bare Ruined Choirs*, Cambridge University Press, Cambridge, 1959, p 189.

10 Chadwick, p 105.

11 Knowles, p 286.

12 Knowles, p 206.

13 R Warnicke, *Women of the English Renaissance and Reformation*, Greenwood Press, Connecticut, p 97. Elizabeth I was fluent in French and produced her version of the work of the Calvinist, Margaret of Navarre, that appeared in 1548.

14 William Trimble, *The Catholic Laity in Elizabethan England*, Belknap Press, Cambridge (Mass), 1964, p 9.

15 Gilles, p 89.

16 Marvin O'Connell, *The Counter-Reformation 1559-1610*, Harper and Row, New York, 1974, p 3.

17 Edward Norman, *Roman Catholicism in England*, Oxford University Press, Oxford, 1985, p 1.

18 Norman, p 1.

19 Henriette Peters, *Mary Ward: A world in contemplation*, H Butterfield (trans), Gracewing, England, 1994, p 67, and p 68 n 33.

20 Mary CE Chambers, *The Life of Mary Ward*, Vol 1, HJ Coleridge (ed), Burns and Oates, London, 1882, p 89.

21 Norman, p 20.

22 Trimble, pp 107-8.

23 Chadwick, pp 289-90.

24 Norman, p 9.

25 Scarisbrick, p 168.

26 John Bossy, *The English Catholic Community 1570-1850*, Darton, Longman and Todd, London, 1975, p 51.

27 Bossy, p 36.

28 Peter Holmes, *Resistance and Compromise*, Cambridge University Press, Cambridge (Mass), 1982, p 117.

29 Peters, p 35.

30 Trimble, p 108.

31 Holmes, p 117.

32 Holmes, pp 121-4. This section deals at length with the different types of equivocation which were much discussed at that time.

33 Jeanne Cover, *The Significance of Mary Ward's Spirituality and Practice for Moral Theology Today*, unpublished PhD thesis, University of St Michael's College, Toronto, 1993, p 160.

34 Scarisbrick, pp 177, 156.

35 Bossy, p 158.

36 Bossy, p 158.

37 Bossy, p 158.

38 Scarisbrick, pp 151-2.

39 Scarisbrick, p 151.

40   Bossy, p 171.

41   Bossy, p 157.

42   Mary Claridge, *Margaret Clitherow*, Anthony Clarke Books, Hertfordshire, 1966, p 56.

43   Claridge, p 85.

44   Claridge, p 151.

45   Claridge, p 157.

46   Warnicke, p 173.

47   Bossy, p 160.

48   Gilles, p 105. Wars, disputes over location, and the non-attendance of bishops were some of these problems.

49   Hubert Jedin, *Ecumenical Councils of the Catholic Church*, Nelson, Edinburgh, 1960, p 155.

50   JD Holmes and BW Bickers, *A Short History of the Catholic Church*, Burns and Oates, Kent, 1983, p 169.

51   Holmes & Bickers, p 170.

52   Hubert Jedin, *Crisis and Closure of the Council of Trent*, Sheed and Ward, London, 1967, p 135.

53   George Ganss (trans), *The Constitutions of the Society of Jesus*, The Institute of Jesuit Sources, St Louis, 1970, ch 1.

54   Ganss, Constitution 527, p 238.

55   John O'Malley, *The First Jesuits*, Harvard University Press, Cambridge (Mass), 1993, p 299.

Women in the Reformation Period

1   Merry E Wiesner, *Women and Gender in Early Modern Europe*, Cambridge University Press, Cambridge, 1993, p 21.

2   Merry E Wiesner, 'Beyond Women and the Family: Towards a gender analysis of the Reformation' in *Sixteenth Century Journal*, vol 18, no 3, 1987, pp 311-23, p 314.

3   Wiesner, 'Beyond Women and the Family', pp 313-4.

4   Roland H Bainton, *Women of the Reformation in Germany and Italy*, Beacon Press, Boston, 1974, p 56.

5   John Bossy, *The English Catholic Community 1570-1850*, Darton, Longman and Todd, London, 1975, p 159.

6 Roland H Bainton, *Women of the Reformation in France and England*, Beacon Press, Boston, 1975, p 9.

7 Wiesner, *Women and Gender in Early Modern Europe*, p 189.

8 Bainton, *Women of the Reformation in Germany and Italy*, p 42.

9 Bainton, *Women of the Reformation in Germany and Italy*, p 43.

10 Jane Douglass, 'Women and the Continental Reformation' in RR Ruether (ed), *Religion and Sexism*, Simon and Schuster, New York, p 299.

11 Bainton, *Women of the Reformation in France and England*, p 42.

12 Bainton, *Women of the Reformation in Germany and Italy*, p 56.

13 Bainton, *Women of the Reformation in Germany and Italy*, p 72.

14 Douglass, p 307.

15 Douglass, quoted on p 297.

16 Anthony Gilles, *The People of Anguish*, St Anthony Messenger Press, Cincinnati, 1987, p 92.

17 Douglass, p 301.

18 Roland H Bainton, *Women of the Reformation from Spain to Scandinavia*, Augsburg Publishing House, Minneapolis, 1977, p 11.

19 Elise Boulding, *The Underside of History*, Vol 2, Sage Publications, California, p 125.

20 R Tucker and W Liefeld, *Daughters of the Church*, Academic Books, Michigan, 1987, pp 185-90.

21 Debra Parish, 'The Power of Female Pietism: Women as spiritual authorities and religious role models in seventeenth century England' in *The Journal of Religious History*, vol 17, no 1, June 1992, pp 33-46, p 39.

22 Mary B Rose (ed), *Women in the Middle Ages and the Renaissance*, Syracuse University Press, USA, 1986, p 20.

23 Wiesner, *Women and Gender in Early Modern Europe*, p 132.

24 Lavinia Byrne, *Mary Ward: A pilgrim finds her way*, Carmelite Centre of Spirituality, Dublin, 1984, pp 41-2. The Verity Speech is quoted in appendix 3, above.

25 Parish, p 35.

26 *Bull of Suppression.* See appendix 4, above.

27 Wiesner, *Women and Gender in Early Modern Europe*, p 192.
28 BP Levack, *The Witch Hunt in Early Modern Europe*, Longman, London, 1987, introduction.
29 Wiesner, *Women and Gender in Early Modern Europe*, p 133.
30 Wiesner, *Women and Gender in Early Modern Europe*, p 122.
31 Wiesner, *Women and Gender in Early Modern Europe*, p 135. The Dutch woman, Anna Maria Schurman, was granted the rare privilege of attending lectures at the University of Utrecht, but she had to stand behind a curtain.
32 Wiesner, *Women and Gender in Early Modern Europe*, p 122.
33 Wiesner, *Women and Gender in Early Modern Europe*, pp 121, 123.
34 Eileen Power, *Medieval Women*, M Postan (ed), Cambridge University Press, London, 1975, p 80.
35 Power, p 81.
36 Power, p 83.
37 Bossy, p 161.
38 Mary CE Chambers, *The Life of Mary Ward*, Vol 1, HJ Coleridge (ed), Burns and Oates, London, 1882, p 41.
39 Power, p 83.
40 Power, p 84.
41 Antonia Fraser, *The Weaker Vessel: Woman's lot in seventeenth century England*, Weidenfeld and Nicolson, London, 1984, p 137.
42 Fraser, p 129, comments that a good school or benevolent patronage or both might account for sudden high figures of local literacy.
43 Fraser, p 129.
44 Power, p 86.
45 R Warnicke, *Women of the English Renaissance and Reformation*, Greenwood Press, Connecticut, 1983, p 208.
46 Fraser, p 149.
47 Fraser, p 149.
48 Wiesner, *Women and Gender in Early Modern Europe*, p 110.
49 B Anderson and J Zinsser, *A History of Their Own: Women in Europe from prehistory to the present*, Vol 1, Penguin, London, pp 131-2.

50 Fraser, pp 148, 149.

51 Fraser, p 203.

52 Fraser, p 424.

53 Fraser, pp 410-1.

54 Lyndal Roper, *The Holy Household: Women and morals in Reformation Augsburg*, Clarendon Press, Oxford, 1989, p 48.

55 Fraser, p 84.

56 Bainton, *Women of the Reformation from Spain to Scandinavia*, p 9.

57 Fraser, p 84.

58 Fraser, p 84.

59 Jeanne Cover, *Love: The driving force*, Marquette University Press, Milwaukee, 1997, p 26.

60 Fraser, p 101.

61 Boulding, p 116.

62 Boulding, p 117.

63 Fraser, p 5.

64 Wiesner, *Women and Gender in Early Modern Europe*, p 61.

65 Henriette Peters, *Mary Ward: A world in contemplation*, H Butterfield (trans), Gracewing, England, 1994, p 46.

66 Ruth Perry, *The Celebrated Mary Astell*, University of Chicago Press, Chicago, 1993, pp 98-9.

67 Douglass, p 303.

68 Douglass, p 300.

69 Wiesner, *Women and Gender in Early Modern Europe*, p 23.

70 Wiesner, *Women and Gender in Early Modern Europe*, pp 48-9.

71 S Osment, *When Fathers Ruled: Family life in Reformation Europe*, Harvard University Press, Cambridge (Mass), 1983, pp 70-2.

72 Wiesner, *Women and Gender in Early Modern Europe*, p 22.

73 *The Catechism of the Council of Trent*, Q XXVI, pp 302-3.

74 *The Catechism of the Council of Trent*, Q XXVII, p 303.

75 John Scarisbrick, *The Reformation and the English People*, Basil Blackwell, Oxford, 1984, p 168. Some women controlled fairly large sums of money and some (such as Joan Belcher) hired the priest to say Mass on patronal feast days and anniversaries and to bury the dead. (p 166)

76 Paul Johnson, *Elizabeth I*, Weidenfeld and Nicolson, London, 1974, pp 17, 20.

77 Warnicke, p 6.

78 Natalie Davis, *Society and Culture in Early Modern France*, Stanford University Press, Stanford, 1975, quoted by Wiesner, 'Beyond Women and the Family', p 313.

79 Fraser, p 147.

80 Fraser, p 10.

81 MR Beard, *Women as Force in History*, MacMillan and Co, Melbourne, 1987, p 86.

82 Fraser, p 147.

83 Wiesner, 'Beyond Women and the Family', p 314.

84 Warnicke, p 184 n 46.

85 Wiesner, 'Beyond Women and the Family', p 316.

86 Fraser, p 206.

87 Bossy, quoted on p 154.

88 Bossy, pp 154-5.

89 Bainton, *Women of the Reformation in France and England*, p 44.

90 Bainton, *Women of the Reformation in France and England*, p 68.

91 Bainton, *Women of the Reformation in France and England*, p 15.

92 Bainton, *Women of the Reformation in France and England*, p 15.

93 Bainton, *Women of the Reformation in France and England*, p 38.

94 This letter, however, never reached the pope as it mysteriously disappeared. Presumably this association of the Infanta Isabella with Mary Ward was opposed in some quarters. (Peters, p 299)

95 Peters, p 404.

96 Mary CE Chambers, *The Life of Mary Ward*, Vol 2, HJ Coleridge (ed), Burns and Oates, London, 1885, pp 164-5.

97 Leah Marcus, 'Shakespeare's Comic Heroines, Elizabeth I, and the Political Uses of Androgyny' in *Women in the Middle Ages and the Renaissance*, Mary B Rose (ed), Syracuse University Press, USA, 1986, p148.

98 Marcus, p 137.

99 Marcus, p 141.

100 Marcus, p 138.

101 Marcus, p 149.

102 Teresa Ledochowska, *Angela Merici and the Company of St Ursula according to the Historical Documents*, Vol 1, Ancora, Rome, French edition revised 1968, p 36.

103 Bainton, *Women of the Reformation in Germany and Italy*, p 165.

104 Parish, p 45. In this article Parish also comments: 'Anglican clergymen used their funeral sermons for pious women to push for the re-establishment of the Church of England and religious uniformity.' (p 45)

Mary Ward: Beginnings

1 Henriette Peters, *Mary Ward: A world in contemplation*, H Butterfield (trans), Gracewing, England, 1994, p 7; and Emmanuel Orchard (ed), *Till God Will: Mary Ward through her writings*, Darton, Longman and Todd, London, 1985, p 7.

2 Peters, p 28.

3 Peters, pp 28-9, nn 4 and 6.

4 Immolata Wetter, *Mary Ward's Devotion to Our Blessed Lady*, private circulation, Rome, 1974, p 2.

5 Jeanne Cover, *Love: The driving force*, Marquette University Press, Milwaukee, 1997, p 26.

6 Peters, p 22.

7 Peters, pp 19-20.

8 Mary CE Chambers, *The Life of Mary Ward*, Vol 1, HJ Coleridge (ed), Burns and Oates, London, 1882, p 5 n 10.

9 Peters, p 20.

10 Orchard, p 5.

11 Peters, p 37.

12 Peters, p 24.

13 Orchard, p 60.

14 Peters, p 35.

15 Orchard, p 6.

16 Mary relates the playing of the game 'sieve and scissors' apparently initiated by Alice. In this game one had to try to

hold both the sieve and the scissors high up in equal balance,while uttering a special formula and the name of the person suspected or desired. If the sieve moved during this operation, the person named was held as the guilty one, or the person sought. (Peters, p 51 n 41.)

17 Orchard, p 6.

18 Chambers, p 22.

19 Peters, p 41.

20 Unpublished tour notes of Mary Ward Country, p 70.

21 Peters, p 44.

22 Peters, p 45.

23 Peters, p 46.

24 Orchard, p 9.

25 Orchard, p 9.

26 Peters, p 42.

27 Peters, p 53-4 n 99.

28 Peters, p 66.

29 Peters, p 66.

30 Orchard, p 14. Peters, p 70, notes that the seven northern provinces of the Netherlands (the majority of modern-day Holland) had become Calvinist and had adopted a republican form of government. The southern Netherlands (most of today's Belgium) remained Catholic and Spanish.

31 Peters, pp 70-1.

32 Peters, p 73.

33 Peters, p 73.

34 One example was the bishop's letter supporting Mary Ward in 1615. (Peters, p 147.)

35 Peters, p 73 n 12, p 78.

36 Mary Wright, *Mary Ward's Institute*, Crossing Press, Sydney, 1997, p 4.

37 Peters, p 79.

38 Wright, p 5 n 17.

39 Peters, p 86.

40 Orchard, p 24.

41 Orchard, p 26.

42   Peters, p 98. Claudio Aquaviva was elected Jesuit General at thirty-nineyears of age. He was the longest serving General to that stage — for thirty-three years from 1542 to 1615. (George Ganss (trans), *The Constitutions of the Society of Jesus*, The Institute of Jesuit Sources, St Louis, 1970, p 71.)

43   Peters, p 102. From England these Poor Clares established foundations in Ireland (as Colettines). They came to Australia in 1883 and are now at Waverley and Campbelltown in New South Wales.

44   Orchard, p 27.

45   Peters, pp 108-9.

46   Peters, p 110.

47   Orchard, p 28.

48   Orchard, p 29.

49   Peters, p 73.

50   Peters, p 73.

51   Chambers, p 268.

52   Peters, p 111.

53   Orchard, p 28.

54   Peters, p 110.

55   Orchard, p 28.

56   Chambers, pp 236-40.

57   Chambers, p 242.

58   Chambers, p 240.

59   Orchard, p 62.

60   Mary CE Chambers, *The Life of Mary Ward*, Vol 2, HJ Coleridge (ed), Burns and Oates, London, 1885, p 520.

61   Chambers, Vol 2, p 520.

62   Chambers, Vol 1, p 244.

63   Chambers, Vol 1, p 246 - quotation from the French obituary.

Significant Initiatives of Catholic Women in Europe

1   Marygrace Peters, 'Beguine Women: Medieval spirituality,

modern implications' in *Review for Religious*, vol 54 no 2, March-April 1995, p 228.

2   Peters, pp 228-9.

3   Peters, p 234.

4   Mary CE Chambers, *The Life of Mary Ward*, Vol 2, HJ Coleridge (ed), Burns and Oates, London, 1885, p 294.

5   M Dortel-Claudot, *The Evolution of the Canonical Status of Religious Institutes with Simple Vows from the Sixteenth Century until the New Code*, trans M Rosa MacGinley, Institute of Religious Studies, Strathfield (New South Wales), 1989, p 11.

6   J Grisar, *Mary Ward's Institute before Roman Congregations (1616-1630)*, Section 1, pp 113-4 n 155. They were Benedictine oblates, analogous to the tertiaries of the Franciscans and Dominicans, hence they had essentially simple vows.

7   Grisar, p 104.

8   Chambers, p 77. Barbara did not recover, despite also leaving the hot Roman weather, and she died on 25 January 1623. She was buried at the English College in Rome.

9   M Rosa MacGinley, *A Dynamic of Hope*, Crossing Press, Sydney, 1996, pp 23-4.

10   MacGinley, *A Dynamic of Hope*, p 23.

11   *Rule*, Chapter XII. Early Italian Text and modern translation, Ursulines of the Roman Union, 1985.

12   Teresa Ledochowska, *St Angela Merici* (abridged edn), Catholic Press, Ranchi, 1990, p 25.

13   Philip Caraman, *St Angela*, Green and Co Ltd, London, 1963, p 132.

14   Caraman, p 132.

15   Peter M Waters, *The Ursuline Achievement*, Colonna, Melbourne, 1994, p 40 n 91.

16   Caraman, p 184.

17   Mary Wright, *Mary Ward's Institute*, Crossing Press, Sydney, 1997, p 3.

18   Francoise Soury-Lavergne, *A Pathway in Education: Jeanne de Lestonnac 1556-1640*, translated from the French, Rome, 1984, p 125.

19 Soury-Lavergne, pp 26-47.

20 Soury-Lavergne, p 236.

21 Soury-Lavergne, p 151.

22 Soury-Lavergne, p 201.

23 Soury-Lavergne, p 204.

24 Soury-Lavergne, p 211.

25 Soury-Lavergne, p 225.

26 Jeanne de Lestonnac was canonised by Pope Pius XII in 1949. (*New Catholic Encyclopedia*, Vol 8, McGraw Hill, New York, 1967, p 678.)

27 Merry E Wiesner, *Women and Gender in Early Modern Europe*, Cambridge University Press, Cambridge, 1993, p 197.

28 Henriette Peters, *Mary Ward: A world in contemplation*, H Butterfield (trans), Gracewing, England, 1994, pp 106-7.

29 Wiesner, p 198.

30 Peters, *Mary Ward*, p 159.

31 After Soury-Lavergne, p 119, especially n 28.

32 Waters, p 40 n 90.

33 Waters, p 40.

34 Grisar, p 216 n 103.

35 Soury-Lavergne, p 121.

36 Soury-Lavergne, p 114.

37 Soury-Lavergne, p 114.

38 Soury-Lavergne, p 116.

39 Soury-Lavergne, p 116.

40 Alix Le Clerc died at Nancy aged 45 in 1622. She was beatified by Pius XII in 1947. Refer to *Whisps of Straw*, Catholic Truth Society pamphlet, London, undated.

41 Grisar, p 115 n 166.

42 Joseph J Dirvin, *Louise de Marillac*, Doubleday, Toronto, 1970, p 386.

43 Dirvin, p 153.

44 Dirvin, p 210.

Mary Ward: Early attempts to establish the Institute

1   Emmanuel Orchard (ed), *Till God Will: Mary Ward through her writings*, Darton, Longman and Todd, London, 1985, p 29.

2   Agnes Walsh (ed), *A Soul Wholly God's*, Don Bosco Graphic Arts, Calcutta, undated, p 45.

3   George Ganss (trans), *The Constitutions of the Society of Jesus*, The Institute of Jesuit Resources, St Louis, 1970, pp 35-6.

4   Ganss, p 36.

5   Mary Wright, *Mary Ward's Institute*, Crossing Press, Sydney, 1997, p 14, with reference to the source in n 58.

6   Wright, p 15, with relevant n 63.

7   Wright, p 165.

8   Henriette Peters, *Mary Ward: A world in contemplation*, H Butterfield (trans), Gracewing, England, 1994, p 117.

9   Peters, p 120.

10 Orchard, p 33.

11 Peters, p 124 n 14.

12 Peters, p 122.

13 Peters, pp 121-2.

14 Peters, p 123.

15 Peters, p 154.

16 Peters, p 134.

17 Peters, p 137.

18 John O'Malley, *The First Jesuits*, Harvard University Press, Cambridge (Mass), 1993, p 75.

19 Ganss, p 263 n 5.

20 Hugo Rahner, *St Ignatius Loyola: Letters to women*, K Pond and S Weetman (trans), Nelson, Edinburgh, 1960, p 287.

21 Rahner, p 287.

22 Ganss, pp 262-3.

23 Ganss, p 263 n 5.

24 O'Malley, pp 75-6.

25 Rahner, p 57.

26 Rahner, p 56. Francis Borgia was beatified on 24 November 1624 by Pope Urban VIII and canonised on 12 April 1671 by Clement X. (*New Catholic Encyclopedia*, Vol 2, p 710.)

27 O'Malley, p 10. A comprehensive coverage of the status of women in the Society of Jesus is given in *Studies in the Spirituality of Jesuits*, November 1999, vol 31 no 5.

28 This was included in Ingoli's accusations. Peters, p 468 n 2.

29 Peters, p 145 n 3.

30 Peters, p 145.

31 Peters, p 145.

32 Peters, pp 145-7.

33 It is not known who commissioned this further report. (Peters, p 154.)

34 Peters, p 154.

35 Peters, p 156.

36 Peters, p 160.

37 Peters, p 161.

38 Peters, p 374 n 18.

39 Mary CE Chambers, *The Life of Mary Ward*, Vol 2, HJ Coleridge (ed), Burns and Oates, London, 1885, p 25.

40 Chambers, p 28.

41 Chambers, p 29.

42 Antonia Fraser, *The Weaker Vessel: Woman's lot in seventeenth century England*, Weidenfeld and Nicolson, London, 1984, p 146.

43 Fraser, p 148.

44 Chambers, p 37.

45 Chambers, p 38.

46 Chambers, p 39.

47 Margaret M Littlehales, *Mary Ward: A woman for all seasons*, Catholic Truth Society, England, 1974, p 14.

48 Paul Johnson, *Elizabeth I*, Weidenfeld and Nicolson, London, 1997, p 40.

49 Johnson, pp 40-1.

50 Orchard, p 39.

51 Peters, p 108.

52 Peters, p 114.

53 Peters, p 174.

54 Peters, p 174.

55 Wright, p 122, n 178, quoting the minutes of the Rome Meeting.

56 Unpublished paper entitled *The Name of the Institute* by Dr Mary Wright IBVM, January, 1992.

Period of Expansion of the Institute (1615-1621)

1 Emmanuel Orchard (ed), *Till God Will: Mary Ward through her writings*, Darton, Longman and Todd, London, 1985, pp 72, 92.

2 Two copies of the 'Petition' now make it difficult to know what were its true contents. Henriette Peters, *Mary Ward: A world in contemplation*, H Butterfield (trans), Gracewing, England, 1994, p 179.

3 Orchard, p 34-5.

4 J Grisar, *Mary Ward's Institute before Roman Congregations (1616-1630)*, Pontifical Gregorian University, Rome, 1966, Section 1, p 33.

5 Peters, p 183.

6 Grisar, p 48.

7 Peters, pp 183-7.

8 Peters, p 184.

9 Peters, p 186.

10 Peters, p 187.

11 Peters, p 190.

12 Peters, p 192.

13 Peters, p 212.

14 Peters, p 217.

15 Peters, p 218.

16 Peters, p 219.

17 Peters, p 219. Philip Caraman tells his story graphically in the autobiography of John Gerard called *The Hunted Priest* (Fontana Books, Great Britain, 1959).

18 Peters, p 220.

19 According to Peters' speculation this may have been in connection with his mother's death, as she died in 1615. (Peters, p 232.)

20 Peters, p179.

21 Mary CE Chambers, *The Life of Mary Ward*, Vol 1, HJ Coleridge (ed), Burns and Oates, London, 1882, p 365 n 2.

22 Grisar, Section I, p 40 n 4.

23 Peters, p 225 n 40.

24 Peters, p 232.

25 Peters, p 230.

26 Several years previously Mary's confessor, Father Roger Lee SJ, had instructed her to write her biography. (Orchard, p 3.)

27 Chambers, p 406.

28 Chambers, p 407.

29 Chambers, p 437.

30 Chambers, p 442.

31 Chambers, p 443.

32 Orchard, p 61 n 24.

33 Mary Poyntz, and Winifred Wigmore, *A Briefe Relation*, Institute circulation (unpublished), 1645, p 22.

34 Peters, p 259.

35 Chambers, p 459.

36 Tom O'Hara, *At Home with the Spirit*, Aurora Books, Melbourne, 1992, pp 91-2.

37 Orchard, p 60.

38 Peters, p 286.

39 Peters, p 287.

40 Chambers, p 476.

41 Chambers, p 476.

Roman Venture

1   Henriette Peters, *Mary Ward: A world in contemplation*, H Butterfield (trans), Gracewing, England, 1994, p 297.

2   Mary CE Chambers, *The Life of Mary Ward*, Vol 1, HJ Coleridge (ed), Burns and Oates, London, 1882, p 485 n 2.

3   Peters, p 312-3.

4   Emmanuel Orchard (ed), *Till God Will: Mary Ward through her writings*, Darton, Longman and Todd, London, 1985, p 61 n 1.

5   Peters, p 317 n 63.

6   Peters, pp 318-9.

7   Peters, p 323.

8   Adapted from Peters, p 324.

9   Elizabeth Rapley, *The Devotes: Women and Church in seventeenth-century France*, McGill-Queen's University Press, Montreal, 1990, p 27.

10   Rapley, p 27 n 15.

11   Rapley, pp 27-8.

12   Peters, p 325.

13   Mary Wright, *Mary Ward's Institute*, Crossing Press, Sydney, 1997, pp 23-4.

14   J Grisar, *Mary Ward's Institute before Roman Congregations (1616 -1630)*, Pontifical Gregorian University, Rome, 1966, Section 1, p 68.

15   Peters, p 320.

16   Grisar, p 70 n 32.

17   Grisar, p 86.

18   Grisar, pp 88-9.

19   JND Kelly, *The Oxford Dictionary of Popes*, Oxford University Press, Oxford,   1986, p 280.

20   Peters (p 332 n 56) states that the manuscript is held in the Institute Archives in Munich.

21   Peters, p 332.

22   Peters, p 334.

23 Peters, p 334.
24 Peters, p 335.
25 Grisar, p 143 n 36.
26 Grisar, p 144 n 40.
27 Mary CE Chambers, *The Life of Mary Ward*, Vol 2, HJ Coleridge (ed), Burns and Oates, London, 1885, p 87.
28 Grisar, p 145 n 46.
29 Peters, pp 352-3 n 95.
30 Summarised from Peters, p 340.
31 Peters, p 389.
32 Grisar, p 188 n 33. Grisar notes also that Mr Rant left Rome to go to England or France in 1625 and that he died in 1626.
33 Peters, pp 341, 343.
34 Peters, p 343.
35 Peters, p 344.
36 Peters, p 346.
37 Merry E Wiesner, *Women and Gender in Early Modern Europe*, Cambridge University Press, Cambridge, 1993, p 198.
38 Wiesner, p 189.
39 Peters, p 247.
40 Peters, p 326.
41 Peters, pp 485, 522.
42 Her remains are still venerated in the English College in Rome.
43 Chambers, pp 77-80.
44 Peters, p 378.
45 Paul Johnson, *The Papacy*, Weidenfeld and Nicolson, London, 1997, p12.
46 Peters, p 378 n 1, quoting Ludwig v Pastor, *Geschichte der Päpste* Bd XIII/I, Freiburg/Br, 1928.
47 JND Kelly, p 280.

Further Expansion of the Institute

1 Henriette Peters, *Mary Ward: A world in contemplation*, H Butterfield (trans), Gracewing, England, 1994, p 399 n 24.

2   Peters, pp 381-2.

3   Peters, p 284.

4   Peters, p 386.

5   Mary Wright, *Mary Ward's Institute*, Crossing Press, Sydney, 1997, p11.

6   Peters, p 388.

7   Peters, p 393.

8   Peters, p 393.

9   Peters, p 394.

10   J Grisar, *Mary Ward's Institute before Roman Congregations (1616-1630)*, Pontifical Gregorian University, Rome, 1966, Section 1, p165.

11   Peters, p 403.

12   Grisar, p 170.

13   Peters, p 416.

14   Mary CE Chambers, *The Life of Mary Ward*, Vol 1, HJ Coleridge (ed), Burns and Oates, London, 1882, p 172.

15   Peters, p 407.

16   Grisar, p 171.

17   Peters, p 408.

18   Peters, p 432.

19   Mary CE Chambers, *The Life of Mary Ward*, Vol 2, HJ Coleridge (ed), Burns and Oates, London, 1885, p 207. Charles Borromeo was the great reforming bishop of the Counter-Reformation, who was later canonised.

20   Peters, p 433.

21   Chambers, Vol 2, p 198.

22   Wright, p 44.

23   Peters, p 436.

24   Peters, p 436.

25   Cf chapter 5.

26   Grisar, Section 2, p 6 n 19.

27   Peters, p 440 and p 463 n 67.

28   Peters, p 446.

29 Grisar, Section 2, p 237 n 50.

30 Grisar, Section 2, p 10.

31 Chambers, Vol 2, p 441.

32 Chambers, Vol 2 p 441.

33 Peters, p 444.

34 Peters, p 447 n 91.

35 Chambers, Vol 2, pp 255-8.

36 Peters, p 451.

37 Peters, p 452.

38 Grisar, Section 2, p 40.

39 Peters, p 460.

40 Grisar, Section 2, p 57.

41 Chambers, Vol 2, p 274.

Further Roman Developments

1 Henriette Peters, *Mary Ward: A world in contemplation*, H Butterfield (trans), Gracewing, England, 1994, p 467 n 6 has it placed from Rome in 1628.

2 Peters, p 467.

3 J Grisar, *Mary Ward's Institute before Roman Congregations (1616-1630)*, Pontifical Gregorian University, Rome, 1966, Section 2, pp 94-5.

4 Peters, p 471.

5 Peters, p 481.

6 Peters, p 492.

7 Peters, p 494.

8 Peters, p 494.

9 Peters, p 496.

10 Peters, p 496.

11 Peters, p 495.

12 Grisar, p 207.

13 Grisar, p 208.

14 Peters, p 496.

15 Grisar, p 284 n 126.

16 Peters, p 509.

17 Peters, p 525. (This is a translation of the letter.)

18 Peters, p 531.

19 Peters, p 530.

20 Grisar, p 329.

21 Peters, p 548.

22 In the Bull of Suppression the term 'zizania', or weeds, was used. See appendix 4.

23 Peters, p 548.

24 Peters, p 554.

25 Peters, p 555.

26 Peters, p 560.

27 Grisar, p 300.

28 Peters, p 514.

29 Peters, p 517.

30 Peters, p 73.

31 Grisar, p 197.

32 In 1628 the Daughters of St Agnes had financial difficulties and finally broke up as a result of the Franco-Spanish war. (Francoise Soury-Lavergne, *A Pathway in Education: Jeanne de Lestonnac 1556-1640*, translated from the French, Sisters of the Company of Mary (Province of England and Ireland), Rome 1984, p 118.)

33 Peters, p 522.

34 The full text of the bull appears in appendix 4.

35 Peters, p 565.

36 Paul Johnson, *The Papacy*, Weidenfeld and Nicolson, London, 1997, p 13.

37 Appendix 4 contains the Bull of Suppression.

38 Peters, p 566.

39 Peters, p 567.

40 Peters, p 567.

41 Peters, p 579. The full text of Mary's declaration appears in appendix 5.

42 Peters, p 580.

43 Peters, p 555.

44 Emmanuel Orchard (ed), *Till God Will: Mary Ward through her writings*, Darton, Longman and Todd, London, 1985, p 62.

45 Orchard, pp 94-5.

Last Years of Mary Ward and the Aftermath (1631-1645)

1 Henriette Peters, *Mary Ward: A world in contemplation*, H Butterfield (trans), Gracewing, England, 1994, p 578.

2 Peters, p 585.

3 Peters, p 586.

4 Anthony Gilles, *The People of Anguish*, St Anthony Messenger Press, Cincinatti, 1987, p 113.

5 Peters, p 586.

6 Peters, p 587 n 5, with reference to the English Vita, known as *A Briefe Relation*. See appendix 6, p 253.

7 Emmanuel Orchard (ed), *Till God Will*, p 114, with acknowledgment to Mary CE Chambers, *The Life of Mary Ward*, Vol 2, HJ Coleridge (ed), Burns and Oates, 1885, pp 410-1.

8 Peters, p 587.

9 Chambers, p 410.

10 Chambers, p 411.

11 Peters, p 591.

12 Orchard, p 115.

13 Orchard, pp 120-1.

14 Chambers, p 519.

15 Peters, p 600.

16 Peters, p 606.

17 Peters, p 603.

18 Gilles, p 122.

19 Peters, p 606.

20 Orchard, p118.

21 Unpublished tour notes on Mary Ward Country, p 3.

22 Peters, p 613 n 61.

23 Peters, pp 610-1, quoting Mary's words.

24 Chambers, p 502.

25 Peters, p 611.

26 Peters, p 611.

27 Chambers, p 514.

28 Chambers, p 513-8.

29 Wright, 'The Bar Convent York' in the *History of Women Religious*, Institute of Religious Studies, Strathfield (New South Wales), 1992, p 56.

30 Chambers, p 541.

31 Chambers, p 510.

32 M Rosa MacGinley, *A Dynamic of Hope: Institutes of women religious in Australia*, Crossing Press, Sydney, 1996, p 46.

33 Mary Wright, *Mary Ward's Institute*, Crossing Press, Sydney, 1997, p 72.

34 MacGinley, p 46.

35 MacGinley, p 46.

36 MacGinley, p 46.

37 Peters, p x.

38 Letter from canon lawyer, Dr Mary Wright, dated 7 October 1994.

39 *Constitutions of the Institute of the Blessed Virgin Mary*, p 7.

Mary Ward's Spirituality

1 Emmanuel Orchard (ed), *Till God Will: Mary Ward through her writings*, Darton, Longman and Todd, London, 1985, p 5.

2 Immolata Wetter, *Mary Ward*, B Ganne (trans), Regenberg, Verlag Schnell and Steiner, Germany, 1995, p 5.

3 R Warnicke, *Women of the English Renaissance and Reformation*, Greenwood Press, Connecticut, 1983, p 175.

4 Jeanne Cover, *The Significance of Mary Ward's Spirituality and Practice for Moral Theology Today*, unpublished PhD thesis, University of St Michael's College, Toronto, 1993, pp 73-5.

5 Orchard, p 10 n 28.

6   Anthony Gilles, *The People of Anguish*, St Anthony Messenger Press, Cincinnati, 1987, p 164.

7   Gilles, pp 164-5.

8   Mary Wright, *Mary Ward's Institute*, Crossing Press, Sydney, 1997, p16.

9   Orchard, p 27.

10 Agnes Walsh (ed), *A Soul Wholly God's*, Don Bosco Graphic Arts, Calcutta, undated, p 43.

11 Cover, p 215.

12 Walsh, p 44.

13 Cover, p 269.

14 Cover, p 269.

15 Walsh, pp 19 and 35.

16 Immolata Wetter, *Mary Ward's Prayer*, Rome, 1974 (private circulation), p 89.

17 Orchard, p10.

18 Orchard, p xviii.

19 Full text in appendix 3.

20 The full text of this address is in appendix 3.

21 The full text of the *Bull of Suppression* is in appendix 4.

22 Wetter, *Mary Ward*, p 24.

23 Mary CE Chambers, *The Life of Mary Ward*, Vol 2, HJ Coleridge (ed), Burns and Oates, London, 1885, p 496.

24 Mary B Rose (ed), *Women in the Middle Ages and the Renaissance*, Syracuse University Press, USA, 1986, p 137.

25 Eamon Duffy, *The Stripping of the Altars*, Yale University Press, London, p 256.

26 Orchard, p 7.

27 Mary Poyntz and Winifred Wigmore, *A Briefe Relation*, 1645 (Institute circulation), p 89.

28 Walsh, cover page.

Some Cultural Aspects of the Reformation Period

1   Hubert Jedin, *Ecumenical Councils of the Catholic Church*, Nelson, Edinburgh/ London, 1960, p 155.

2   Henriette Peters, *Mary Ward: A world in contemplation*, H Butterfield (trans), Gracewing, England, 1994, p 434.

3   *The New Catholic Encyclopedia*, Vol 9, McGraw-Hill Book Co, New York, 1967, pp 319-32.

4   Howard Loxton, *The Encyclopedia of Saints*, Brockhampton Press, London, 1996, p 30.

5   John Cuming (ed), *Letters from Saints to Sinners*, Crossroad, New York, 1996, p 270.

6   Philip Caraman, *A Study in Friendship*, The Institute of Jesuit Sources, St Louis (MO), 1995, p 53.

7   Cuming, p 275.

8   Caraman, pp 54, ix.

9   Caraman, p 91.

10   *The Tablet*, 21 November 1987, p 1273.

11   Anthony Gilles, *The People of Anguish*, St Anthony Messenger Press, Cincinnati, 1987, pp 115, 125.

12   Kenneth Clark, *Civilisation*, Penguin, England, 1969, p 128.

13   Clark, p 134.

14   Clark, p 131.

15   Clark, p 128.

16   Clark, p 132.

17   Australian Broadcasting Commission (ABC), *A History of British Art – North   and South*, telecast on 22 June 1997.

18   HG Koenigsberger, and GL Mosse, *Europe in the Sixteenth Century*, Longman, London, 1973, p 337.

19   Koenigsberger and Mosse, p 346.

20   Clark, p 128.

21   Koenigsberger and Mosse, p 343.

22   Henry Raynor, *A Social History of Music*, Tapliner Publishing Company, New York, 1978, p 154.

23   W and A Durant, *The Story of Civilization, VII: The Age of Reason*, Simon and Schuster, New YOrk, 1961, pp 59-60.

24   Will and A Durant, pp 65-7.

25   Koenigsberger and Mosse, p 316.

26   Koenigsberger and Mosse, p 317.

27   Koenigsberger and Mosse, p 366.

Educational Aspects of the Reformation Period

1   John O'Malley, *The First Jesuits*, Harvard University Press, Cambridge (Mass), 1993, p 232.

2   O'Malley, p 204.

3   O'Malley, p 204.

4   O'Malley, p 324.

5   O'Malley, p 324.

6   George Ganss (trans), *The Constitutions of the Society of Jesus*, The Institute of Jesuit Sources, St Louis, 1970, p x.

7   G Ganss (ed), *Ignatius of Loyola: The Spiritual Exercises and selected works*, Paulist Press, New York, 1991, p 49.

8   Ganss, *The Constitutions of the Society of Jesus*, p 216 n 4.

9   Ganss, *The Constitutions of the Society of Jesus*, p 216 n 4.

10   O'Malley, p 229.

11   O'Malley, p 230.

12   O'Malley, p 223.

13   O'Malley, p 225.

14   O'Malley, pp 226-7.

15   Elizabeth Rapley, *The Devotes: Women and Church in seventeenth-century France*, McGill-Queen's University Press, Montreal, 1990, p 151.

16   Rapley, p 151.

17   Rapley, p 159.

18   Emmanuel Orchard (ed), *Till God Will: Mary Ward through her writings*, Darton, Longman and Todd, London, 1985, pp 34-5.

19   Orchard, p 56.

20   Orchard, p 58.

21   Henriette Peters, *Mary Ward: A world in contemplation*, H Butterfield (trans), Gracewing, England, p 436.

22   J Grisar, *Mary Ward's Institute before Roman Congregations (1616-1630)*, Pontifical Gregorian University, Rome, 1966 (private Institute circulation), Section 2, p 10.

23   Peters, p 381-2.

24   Grisar, Section 1, p 127.
25   Grisar, Section 1, p 144 n 40.
26   Grisar, Section 1, p 139 n 5.
27   Grisar, Section I, p 50 n 7.
28   Orchard, p 82 n 6.
29   WJ Battersby, *Educational Work of the English Religious Orders of Women*, (unpublished work), p 209.
30   Mary CE Chambers, *The Life of Mary Ward*, Vol 2, HJ Coleridge (ed), Burns and Oates, London, 1885, p 45.
31   Chambers, p 186.
32   Chambers, p 531.
33   Orchard, p 96.
34   Orchard, p 95 n 32, says that Winifred Bedingfield (1606-1660) entered the   Institute at Cologne. She became a founding member of the Munich   community, headmistress of the school and superior there. Her sister, Frances, founded the Bar Convent, York, in 1686.
35   R Warnicke, *Women of the English Renaissance and Reformation*, Greenwood   Press, Connecticut, 1983, p 208.
36   O'Malley, p 242.
37   Orchard, p 49 n 5.
38   Peters, p 342.
39   ACF Beales, *Education under Penalty*, Athlone, London, 1963, p 203.
40   Marion Norman, *Mary Ward as Educator*, (unpublished work) p 17.

An Incomparable Woman

1   Antonia Fraser, *The Weaker Vessel: Woman's lot in seventeenth-century England*, Weidenfeld and Nicolson, London, 1984, p 370.
2   Merry E Wiesner, *Women and Gender in Early Modern Europe*, Cambridge University Press, Cambridge, 1993, pp 206-7.
3   Mary CE Chambers, *The Life of Mary Ward*, Vol 2, HJ Coleridge (ed), Burns and Oates, London, 1885, p 563 n 2.

4   M Rosa MacGinley, *A Dynamic of Hope*, Crossing Press, Sydney, 1996, p 35.

5   Henriette Peters, *Mary Ward: A world in contemplation*, H Butterfield (trans), Gracewing, England, 1994, p 456.

6   Mary CE Chambers, *The Life of Mary Ward*, Vol 1, HJ Coleridge (ed), Burns and Oates, London, 1882, p 27.

7   Chambers, Vol 1, p 465.

8   Peters, p 162 n 19.

9   Emmanuel Orchard (ed), *Till God Will: Mary Ward through her writings*, Darton, Longman and Todd, London, 1985, p 55 n 5.

10   Peters, p 611.

11   Immolata Wetter, *Mary Ward*, B Ganne (trans), Regenburg, Verlag Schnell and Steiner, 1995, p 5.

12   MacGinley, p 45.

13   Mary Wright, *Mary Ward's Institute*, Crossing Press, Sydney, 1997, p 70.

14   MacGinley, p 46.

15   MacGinley, p 46.

16   MacGinley, p 46.

17   MacGinley, p 46.

18   *Bull of Suppression*, no 10. See appendix 4.

19   The nucleus members of the Grail movement were originally called the 'Women of Nazareth'. Ginneken indicates that he thought that Mary Ward was naive in her tactics in dealing with Rome. This Grail Manuscript is held by the Grail, 22 McHatton St, North Sydney, New South Wales.

20   *L'Osservatore Romano*, October 1951.

21   John Paul II, *On the Dignity and Vocation of Women*, St Paul Publications, Homebush, 1988, p 99.

22   Chambers, Vol 2, p 562 n 2.

23   Chambers, Vol 2 p 563 n 2.

24   Chambers, Vol 2, pp 285, 294.

25   Chambers, Vol 2, p 499.

26 EM Sunstein, *A Different Face: The life of Mary Wollstonecraft*, p 340, quoted in S McGrath, 'Mary Wollstonecraft: Natural theologian?' *Compass*, vol 26 no 3, 1992, p 42.

27 Orchard, p 105.

28 Chambers, Vol 1, p 468.

29 Orchard, p 117.

30 Orchard, p 107.

Afterword: 'Galloping Girls'

1 Mary CE Chambers, *The Life of Mary Ward*, Vol 2, HJ Coleridge (ed), Burns and Oates, London, 1885, pp 385-6.

2 Mary CE Chambers, *The Life of Mary Ward*, Vol 1, HJ Coleridge (ed), Burns and Oates, London, 1885, p 234-5.

3 Mary Philip, *Companions of Mary Ward*, Burns, Oates and Washbourne, London, 1939, p 109.

4 Philip, p 110.

5 Henriette Peters, *Mary Ward: A world in contemplation*, H Butterfield (trans), Gracewing, England, 1994, p538.

6 Peters, p 594 .

7 Chambers, Vol 2, p 511.

8 FL Carsten (ed), *The New Cambridge Modern History*, Vol 5, Cambridge University Press, Cambridge, 1969, p 246.

9 Anthony Gilles, *The People of Anguish*, St Anthony Messenger Press, Cincinnati, 1987, pp 152-3.

10 Chambers, Vol 2, p 167.

11 Chambers, Vol 2, p 174.

12 Philip, pp 169-70.

13 Philip, p 138.

14 Mary Wright, *Mary Ward's Institute*, Crossing Press, Sydney, 1997, p 45.

15 Philip, p 142.

16 Philip, p 158.

17 Philip, p 162.

18 Wright, p 49.

19 Peters, p 51 n 34.

20 Peters, p 355.
21 Chambers, Vol 1, p 424.
22 Peters, p 374 n 12.
23 Chambers, Vol 1, p 485.
24 Chambers, Vol 2, p 67.
25 Chambers, Vol 1, p 262.
26 Chambers, Vol 1, p 261.
27 Chambers, Vol 1, pp 248-9.
28 Peters, p 514.
29 Philip, p 73.
30 Chambers, Vol 1, p 249.
31 Chambers, Vol 1, p 248.
32 Peters, p 160.
33 Philip, p 68.
34 Chambers, Vol 2, p 425.
35 Chambers, Vol 2, p 424.
36 Chambers, Vol 2, pp 424-5.
37 Chambers, Vol 1, p 89.
38 Chambers, Vol 1, p 251.
39 Philip, p 57.
40 Chambers, Vol 1, p 249.
41 Chambers, Vol 1, p 443.
42 Chambers, Vol 1, p 338.
43 Philip, p 60.
44 Peters, p 313.
45 Peters, p 379.
46 Chambers, Vol 2, p 120.
47 Chambers, Vol 2, p 121.
48 Peters, p 399 n 24.
49 Emmanuel Orchard (ed), *Till God Will: Mary Ward through her writings*, Darton, Longman and Todd, London, 1985, pp 91-2.
50 Peters, p 399 n 24, and Chambers, Vol 2, p 121.
51 Peters, p 45.
52 Chambers, Vol 1, p 258.
53 Peters, p 45.

54 Peters, p 45.

55 Peters, p 45.

56 Peters, p 45.

57 Philip, p 86.

58 Peters, p 46.

59 Chambers, Vol 1, pp 257-8.

60 Peters, p 110.

61 Chambers, Vol 1, p 299.

62 Philip, p 89.

63 Peters, p 592.

64 Peters, p 604.

65 Chambers, Vol 2, p 495.

66 Philip, p 106.

Appendix 5

1 Mary Ward had been imprisoned on 7 February 1631, on the accusations of heresy, schism, and rebellion against the Church.

Appendix 6

1 Mary CE Chambers, *The Life of Mary Ward*, Vol 1, HJ Coleridge (ed), Burns and Oates, London, 1882, p xlii.

2 Chambers, pp xliii-xlv.

3 Immolata Wetter, *Tenth Letter of Instruction*, (Institute circulation), pp i-x.

4 Wetter, p i-x.

5 Wetter, p i-x.

6 Chambers, Vol 1, p xlvi.

7 (Sr) Gregory Kirkus, *The Portraits at the Bar Convent*, unpublished paper, 1993, pp 22-3.

8 Mary CE Chambers, *The Life of Mary Ward*, Vol 2, HJ Coleridge (ed), Burns and Oates, London, 1885, p v-vi.

9 Henriette Peters, *Mary Ward: A world in contemplation*, H Butterfield (trans), Gracewing, England, 1994, p ix.

10 Peters, p xi.

Bibliography

Primary references

Chambers, Mary CE. *The Life of Mary Ward*, 2 vols, (edited by HJ Coleridge). Burns and Oates, London, 1882 (Vol 1), 1885 (Vol 2).

Ganss, G (translator). *The Constitutions of the Society of Jesus.* The Institute of Jesuit Sources, St Louis, 1970.

Grisar, J. *Mary Ward's Institute before Roman Congregations (1616-1630).* Pontifical Gregorian University, Rome, 1966 (private Institute circulation).

Littlehales, Mary M. *Mary Ward: Pilgrim and Mystic.* Burns and Oates, Kent, 1998.

Orchard, Emmanuel (ed). *Till God Will: Mary Ward through her writings.* Darton, Longman and Todd, London, 1985.

Peters, Henriette. *Mary Ward: A world in contemplation.* Translated by H. Butterfield. Gracewing, England, 1994.

Poyntz, Mary, and **Wigmore**,Winifred. *A Briefe Relation.* Written soon after Mary Ward's death in 1645. Institute circulation.

Wetter, Immolata. *Letters of Instruction.* Institute circulation.

Secondary references: books

Alexander, JH. *Ladies of the Reformation.* Gospel Standard Strict Baptist Trust Ltd, Herts, 1978.

Anderson, B, and **Zinsser**, J. *A History of Their Own: Women in Europe from prehistory to the present*, Vol 1. Penguin, London, 1990.

Bainton, Roland H. *The Age of the Reformation.* Van Rostrand Reinhold Co, New York, 1956.

Bainton, Roland H. *Women of the Reformation in Germany and Italy*. Beacon Press, Boston, 1974.

_____. *Women of the Reformation in France and England*. Beacon Press, Boston, 1975.

_____. *Women of the Reformation from Spain to Scandinavia*. Augsburg Publishing House, Minneapolis, 1977.

Beales, ACF. *Education Under Penalty*. Athlone, London, 1963.

Beard, MR. *Women as Force in History*. Macmillan Co, Melbourne, 1987. (First published in 1946).

Bossy, John. *The English Catholic Community 1570-1850*. Darton, Longman and Todd, London, 1975.

Boulding, Elise. *The Underside of History*, Vol 2. Sage Publications, California, 1992.

Byrne, Lavinia. *Mary Ward: A pilgrim finds her way*. Carmelite Centre of Spirituality, Dublin, 1984.

Caraman, Philip. *St Angela*. Green and Co Ltd, London, 1963.

_____. *A Study in Friendship*. The Institute of Jesuit Sources, St Louis MO, 1995.

Carsten, FL (ed). *The New Cambridge Modern History*, Vol 5. Cambridge University Press, Cambridge, 1969.

Chadwick, Owen. *The Reformation*. Penguin Books, Middlesex, 1964.

Chittister, Joan. *Winds of Change: Women challenge Church*. Sheed and Ward, Kansas City, 1986.

Claridge, Mary. *Margaret Clitherow*. Anthony Clarke Books, Hertfordshire, 1966.

Clark, Kenneth. *Civilisation*. Penguin Books Ltd, England, 1969.

Cover, Jeanne. *Love: The driving force*. Marquette University Press, Milwaukee, 1997.

Cuming, John (ed). *Letters from Saints to Sinners*. Crossroad, New York, 1996.

Delumeau, J. *Catholicism between Luther and Voltaire: A new view on the Counter-Reformation*. Burns and Oates Ltd, Great Britain, 1977.

Dempsey, T. *Richard Gwyn, Man of Maelor: Martyr or traitor?* The Catholic Printing Co of Farnworth, England, 1970.

Dickens, A, and **Tonkin**, J. *The Reformation in Historical Thought*. Basil Blackwell, Oxford, 1985.

Dickens, AG. *Reformation and Society in Sixteenth Century Europe*. Thames and Hudson, London, 1966.

_____. *The Counter Reformation*. Thames and Hudson, London, 1968.

Dirvin, Joseph J. *Louise de Marillac*. Doubleday Canada Ltd, Toronto, 1970.

Dortel-Claudot, M. *The Evolution of the Canonical Status of Religious Institutes with Simple Vows from the Sixteenth Century until the New Code*, trans M R MacGinley, Institute of Religious Studies, Strathfield (New South Wales), 1989.

Duffy, Eamon. *The Stripping of the Altars*. Yale University Press, London, 1992.

Durant, Will. *The Story of Civilization*, Volume 6. Simon and Schuster, New York, 1961.

Elton, GR (ed). *The New Cambridge Modern History, Vol 2: The Reformation 1520-1559*. Cambridge University Press, Cambridge, 1990.

Fraser, Antonia. *The Weaker Vessel: Woman's lot in seventeenth-century England*. Weidenfeld and Nicolson, London, 1984.

_____. *The Gunpowder Plot*. Weidenfeld and Nicolson, London, 1996.

Ganss, George (ed). *Ignatius of Loyola: The Spiritual Exercises and selected works.* Paulist Press, New York, 1991.

Gerard, J. *The Hunted Priest.* Translated by Philip Caraman SJ. Fontana Books, Great Britain, 1959.

Gilles, Anthony. *The People of Anguish.* St Anthony Messenger Press, Cincinnati, 1987.

Gonne, Francis. *Wisps of Straw.* Catholic Truth Society, London, no date.

Green, VHH. *Renaissance and Reformation.* Edward Arnold, London, 1977.

Haigh, C (ed). *The English Reformation Revised.* Cambridge University Press, Cambridge, 1987.

Holmes, J, and **Bickers**, B. *A Short History of the Catholic Church.* Burns and Oates, Kent, 1983.

Holmes, Peter. *Resistance and Compromise.* Cambridge University Press, Cambridge (Mass), 1982.

Hostie, R. *The Life and Death of Religious Orders.* Centre for the Applied Research in the Apostolate, Washington DC, 1983.

Jedin, Hubert. *Ecumenical Councils of the Catholic Church.* Nelson, Edinburgh/London, 1960.

_____. *Crisis and Closure of the Council of Trent.* Sheed and Ward, London, 1967.

Johnson, Paul. *Elizabeth I.* Weidenfeld and Nicolson, London, 1974.

_____. *The Papacy.* Weidenfeld and Nicolson, London, 1997.

Jones, Tudor R. *The Great Reformation.* Inter-Varsity Press, England, 1985.

Kelly, JND. *The Oxford Dictionary of Popes*. Oxford University Press, Oxford, 1986.

Kirkus, Sr Gregory. *The Portraits at the Bar Convent*, unpublished paper, 1993.

Knowles, David. *Bare Ruined Choirs*, Cambridge University Press, Cambridge, 1959.

Koenigsberger, HG, and **Mosse**, GL. *Europe in the Sixteenth Century*, 5th impression. Longman, London, 1973.

Leach, A. *English Schools at the Reformation 1546-8*. Russell and Russell, New York, 1896. Revised 1968.

Ledochowska, Teresa. *Angela Merici and the Company of St Ursula according to the Historical Documents, Vols 1 and 2*. French edition. Ancora, Rome, revised 1968.

_____. *In Search of the Charism of the Institute*. Ursulines of the Roman Union, Rome, no date.

_____. *St Angela Merici* (abridged edition). Catholic Press, Ranchi, 1990.

Levack, BP. *The Witch Hunt in Early Modern Europe*. Longman, London, 1987.

Lonergan, Bernard. *Method in Theology*. Darton Longman and Todd, London, 1972.

Lonsdale, D. *Eyes to See, Ears to Hear*. Darton Longman and Todd, London, 1990.

MacGinley, M Rosa. *A Dynamic of Hope: Institutes of women religious in Australia*. Crossing Press, Sydney, 1996.

Marshall, S (ed). *Women and Reformation and Counter-Reformation Europe*. Indiana University Press, Indianapolis, 1989.

Maurice, H. *St Francis de Sales and his Friends.* Translated by Veronica Morrow. Scepter, Dublin, 1964.

Norman, Edward. *Roman Catholicism in England.* Oxford University Press, Oxford, 1985.

O'Connell, Marvin. *The Counter-Reformation 1559-1610.* Harper and Row, New York, 1974.

O'Dea, R. *The Debate on the English Reformation.* Methuen, London, 1986.

O'Hara, Tom. *At Home with the Spirit.* Aurora Books, Melbourne, 1992.

Oliver, M. *Mary Ward 1585-1645.* Sheed and Ward, New York, 1959.

O'Malley, John. *The First Jesuits.* Harvard University Press, Cambridge (Mass), 1993.

Osment, S. *When Fathers Ruled: Family life in Reformation Europe.* Harvard University Press, Cambridge (Mass), 1983.

Perry, Ruth. *The Celebrated Mary Astell.* University of Chicago Press, Chicago, 1993.

Philip, Mary. *Companions of Mary Ward.* Burns, Oates and Washbourne, London, 1939.

Power, Eileen. *Medieval Women.* Edited by M Postan. Cambridge University Press, London, 1975.

Rahner, Hugo. *St Ignatius Loyola: Letters to women.* Translated by K Pond and S Weetman, Nelson, Edinburgh/London, 1960.

Rapley, Elizabeth. *The Dévotes: Women and Church in seventeenth-century France.* McGill-Queen's University Press, Montreal, 1990.

Raynor, Henry. *A Social History of Music.* Tapliner Publishing Company, New York, 1978.

Rogers, H (ed). *The Oxford Illustrated History of English Literature.* Oxford University Press, Oxford, 1987.

Roper, Lyndal. *The Holy Household: Women and morals in Reformation Augsburg.* Clarendon Press, Oxford, 1989.

Rose, Mary B (ed). *Women in the Middle Ages and the Renaissance.* Syracuse University Press, USA, 1986.

Rosenthal, Koonz, Stuard (eds). *Becoming Visible: Women in European history,* Haughton Mifflin Co, Boston, 1987.

Ruether, Rosemary R. *Religion and Sexism.* New York, Simon and Schuster, 1974.

Scarisbrick, John. *The Reformation and the English People.* Basil Blackwell, Oxford, 1984.

Sheldrake, P. *The Way of Ignatius Loyola.* SPCK, London, 1991.

Soury-Lavergne, Francoise. *A Pathway in Education: Jeanne de Lestonnac, 1556-1640.* Translated from the French. Sisters of the Company of Mary, Rome, 1984.

_____. *Ignatian Origin of the Spiritual Instruction.* Rome, 1983.

Sykes, N. *The English Religious Tradition.* SCM Press, London, 1985.

Trevor-Roper, HR. *The European Witch-Craze of the Sixteenth and Seventeenth Century.* Penguin Books, England, 1969.

Trimble, William. *The Catholic Laity in Elizabethan England.* Belknap Press, Cambridge (Mass), 1964.

Tucker, R, and **Liefeld**, W. *Daughters of the Church.* Academic Books, Michigan, 1987.

Warnicke, R. *Women of the English Renaissance and Reformation.* Greenwood Press, Connecticut, 1983.

Waters, Peter M. *The Ursuline Achievement.* Colonna, Melbourne, 1994.

Wetter, Immolata. *Mary Ward's Prayer.* Talks given to the General Chapter, IBVM, at Loyola, Spain, 1994.

Wiesner, Merry E. *Women and Gender in Early Modern Europe.* Cambridge University Press, Cambridge, 1993.

Wright, Mary. *Mary Ward's Institute.* Crossing Press, Sydney, 1997.

Encyclopedias

Grazier, M, **Hellwig**, M (eds). *The New Modern Encyclopedia.* EJ Dwyer, Sydney,1994

Hale, JR (ed). *Encyclopedia of the Italian Renaissance.* Thames and Hudson, London, 1989.

Loxton, H. *The Encyclopedia of Saints.* Brockhampton Press, London, 1996.

The New Catholic Encyclopedia. McGraw Hill Book Co, New York, 1967.

Catechism

Donovan, J (trans). *Catechism of the Council of Trent.* James Duffy and Co, Dublin, 1914.

Pamphlets

Burke, C. *A Wisdom Figure from Our Past.* Reprinted from Women-Church, Sydney, 1993.

Dempsey, T. *Richard Gwynn*. Catholic Printing Co of Farnworth, Lancashire, 1970.

Grisar, J. *Mary Ward 1585-1645*. Reprinted from *The Month*. London, no date.

John Paul II. *On the Dignity and Vocation of Women*. St Paul Publications, Homebush, 1988.

Littlehales, Mary M. *Mary Ward: A woman for all seasons*. Catholic Truth Society, England, 1974.

McDonald, E. *Short Summary of the History of the Constitutions of the IBVM*. Printing Services, Calcutta, 1970.

Orchard, Emmanuel. *Mary Ward: Once and future foundress*. Incorporated Catholic Truth Society, London, 1985.

Walsh, A (ed). *A Soul Wholly God's*. Don Bosco Graphic Arts, Calcutta, no date.

Wetter, Immolata. *Mary Ward*. Translated by B Ganne. Regenburg, Verlag Schnell and Steiner, Germany, 1995.

————. *Mary Ward's Prayer*. Private Circulation, Rome, 1974.

Articles and theses

Amaladoss, M. 'Inculturation and Ignatian Spirituality'. *The Way Supplement 79*, Spring 1994: 39-47.

Battersby, WJ. 'Educational Work of the English Religious Orders of Women'. Unpublished manuscript.

Buxton, P, and others. 'Mary Ward: Journey into freedom. Essays in honour of the fourth centenary of her birth', *The Way Supplement 53*, Summer 1985: 4-132.

Cover, Jeanne. *The Significance of Mary Ward's Spirituality and Practice for Moral Theology Today*, unpublished PhD thesis, University of St Michael's College, Toronto, 1993.

298 ❖ *A DANGEROUS INNOVATOR*

Fraser, A. 'Mary Ward: A seventeenth century reformer', *History Today*, May 1981:14-8.

Fullam, L. 'Juana, SJ: The past (and future?) status of women in the Society of Jesus', *Studies in the Spirituality of Jesuits*, vol 31 no 5, November 1999.

McGrath, S. 'Mary Wollstonecraft: Natural theologian?', *Compass*, vol 26 no 3, 1992.

O'Reilly, T. 'The Spiritual Exercises and the Crisis of Medieval Piety', *The Way Supplement 70*, Spring 1991: 101-10.

Parish, Debra. 'The Power of Female Pietism: Women as spiritual authorities and religious role models in seventeenth century England', *The Journal of Religious History*, vol 17 no 1, June 1992: 33-46.

Peters, Marygrace. 'Beguine Women: Medieval spirituality, modern implications', *Review for Religious*, vol 54 no 2, March-April, 1995.

Press, M. 'An Enquirer Mumbling Surmises', *Compass Theology Review*, vol 20, Autumn 1986.

Weaver, MJ. 'The Most Adventurous of Nuns: Ursulines and the future', *Review for Religious*, vol 52, no 4, July-August, 1993.

Wetter, Immolata. 'Mary Ward's Apostolic Vocation', *The Way Supplement 17*, Autumn 1972: 69-91.

Wiesner, ME. 'Beyond Women and the Family: Towards a gender analysis of the Reformation', *Sixteenth Century Journal*, vol 18 no 3, 1987: 311-23.

Index